Peanut Butter Memoirs

A (Sometimes) Satirical Story
A (Sometimes) Cynical Story
But (Always) a Human Story of
the Journey to Becoming a
Law Enforcement Officer in
(Very) Rural Maine

by

David Wilson

"…Let us relive our lives in what we tell you…"

-Phil Collins

TABLE OF CONTENTS

PROLOGUE

Death by peanut butter. What an interesting way to begin a story, don't you think? Every book needs an opening line that grabs the reader and holds on for the duration. It's not easy thinking about a good opening line, many have been used and very few are left nowadays that we haven't already read. And what does it mean, death by peanut butter? It almost sounds like the title of a local live theater company's production of some sort of play. Perhaps a comedic play, perhaps a murder mystery. Anyway, I'll tell you later what it means. Why later? Because just like in any good movie, if you give away all the good stuff in the first act, by the third act everyone's fallen asleep or walked out of the theater. We can't have that now, can we? So, what makes my story something worth writing down or interesting to the reader? What does it take to make us good storytellers? Is it sitting around a campfire and not having your buddies walk away to go pee in the woods while you're telling a story? Maybe. As a law enforcement officer, I've found that people want to hear about particular calls that I've responded to, especially if the call was important enough to make the local newspapers. I've sat around many-a-campfire where people have asked me about a particular call I'd been on and then listened intently as I told the tale. I've also listened to others in my profession who've had stories of their own to tell. I believe you must be a good listener to ultimately be a good storyteller. There's a bit of a storyteller in all of us, it just depends on whether they're interesting enough to write about or enough of them to complete a book that someone will want to read.

Have you ever had someone say to you after telling them a story about something that happened to you, "You know, you should write a book?" I know many of you have, in fact, had someone say this very thing to you. I have as well. So, this one's about my journey in becoming a law enforcement officer in rural Maine. It's only my story, no other, and it's all true. I hope some parts are amusing for you to read about and maybe get a chuckle or two. We all need to laugh at something nowadays.

I know some parts won't be funny; there's certainly not always humor in this line of work and not every moment of our lives are necessarily something to laugh about, many are quite sad. I also have to be honest about a few things. This story is primarily about my years in law enforcement, but I do have to go back a bit to show the evolution of the journey. No, I'm not going to go back to my birth and talk about my memories of tumbling out of my baby crib and landing in the cat box. I truly have no memories about that, even if it did occur, and there are no photos to prove it ever happened anyway. Nor am I going to bore you with my earliest childhood years, those were normal and traumatic-free, so I can't blame all the insanity on my parents.

Therefore, it's called *Peanut Butter Memoirs* because I don't believe there are any other books with this title. This way I won't get letters telling me to appear in court with a bag of cash in my arms ready to hand it over to someone else who didn't make enough money from their books of the same title. I also don't believe there are any movies of this title, none at least under a rating of NC-17.

Actually, it's called this for a reason, and I'm still not telling you why quite yet.

I do feel it necessary to warn all of you, well, at least the one reading this book, right away of a couple of things. First, you've probably heard the rumors about the warped sense of humor that cops possess. Well, it's true. Whether it be police, fire, or ambulance, we all have a sense of humor that some may consider twisted. The truth is we're required to have a warped sense of humor. We're not attempting to be cruel in referring to the sometimes gruesome and violent situations that we're forced to deal with as part of the job, we simply have to make a joke about some of it, otherwise, we'd all end up spending years in very expensive therapy sessions. Which by the way is, in fact, where some of us do end up.

So, yes, I'll admit, the humor is at someone else's expense. But really, have you seen the sick crap on social media where everyone can, and does, offer their opinions and make sick jokes at other people's expense? At least the jokes that we make about a situation help us stay sane and are normally only spoken amidst the circle of those who experienced the situation along with us. Well, except for the ones I've written about here, but there's no guarantee that anyone will read this book, so I'm not overly worried about it. The sense of humor we display isn't to offend, it's to help us cope with what occurred and to get us through each day without going 'postal' on everyone. My apologies to everyone in the postal service, that's an old cliché.

So, you've been warned.

And speaking of opinions, not that I was, this brings me to disclaimer number two. I am very opinionated, especially when it comes to matters of drugs, crime, and punishment. I've found that everyone has an opinion. Yes, I know, you've heard the saying before. Everyone wants to give you their opinion, and theirs is the only opinion that matters. They don't want to hear *your* opinion and they get upset when you disagree with *their* opinion. Well, one of the things that makes life great is we're all entitled to our own opinions. However, I'm not going to give you my opinion right now on any of it. Why? Because if I provide my opinions to you now and you don't like them, then you're going to stop reading my book on page three. If I wait a while until you're further into the book and possibly enjoying the stories, then

I'll get to hear you cursing from where I'm sitting when I provide an opinion and you don't agree with it, and you're upset because by then you just can't stop reading and must continue to see how it all ends.

Now, as far as changing names to protect the innocent, let's clarify this. No one is innocent. I will, however, change the names of almost everyone in this book because again, I don't want anyone to sue me if I paint them in a less-than-favorable light, which I probably will at times. Why? Because remember these are true stories, and by virtue of that fact, there are times when decisions made aren't the best ones that could have been in the moment. Some people are simply poor decision-makers or have difficulty thinking quickly on their feet. I also want to protect those innocent people whose part in these tales I'll need to talk about if I'm to tell true stories about my career as a cop, and I don't want to hurt or offend these people by providing their actual names. On the flip side, I may use real names for those who have been my true friends, and they certainly deserve the recognition. And no, I didn't ask their permission, so tough noogies if they don't like it.

I'd also like to say right up front that I'm not a racist as many police officers have recently been made out to be. I realize there's a great deal in the media lately about law enforcement and race, and yes, I make light of certain situations to bring humor to them, but never to cause them to appear racially motivated. I truly think there's far too much drama in the world today, and we all need to go back to a time when it was okay to make fun of ourselves. I think it's far too easy to take something that someone says and twist it into something it was never intended to be. I also believe we'd all get along much better if we eased up on the drama. I offer no apologies. If you get offended by the stories that I'm about to tell you, suck it up, buttercup. Yes, I know, your name isn't Buttercup, or maybe it is, I don't know.

Let's get started... ♦

CHAPTER 1

I STARTED OUT AS A CHILD

Wait, I promised I wouldn't do that. Fast forward to 1980 when I was thirteen years old. As I said, anything before this was mundane and fairly normal, as normal is. My parents both had jobs and worked hard, and I was the typical child who grew up without cellular telephones and video games. I do, however, remember when Atari came out and we all thought Pong was a game of intense skill. That's right, folks, a small dot bouncing back and forth on our big Zenith television screen that you had to hit with an up-and-down dash using a hand controller that was no more than a small wheel on a tiny plastic box that wore out fairly quickly. This was our 'Call of Duty' and 'Grand Theft Auto' of the time.

Simpler times they were.

My mother owned and operated a very successful catering service in the Greater Bangor area. In the local print media, her business was ranked number two in the area. I'm not certain what it took to be number one, possibly placing an extra cupcake on the bride's dinner plate would've done it. Now, Greater Bangor, for anyone that isn't familiar with where that is, is basically a fancy term for Bangor, Maine, except that they include all the surrounding little towns to make Bangor appear bigger. Probably a census trick to get more grant money for economic development. Anyway, I went to work for my mother, obviously prior to any child labor laws because nobody came to investigate her for putting me to work at such an early age. I was earning a decent hourly income for a kid of thirteen years old, too. I'd perform set up of the food area, constant dishwashing, and clean up after the events were over. We averaged one to two events per week, mostly on Friday and Saturday evenings. There was lots of prep work and no, I didn't touch all of the food with my filthy teenage hands, just some of it, mostly the desserts. And this is also where I had my first taste of champagne. All of the events had champagne, especially weddings. I'd grab a sip here and there when no one was looking. This is probably why I didn't mind doing the dishes every night.

Three years into the job my mother noticed that the disc jockeys who were hired to blast loud music during these events drank more free alcohol than most of the guests at the open bar, and were still making some pretty serious coin even though they were so drunk that you couldn't understand any of their mandatory announcements. You know, important stuff like announcing the new bride and groom's name as they entered the party. Unimportant things like that. Mom asked me if I'd consider deejaying her events and she'd hire me through her company and advertise us as a package deal to potential customers. I agreed, even though I had no idea about how to start a business. Play music, and get paid, that was about all my teenage mind could process at the time. Seemed reasonable.

At that time in the early 1980s, CDs hadn't been invented yet, so I bought a top-of-the-line tape deck that had the ability to play two cassette tapes. I also purchased a very expensive turntable. Yes, in 1980 vinyl records were still in existence and still popular, with cassette tapes being fairly new and having evolved from the basic failure of the unpopular eight-track tapes. I also bought a small mixing board and two tower speakers, each capable of putting out 100 watts of sound, which was a lot for those days. I also built myself two additional very large, high-wattage bass speakers because I found that people really wanted the music to be loud, the bass to thunder, and shake the floor under their intoxicated dancing feet.

I had learned electronics from my dad, who for many years was one of only two television repairmen in the Greater Bangor area. Dad had been an electronics specialist in the armed services, and after being discharged, he found that television repair was in demand. Yes, I'm being serious, we're talking about the 1950s and 60s here. For the next couple of decades, television sets were fairly high maintenance with their cathode ray picture tubes and vacuum tube designs. Dad had the contracts for all the major hotels in the area and would take me along on service calls to repair the television sets on-site. I learned basic wiring and soldering at a very young age, so throwing together a couple of mondo speakers was pretty simple, and the bigger the wooden box that I'd built and painted jet black to house them in, the louder and more professional people *thought* they were and made the business look better and brought in more customers. By the way, more on what Dad did for work after televisions became zero maintenance in the 1990s later. Stay tuned, pun certainly intended.

So, at age sixteen, there I was on my way to entrepreneurship with my own in-house disc jockey-for-wedding service. I called myself *Magic Sounds*. I had a pretty good voice for announcements and heavy base on the speakers to make the music *felt*, as well as heard, and made my voice sound even deeper, which helped. I had a big rotating disco-light ball with multiple-colored spotlights illuminating the dance floors. Loud music and a light show, what a spectacle it was. I specialized in sixties and seventies rock, plus the standard "first dance" songs, like Anne Murray's *Could I Have This Dance*, which made me deathly sick to listen to over and over to the point I could vomit each time I had to play it. There were other standards that I had to play each time that I eventually equally learned to hate, like Jim Croce's *Bad Leeroy Brown* and Foghat's *Slow Ride*. I'd play two fast tunes to boogie to and then mix in a slow one for the up-close dancing and take requests from the room in between.

Apparently, I wasn't bad at my job either because I quickly began receiving referrals to play gigs outside of Mom's catering service. And for a kid at age sixteen in the early 1980s, pulling down a C-note for each hour I played for a few hours a night wasn't bad coin. I also did something the other local DJs didn't do, I dressed professionally. Dress pants, a dress shirt, and a tie whereas most of your local DJs looked like beach bums, and I figured out quickly that if I was courteous and looked at least as good as someone in the wedding party, I'd get more referrals for other gigs. I was also able to hire my best friend James, aka "Butch" to help me out. By the way, as promised, this is his real name.

I was required to juggle private gigs around Mom's business, so I could use her Ford Econoline van to truck my equipment around on nights that I wasn't working one of her events. More gigs came in along with more money. The only problem was how to spend the money. You see, in any business, a portion must be re-invested back into the business to keep up with current trends and demand. Now try telling that to a seventeen-year-old. New music comes out every day that everyone wants to hear at their parties, even if you choose a genre to specialize in and advertise yourself as. Equipment breaks down, new equipment needs purchasing, paying help, gas money for the shag wagon, and so on. Although I did earn enough to buy my first motorized vehicle, a motorcycle, and still put a little cash in my pocket. In fact, enough cash that in a way it blurred my vision of the term "continued education" and gave me a false sense of reality when it came to success without a college degree. At the time, easy cash spoke louder than an education after high school, and college came with a high price tag.

The other problem was the type of gigs I was accepting. Fewer formal weddings were coming my way, and by 1986, more private functions and college parties were the norm. Which, oddly enough, turned me off to the idea of college even more when I saw what kind of behavior a lot of alcohol was causing these bright young minds who were hiring me to play their parties. I guess I was a bit more mature, or maybe it was the drunken assholes who were dancing on top of my speakers and puking on my equipment, but this changed my mind about wanting to join their organization. And I also came to the realization there had to be better-smelling jobs out there, so with 1986 coming to an end, so did *Magic Sounds*.

Not to mention, again, college costs a lot of money, and my goal was to make money and spend it the way I wanted. Even though my parents had decent jobs, they certainly weren't making enough money to send me to college, and up to this point no one else in my family had ever attended college, so why break tradition?

It's 1987, one year after I graduated from Bangor High School. I had taken a year off from doing anything, and the music business money had run out. No, I didn't take the time off in need of *finding myself*, I knew where I was; I was broke, and my first car, a 1978 Ford Fairmount that I'd paid $800 for two years earlier was in serious need of repairs. I was also hanging out with friends who had the same goals in life, to see how far we could go in my car on a tank of gas and no cash. The day I nearly got caught siphoning gas out of my sister's 1980 Plymouth bomb to fill my car, I decided I better get my rear-end back to work.

I picked up a job for a company that catered the airlines at Bangor International Airport, or BIA for short. This was a fairly cool job, except that I had to lie on my application and say that I knew how to drive a large box truck with a five-speed stick shift, which I didn't. The trucks were unique in that the box rose to the galley doors of the plane, some as high as forty feet in the air while the frame and cab remained grounded. The problem was that to get up to the box, you had to climb a ten-inch wide metal ladder with half mounted to the box and half mounted to the frame of the truck. Any height above the ladder mounted to the frame, and you had a gap to get to the other half mounted to the box, this was a challenge. And with no safety equipment to speak of, which I don't think the company owned any, we scaled this ladder, made the jump between the gaps, and continued up to the level of the galley. Keep in mind that box trucks are fairly narrow, and the only thing keeping the top-heavy truck frame from tipping over in the wind when the box was forty feet in the air were small outriggers on either side of the truck frame if you remembered to put them down before raising the box in the first place. I think there was an alarm to let you know if the outriggers weren't down, but they didn't work in any of the aging vehicles.

Next, you had to transfer the food containers on a slippery metal four-foot by four-foot ramp between the box and the plane that normally didn't have safety rails. So, there was nothing mounted to the ramp, which wasn't supposed to touch the plane, thus creating a gap between the two some forty feet in the air. Even if it wasn't raining, the diamond-plated ramp was as slippery as winter ice. This doesn't include the fact that the doors on the plane have a safety catch that releases the inflatable emergency slide. If the airline attendant, for whatever reason, forgot to release the safety catch from inside the plane after it landed before opening the door, there was a good chance you were going to get shot out the back of the truck box by the slide instantly inflating when the airplane door was opened.

Now in addition to all this, the trucks had to be guided into the plane with one person driving and one standing beneath the galley doors to make sure that the ramp, when raised with the box, didn't touch the plane and poke a huge hole in the side of it. This was something the airlines frowned upon greatly when you tore a hole in the side of an airplane built by McDonald Douglas or Rolls Royce, which believe it or not, many of the airlines were built by them. Also, not to mention that when you puncture a commercial jet, it really messes up their flight schedule, which brings me to another fun fact. I'm surprised that I even dare to fly today when during the time I worked for this company, I had the pleasure of watching the pilots do their *safety walk* around the airplane prior to flight. I don't think, "That looks like it will make it to the next stop," is quite the statement the passengers would have wanted to hear. Think about it, what did these guys care? They fly the plane once and then get in a different plane at the next stop and fly that one somewhere else on a daily basis. They only need to care about the next few hours on one flight. If they bothered to think about it, they'd realize the pilots before them didn't put any more effort into their pre-flight checks either on the same airplane they were now inspecting. It was like pilot Russian Roulette, who's going to get the farthest with this plane before it disappears into the ocean?

Oh, and if all this hasn't scared you away from this job enough, think about this. On smaller airlines, the engine intake is literally right beside the galley door. The intake is where the air flows into the engine before it goes through the turbines and out the rear at high velocity, so the plane can take off and maintain airspeed to keep it in the sky. So, we had to carry a large, circular piece of plastic to put over the intake, so in the event the pilot doesn't know that we're out there and they start the engines, this piece of plastic was supposed to keep us from being sucked into the engine and spit out the other side at high speed and in little pieces like a bird going through it and only feathers thrown out the other end.

All this for minimum wage in the late eighties, which was about $4 an hour.

Now there are certainly a few amusing and interesting things that occurred during my time with this company, but that's not why you're here, so I'll keep this time brief, and I sincerely apologize. Well, okay, I don't apologize. Anyway, here are a few stories that I'd like to include that stand out each time I reflect on this particular period in my life that you may find amusing, and it sort of sums up the job at BIA as a whole.

◆ ◆ ◆

BIA was known as an international stopover for fuel, so we received a lot of overseas flights simply touching down for food and fuel.

I had gotten James a job working with me for the company. Let's face it, we both needed gas and Saturday night movie money. For the moment, these were our primary motivators for working. Although mine also included my rent for the crappy little apartment I had by this time. Yes, believe it or not, I didn't live with my parents until I was thirty years old like many do, I moved out at age nineteen.

James and I had the night shift, and it was only the two of us on duty during the week. I was named supervisor of the night shift. Big deal, supervisor of one other person. And for some reason, they trusted to leave me alone to take care of all incoming flights during the night hours. James and I would put up the orders, which were usually called in far in advance, and the food was prepared by the company chef. And when I say chef, I mean a dude that we guessed was certifiably insane and probably wouldn't have lasted in most of the local fast-food joints. In fact, in today's world, he's probably on every "No Flight" list in America. It's more than likely that he had this job just to satisfy his probation requirements.

Anyway, most of the airline meals consisted of some type of mystery meat, powdered mashed potatoes, and a frozen veggie that had been taken from the freezer, pre-packaged and pre-cooked, and that's what they got from us. There were also those flights that for whatever reason didn't call ahead and order a meal in advance.

Every so often we'd get calls from an inbound overseas flight and had nothing prepared for them. So, one slow night that I was working alone and getting ready to close shop, I got a call from an incoming flight based in the Middle East somewhere that was landing for a refueling stop before continuing on to their ultimate destination. The requestor, obviously of a Middle Eastern background due to his heavy accent, asked if they could place an order.

After attempting to explain that there was nothing prepared and not much I could do for them, the caller asked, "Do you have a McDonald's in your city?" It appeared that our foreign friends had not had the pleasure of experiencing American fast food, and word gets around that Mickey-Dees is some good-tasting stuff. I can't say I blame them. It's worth a trip across the ocean for some tasty takeout, especially considering everything else was closed this time of night except the gas stations and their food was worse than anything our chef could concoct.

"Yes, there's a McDonald's in town."

"Can you please get Mcdonald's for us? Sixty cheeseburgers, sixty French fries, and sixty Cokes. Can you bring that to us?"

"Um…Okay."

Well, unfortunately for me, you couldn't just call in a takeout order to McDonald's in the 1980s. No phone apps, no curbside pickup. Not quite the definition of fast food back then. I drove to the local establishment, parked the truck, and went inside. It was late, almost their closing time. There was only one young lady at the customer counter and one guy putting up the orders in the kitchen. I walked up to the counter, and while smiling, she asked in a tired but perky voice, "Can I take your order?"

"Sixty cheeseburgers, sixty medium fries, and sixty medium Cokes please."

She leaned sideways to look behind me to see if I had fifty-nine others who were with me that she hadn't immediately noticed. Not seeing any, she asked, "Did you say sixty cheeseburgers, sixty medium fries, and sixty medium Cokes?"

"Yes, I did."

She leaned again, still not seeing anyone else, she looked back at me and frowned, "Are you kidding?"

"No, I'm not." I was actually beginning to get a bit annoyed.

She leaned into her microphone, *"Sixty cheeseburgers, sixty medium fries."* And lucky me, this was before self-service, so she was going to have to fill the sixty Cokes herself. It took her several minutes to type the order into the register. "That'll be $105," she said in a way that let me know she still didn't believe me and probably thought I was going to bolt out the door after having played a prank on her. She appeared surprised when I handed her cash from the company till.

Then she asked the magic question as she reached out her hand to take the cash, "Is that for here or to go?"

"I think I'll eat them all here if you don't mind," I said with a straight face. She immediately realized what she was programmed to ask every customer, sounding quite ridiculous in this particular situation.

"I'm sorry, do you want a box for that order?" An equally stupid question. *No, sweetie, I'll just juggle the burgers and tie all the fries together. I don't know what I'll do with the Cokes yet.*

"Yes, I want a box, maybe two of them please," is what I actually said.

After about twenty minutes, the order was ready, and I was on my way to the tarmac. The airplane was on the ground and several crew from the plane were standing around it. They were pleased to be eating the fast food they'd heard so much about. They were as happy as kids in a candy store. It was all about the experience, although the food probably tasted great, too. They happily paid the bill, provided a decent tip, and I was on my way.

This was just one of many misadventures during my brief career in airline catering. Maybe I'll write a book about all of them someday.

Time to carry on… ♦

CHAPTER 2

THE GREATER HAMDONIA YEARS

So, as we've discovered so far, I had the drive to work but not necessarily the most desirable of jobs, but it was a start. Over the next couple of years, I'd continue to drive trucks for various companies, not really going anywhere, and just getting by. Luckily during this time, I had a friend who was working as a cop for the Hampden Police Department.

T. Daniel Stewart (*yes, his real name*). Dan's mother was my mother's best friend, and for lack of better terms, was my second mom. Our families lived directly across the street from each other in Bangor when I was born. Edith "Edie" Stewart, who had three children of her own, would take care of me quite often. I spent as much time in the Stewart household as I did my own.

Anyway, just about the time I'd had enough of the airport gig and truck driving, I received a call from T. Dan. The year was 1989.

"What are you doing with your life?" he asked during the conversation.

"Not much."

T. Dan told me there was an opening for a dispatcher at the police department and that I should apply for the job. It must have been my nice, deep, made-for-radio voice because I certainly didn't have any qualifications as a 911 dispatcher. But then again, this was a time prior to *education before experience* was the normal. You didn't need a degree in communications to be a small-town EMS dispatcher. So, I applied for the job, and strangely enough, I got it.

The town of Hampden is one of those "greater" parts that make up Greater Bangor. A small community on the Penobscot River with a small 24/7 police department, which consisted of a chief, sergeant, and several patrol officers. The department was housed on the main road in the basement of the Masonic Lodge. That's right, there was no actual police department. Once down the basement stairs, there was a very small reception area, no larger than your average outhouse and an even smaller dispatch area where one dispatcher handled the Hampden police, fire, and ambulance services. Beyond this were a few tiny offices for the chief, the duty sergeant, an administrative assistant, an interview room, and a patrol office.

The dispatch area was tight, had one phone, one radio, a computer, and a small television to keep you awake during overnight shifts. We even had cable so more than just the three local channels. The small window between the dispatcher and the public was chest high, which meant you weren't able to see anything the public was carrying in their hands like guns, knives, grenades, and whatnot. Not to mention there was no bulletproof glass, in fact, there was no glass in the reception window at all.

Training for the job was minimal. If you had the ability to answer a phone and key a mike, you pretty much were trained to the level of everyone else. There were three other dispatchers to make up the around-the-clock service seven days a week. Rachel, the dispatch supervisor, made up the Monday through Friday day shifts while others worked around her schedule. I was given the swing shift; mid-week, weekend evening, and overnight shifts, which I didn't mind. It wasn't a bad shift, especially if you wanted to learn something because these were generally the busiest shifts, especially the Friday and Saturday nights. It didn't take long to learn the particular quirks of the officers I was working with and also learn the names of the streets and landmarks to provide for the officers to make their jobs easier. I learned the job quickly and became very good at it, which caused a little rift between me and one of the other dispatchers who was hired before me and was seeking to climb the small ladder, but I didn't care, I wasn't out to take anyone's job. The fourth dispatcher was an older gentleman named Henry. I say older in that he was far beyond the normal retirement age, in his seventies. He was a nice guy but very, very laid back. Henry would come in to relieve me on my midnight shift, and the first thing he'd do was check the obituaries in the local newspaper that was delivered each morning. He said if he read his name amongst the other deceased, he was going home. Not much got Henry's energy or anxiety up, which caused some safety issues on certain calls.

I can remember a call he took where a guy was threatening his girlfriend with an axe. Now normally this type of call would raise your awareness and you'd give as much information to the responding officers as necessary for safety reasons. Not with Henry, he dispatched the call as, "Someone having a bad day." Henry was the type of guy that when he came into work, if there was coffee still in the pot that he'd made the day before and probably growing hair on it, he'd pop a cup of it in the microwave and drink it anyway while saying, "No need to waste it."

Nothing seemed to phase Henry, and luckily, he never invited me to his home for coffee and pastries.

Rachel, our leader, was a hip lady in her mid-forties, had a great personality, knew her stuff, and she liked that I caught on quickly because it created trust between me and the officers who were generally all good personal friends of hers. She was like the "mom" of the station, always watching out for everyone around her, especially the cops on the streets.

The calls in the small town were generally low-key and boring. What days are the dump open? What time does the dump close? *Does the town have a dump?* Nothing too severe on average. Generally, the night shift officers would spend their time stopping cars in between the occasional domestic disturbance calls, all the while looking for drunks to arrest. Commonly dispatchers are requested to check driver's license status and car registration information on each traffic stop to see if the driver has a current and active license or the occasional arrest warrant. Again, pretty easy stuff if you generally knew how to use simple motor vehicle computer programs, which weren't difficult to learn. Each time you checked a driver's license, the computer would also automatically run the information through the National Crime Information Center, or NCIC, to see if anyone in the car was wanted or if the vehicle was stolen in the case of registration checks.

Calls were so mundane that when a real emergency call occurred, it sort of took you by surprise and disrupted the complacency of the shift.

◆ ◆ ◆

One of my first bad calls came late one night fairly soon after I was hired. The 911 phone rang around 10:00 P.M., and I asked the standard, "911, what's your emergency?" Which I was completely programmed to say, and then the follow-up statement usually was, "Ma'am, why are you dialing 911 to ask about the dump hours?"

This night, however, was out of the ordinary.

I asked the standard question, to which the person on the other end of the phone said, "I think my husband's been shot!"

Oh shit! No, I didn't say *"Oh shit"* but I was thinking it. This was one of those eyes wide open, take your feet off the counter, sit up straight, and pay attention calls. "What's going on, ma'am?"

In a panicked voice, she said, "I think my husband's been shot! We were in bed when we heard gunshots down the street. My husband took his gun and a flashlight and said he was going to check it out. He said when he got to the end of the street if everything was alright, he was going to flash the light for me to see. He didn't flash the light!"

Wait, what? Am I hearing this correctly? "Your husband heard gunshots, took his own handgun, and went out into the dark to the end of your street to see what, or who, someone else was shooting at?"

"Yes!" Now came the crying with a panicked tone.

After getting the address from her, I dispatched the two officers who were on duty. Now, dispatchers are trained to keep callers on the line as long as possible. The point is to continue to gather information and attempt to keep the caller calm, especially in the event you may have to have them perform some type of medical assistance to someone on the scene. Part of the job is to walk them through simple medical procedures, which is known as Emergency Medical Dispatch, or EMD for short. In this situation, my goal was to reassure this woman that help was on its way and to get updates from her before the officer's arrival. The problem with this was, again, that we were a small dispatch center, so the telephone was literally right beside the radio, which meant the caller could hear everything the officers were saying to me. I really didn't want them to arrive on the scene and confirm over the air that her idiot husband had been shot and was now possibly dead.

And I say *idiot* because this guy was just that. First, he hears gunshots in the night. Duh, this was clue number one to stay inside your house, call 911, and then mind your own business. Next, it was after dark, and he was carrying a gun and a flashlight. If some drunken asshole was shooting at something, or someone, guess what? Here comes a new target complete with a lighted signal at which to shoot at. *Here, right here, shoot towards the light.* And this guy leaves his poor wife all alone to fend for herself? What was this guy thinking?

"Oh my God, two more shots!" she screamed into the phone.

Oh, great. "You heard two more shots, ma'am?"

"Yes!" Now she was fully hysterical and hyperventilating. I probably was, too.

I radioed the information to the responding officers who radioed back how far away they still were with the sounds of sirens behind their voices. I'm certain this wasn't a good feeling for the lady who was also hearing this and knew that help wasn't right outside her door yet.

"More gunshots!" she screamed into the phone. *Jesus, I've got an all-out war happening at the end of that road.* Now at this point, I'm sweating and having a hard time keeping calm. I was definitely breathing as heavily as the woman was. Believe it or not, emergency dispatching is a high-stress job. This is primarily due to the fact of the helplessness the dispatch operator feels in not being able to control the situation. The dispatcher is like a helpless, blind witness to what's happening on the other end of the phone and not the person directly involved or with the ability to drop the phone and respond themselves. I kept the officers apprised of what she was telling me. The call was now sounding so violent that the two officers radioed that they weren't going to drive straight into a shootout and stopped to "stage" at a safer location. This obviously wasn't something that I wanted this woman to hear, that the officers weren't going straight to check on her husband, who was now probably face down and looking like a piece of Swiss cheese at the end of their road.

Moments later the woman said in her panicking voice, "The gunshots have stopped." I advised the officers of her information. After a few more brief moments, one of the officers radioed that they were now going to cautiously continue to the end of the roadway. Now I really didn't want this lady to hear whatever was coming next, but I had to keep her on the line. Several tense minutes went by, and during this time I performed frequent 'patrol checks' on the officers. This is when you simply ask if they're okay and hope like hell you get a positive response, or any response.

Each time I checked, they responded in the affirmative, *"10-4,"* but nothing more yet, which was good enough for me to know they weren't getting shot at, too, and were still alive. Although no details yet of what carnage was to be found at the scene.

Finally, a full sentence from one of the officers broke the silence and tension, *"Hampden Four to dispatch?"* I was wincing, waiting for them to request multiple ambulances or a hearse to respond.

I keyed the mike, "Go ahead."

"All set on the scene."

"Repeat, please. Did you advise all set?"

"10-4."

"Can you advise on what was occurring? I still have the caller on the line."

After a long pause, *"Two guys were working on their car and it was backfiring, that's the sounds they were hearing."*

Uh-oh. I could begin to feel the boiling anger coming through the telephone. Remember, the lady was still live on the line with me and hearing this, too.

"This other guy came down and tried to help them by holding a flashlight under the hood so they could see better."

So, no gunshots, no battle cries, no casualties of war, just incorrect air-to-fuel mixture across the spark plugs. This wasn't going to go over well with this guy's wife. I could actually feel her anger seething through the phone. *Probably should have done as he was told and shined the light back up at your wife.*

"Appears your husband is all set, ma'am," I said delicately.

"So, it appears!" The anxiety and hysteria in her voice had now been replaced with a low, growling sound as if it had come from some demonic ghoul.

"You have a pleasant night, ma'am," I said while hanging up the receiver, thinking this guy should probably go home and keep a tight hold on that gun for the rest of the night. Or maybe just stay put and sleep in that broken-down car.

There were no further calls of shootings that evening. Nor any other type of domestic disturbances from that neighborhood. The latter was a bit surprising.

◆ ◆ ◆

Hampden had its own private landline telephone company, and this was before widespread wireless mobile phones. 911 hang-up calls were frequent. People would program 911 into their telephones and then "test" it. Children would dial 911 and hang up. Guys would try to call phone sex lines and forget they begin with 9-0-0, not 9- 1-1. *Don't ask me how I know that.*

As long as the line made the connection, it was easy to trace a call being that it was on the private system. There were no hoops to jump through with the major telephone companies. No forms to fill out. No privacy issues. We simply had to call the Hampden Telephone Company, which was just a guy and his wife in their own home on their private computer, and they would give us an immediate trace and provide us a telephone number and an address. It was routine, we'd get one or two of these calls per week. You'd barely get the words, "911, what's your emergency?" out of your mouth before the phone hung up. The protocol was to dial the number back and advise the caller that an officer would be stopping by to make certain there was no emergency. Ninety-nine percent of the time it was a simple mistake.

Then there's that other one percent.

It was late afternoon, and my shift was just starting, so Rachel was still in the office, along with the sergeant at his desk in view of dispatch. Two patrolmen were out on the roads. I had just sat down and was being briefed on how mundane the day shift had been. The 911 phone rang, and I picked it up.

"911, what's your…" *click.*

I dialed the phone company and retrieved the name, number, and address of the call. I dialed it back, and someone picked up on the other end. "This is the Hampden Police, you just dialed 911, is there an emer…."

"He's going to kill me!"

So, you don't need the dump hours? No, I wasn't really thinking that, nor did I say that. In fact, I didn't know how to respond to this woman's panicking voice. But the others in the office took notice when I literally jumped to my feet.

"What's going on, ma'am?" I'm certain my voice was elevated, and I was probably shaking a bit with my eyes wide open and scrambling for a pen.

Well, as it turned out, I had a woman on the line who was holding one of her infant children in her arms. At the end of a loaded handgun pointed at her head was her husband with their other infant child in his other arm. It appeared this was the day his wife had told him that she was leaving him for whatever reason, for good, and he apparently didn't take the information well. *Maybe it was the way she said it.*

"Ma'am, I don't suppose I could talk to your husband?" I knew the answer, but it was worth a try.

She had true fear in her voice as she said to her other, and not better, half, "He wants to talk to you," as I'm certain she tried to hold the phone out to him while asking. I didn't quite hear his response, however, she came back, "He doesn't want to talk to you right now." *Great, I'm sure he had plenty to say to his wife a few minutes ago and now I get the silent treatment.*

So, a dilemma. I needed to negotiate with this guy, and he wouldn't take the phone. What the hell was I supposed to do now? I obviously can't just tell her to take her child and leave, that's where she started, and it apparently didn't go over well the first time she tried this.

I quickly wrote down on a piece of paper what was happening as everyone was now looking over my shoulders. Rachel took over the radio and I got as far away from it as possible with what phone cord I had so the woman couldn't hear the radio traffic. The sergeant was already out the door.

During infrequent emergency situations like this, we had the ability to switch other incoming telephone calls directly to the county dispatch center in Bangor, so we didn't have to put people on hold when other calls were coming in. Which, I'm certain, would have been very rude to do to this woman who currently had a loaded handgun pointed at her head. We also had a special ten-code known as a "signal one-thousand" which is transmitted over the primary radio channel. This tells every officer using this channel that there's an emergency that needs radio silence from everyone not involved and to stay off the air. Rachel was taking care of these needs while I remained glued to the caller by phone.

I began to negotiate by proxy. And let me tell you this takes some talent. I needed to talk this guy down through the woman who had threatened to take their children and leave him. And just through experience, I knew the woman's demeanor could switch from fear to anger at any moment and I didn't need her to start yelling at her husband, *"He said to put the goddam gun down, you stupid asshole!"* This probably wouldn't have gone over well.

I told the woman to remain calm. Luckily for me, the children weren't crying, and right now he wasn't telling her to hang up the telephone and he hadn't yanked the phone wires from the wall yet. Over the next several minutes, through her to him, I picked up more of the story and his overall train of thought. He knew she was leaving, and he obviously didn't want her to leave. He also wasn't letting the children go with her. And he realized that he was up shit creek because the police were coming to arrest him for the threats he had made to her life. Oh, and the whole loaded gun to her head thing. Yeah, that was a biggie.

I had his wife tell him that the police were outside of the residence, and they wanted him to put the gun down and come out of the house. Not happening. I had her ask him to put the child down. Also not happening. I did get her to use his first name each time I relayed a request, a tactic to start a more personal connection between us, and more importantly, between her and him. If it works, he'll begin to calm down and become easier to reason with. She did this. I was carrying on a full conversation through her almost as if she wasn't there, which worked to a certain degree. I had to be careful what I said to make it clear that I was speaking to him and not his wife speaking to him, and that it was my words and not hers. It had to have been the most bizarre negotiation to ever have taken place.

Rachel kept the officers on the scene informed by radio. The officers had staged around the residence at safe distances and with cover in case gunplay began. It wasn't long before our Chief and officers from other agencies were on scene, all waiting, and no one attempting to take over the talks, so apparently, I was doing something right. I mean there were infants involved, and this guy, if angry enough, could do anything at this point. None of us wanted this to end up a murder-suicide situation, especially with little ones involved.

After twenty minutes or so, to everyone's surprise, especially mine, I managed to talk him into putting the gun down. Through her, I convinced him to place it on a bed in the next room while still in his sight. This was the best I could do for now to at least get the gun out of his hands, he just needed the ability to see it and have it close enough to get to if he felt he needed it. She confirmed to me the gun was not in his hands and was in the other room for now.

He still had one of the kids in his arm, but now the other hand was free. "Ask him to please take the phone now."

"John, David says please take the phone now," I heard her say calmly. And another surprise, he did. Holy smokes! Now I could speak directly to this scumbag without an interpreter.

One of the most difficult things I found in my career in law enforcement was pretending to make friends with the dirtbags of the earth that I had to deal with. You have to become a tremendously good actor and actually make these people think you're on their side. And let me make it clear, I've *never* been on their side. I just need to get the job done as safely as possible and protect innocent lives in the process. I didn't like this guy at all, but I couldn't let him know that.

"Hello?" He spoke once I finally had him on the line.

"John? How's it going?" I casually inquired.

"Not so good." I could hear the pathetic "poor me" tone in his voice.

We began a calm, rather cordial conversation. I needed to get across the seriousness of the situation he'd caused without getting him excited again. The gun was still too close, and things could turn back to crap very quickly.

"You know you're going to need to come out of the house, don't you, John?"

"I can't."

"Why not?"

"The cops will beat me to the ground."

Okay, I'm not saying that the police at that point wouldn't put him to the ground hard, especially if he put up any resistance. Not to mention the danger he'd put a woman and two infant children in. Police are human, too, with families and children. This stuff makes us mad, and we have adrenalin that needs to be released; we just have to learn to control it better than most. But the reality, which John didn't understand, was that if he came out quietly and did exactly what the officers told him, then he was going to be fine and remain unharmed.

"John, you need to come outside," I calmly said.

"No, I can't, they'll hurt me."

This went back and forth for a brief period of time until I couldn't let this go on any longer. At some point, this guy is going to work himself up again thinking he's in for a fight with the police, or maybe he thinks he won't come out of this alive and we're back to the worst-case scenario again.

"John, do you still have your kid in your arms?" I knew he did. And I knew that part of his motivation was to not lose his kids.

"Yes, I have my son."

"What's his name? How old is he?"

"Mack, he's almost a year."

"Bring him out with you."

"What?" A surprised tone.

"Bring him out with you. The cops won't tackle you with a kid in your arms. They got kids, too, John."

"I can do that?"

"They got kids, too, John, little ones like yours. They won't hurt you with Mack in your arms. Bring Mack out with you. Just walk out, John."

After a long and tedious pause, I heard the words I was looking for, "Okay."

This guy wasn't even thinking about the gun now, or his wife, just his kid. Just the one child he had in his arms that was going to save him from taking a beating and possibly his life. And the cops were now people to him, not just a uniform with a badge. I waved my hand at Rachel. I knew she was on to what was happening now. She radioed the officers and told them he was coming out unarmed with a kid in his arms and not to rush him. Moments later the next radio transmission we heard was, "*One in custody.*"

Smiles and cheers from the room, which had filled up without me even being aware of it with fire, ambulance, and others associated with the department. I slumped down in my chair, exhausted from brain overload and I was finally breathing normally again. People patted my shoulders and told me what a great job I'd done, and everyone in the room felt good about themselves, and the world for a moment. I just wanted a rest. Wasn't it Miller time or something?

The reality was my shift had still only just begun. The next 911 call was someone asking about the dump hours.

◆ ◆ ◆

One of the officers who worked for the Hampden Police Department had a K-9, a German Shepherd named Ninja. Now I truly like police dogs, they're excellent protection and they can sniff out drugs like it's a candy-coated bone. Ninja was a great K-9 partner for Officer Don Brewer, his owner.

Now Ninja was a friendly dog. Well, friendly when Don was right beside him anyway. If Don walked out of the room for any reason and left Ninja alone with you, watch out. In fact, Don couldn't let Ninja out of his sight for this reason alone. If you were left in the room with Ninja alone, you'd better not move or even breathe. One twitch and you saw teeth and heard growling. Stand up from your chair and you become a doggie snack. Don couldn't leave Ninja's side for any reason.

I watched one of Ninja's training sessions. The trainer wore a "red man suit" which is a full-body suit made of thick, red foam padding. The trainer acts as a suspect and pretends to run from the dog's master or pretends to threaten the master. Don then uses a verbal command, which had to be a word out of the normal, that keyed Ninja to attack the suspect. Think about it, if the command was an everyday word, like "hotdog," every trip to the town's lunch wagon could be deadly for the guy who's squirting mustard on your Oscar Myer.

Don's keyword for Ninja was *Fass*, German for "attack." When Don gave the command, it was a good thing that red man suit was thick because Ninja was all over this guy, charging up to and knocking him down hard, sinking his teeth in, and ripping out pieces of foam until Don yelled *Platz*, which is German for "down." It was an impressive sight. Even with the foam suit on, this had to have hurt a little, or maybe a lot.

Don had Ninja commonly ride in the back seat of the cruiser unless a prisoner had to ride there, then the poor schmuck got to watch Ninja staring at him from the front seat, drooling and just hoping that Don would give the command for "lunchtime." It was probably a good thing the K-9 vehicle had a steel mesh cage between the front and back seats, not that this was going to stop Ninja.

I was dispatching one evening shift, and Don was working the road. Also out on the road in a separate cruiser was Jeremy Logan, another one of our patrolmen.

Don had stopped a vehicle with a male driver, probably in his early twenties, and his equally young girlfriend passenger. Now, both had been consuming a few beverages of an alcoholic nature that day. No, I'm not going to use the term *"hair of the dog that bit you."* Not yet at least.

Don proceeded to get the driver out of the vehicle to perform Standard Field Sobriety tests on him. These are standardized divided attention tests like walking in a straight line and standing on one foot type of stuff to check to see if the driver is intoxicated and shouldn't be operating the vehicle Don was performing these tests on the roadside in front of the guy's vehicle with Don's cruiser just behind the dude's car.

In the meantime, Jeremy hears the call. You see, when an officer says on the radio, "I'll be out doing tests," it's a signal to any other officer in the area that you've got a potential drunk on the roadside and other officers should respond automatically for safety reasons. So, Jeremy drives over and parks his cruiser behind Don's and is supposed to stand by in the event someone gets out of hand, or at the very least provide a bit of safety on the roadside so the officer who's performing the tests can concentrate on the field testing rather than the traffic going by. On this occasion, instead of getting out of his car to watch out for Don, Jeremy looks to see that this guy is complying, and he takes the opportunity to get comfortable in his cruiser and chat with another officer that he knows is working in Bangor this night on another radio frequency. So, Jeremy puts his seat back and switches the radio channels. *Great idea.*

And to be fair, the dude was complying and trying to perform the tests for Don to the best of his drunken abilities. The problem was that this was apparently interrupting the girlfriend's plans for the evening because she proceeds to get out of the car and starts giving Don crap for wasting their time. *Another bad idea.*

Now interrupting an officer in the midst of performing his duties was not on the menu for Don that evening, nor was it ever tolerated. Don proceeds to tell the young lady to get back in her car, all the while the boyfriend is trying to apologize to the officer for her behavior because drunk or not, he knew she wasn't helping his current situation at all. Unfortunately for everyone, she didn't heed the warning. In fact, her attitude worsened, and Don was forced to threaten to arrest her, and an argument began between the two.

Three cars down Jeremy is apparently oblivious to the confrontation taking place, busy with his feet up on the dash, staring at the ceiling, and carrying on a radio conversation with his buddy in Bangor. Because Jeremy was three cars back and busy running his mouth on the radio, he wasn't hearing any of the ruckus taking place.

Don quickly grew tired of arguing with the girlfriend and by this time had enough evidence to know that he was going to arrest the guy for DUI, a.k.a. "driving under the influence." And he knew the faster he got this guy in cuffs, the faster he could deal with Little Miss Attitude. Well, telling the man he was under arrest definitely wasn't what the girlfriend wanted to hear at all because as Don was trying to cuff the guy up, she decided to leap onto Don's back, literally. Now she wasn't the heaviest woman, in fact, she was quite skinny but tiny or not when she landed on Don's back, it threw him into the drunk boyfriend who was being arrested, and all three went tumbling to the ground. The arrestee went down face first into a mud puddle with Don second on top of him and Skinny Minnie on Don's back with her tiny arms around Don's neck. Don was an unwilling cop sandwich, complete with mud gravy.

This was quite a site with the girl calling Don names he may or may not have heard before while Don is yelling for her to get off his back, and while still trying to put this guy in cuffs. Plus, the arrestee was still trying to drunkenly apologize while blowing bubbles in the mud puddle.

Jeremy was busy telling his third bad joke to his buddy on the radio while staring up at the ceiling of the cruiser, trying to get the seat to lean back further for maximum comfort and relaxation. And it also wasn't uncommon for Ninja to be barking anytime Don was out of his car on a traffic stop, so the fact that Ninja was going nuts in Don's cruiser and trying to eat his way through the dashboard to help his master went totally unnoticed by Jeremy and just added to the fact that Jeremy was oblivious to the entire situation taking place. Meanwhile, in dispatch, another off-duty officer, Jackson Lombardo, had stopped in to chat with me. I had to interrupt our conversation for a patrol check. As I mentioned earlier, when an officer was out on a traffic stop and we hadn't heard anything from them after several minutes, we were to do a patrol check and repeat them every three minutes thereafter to make certain the officer continued to remain safe. It had been several minutes since hearing from Don.

"Dispatch to Hampden Four, all set?"

Silence.

"Dispatch to Hamden Four, all set?"

Silence. Not that Don could answer me. He was currently in the middle of a muddy battle and couldn't get to his radio with one hand busy holding the guy down and the other hand trying to swat the oversized ladybug off his back that was currently trying to choke him out. Several more tries were all met with radio silence.

"Dispatch to Hampden Five?" Not that Jeremy could answer. He was busy in la-la-land on another frequency and couldn't hear anything that I was transmitting over our primary channel.

Lombardo and I were beginning to get a little worried. It wasn't uncommon for an officer to not immediately respond to a patrol check, especially if they were busy administering field tests, but holy crap, we had two officers on the scene, and no one was answering.

This triggered Lombardo into action, and he was on his way out the door just as Don was finally able to key the mike and we heard him yell for the first time, *"Jesus Christ would someone please come get this skinny drunk bitch off my back!"*

Well, this was odd, Don didn't usually swear on the radio. Now the problem was that the person closest to the scene, Jeremy, never heard this and continued to lounge in his car talking to officer so-and-so about the barbeque they were planning for the weekend.

It didn't take Lombardo long to get to Don's location. However, it wasn't until Lombardo's cruiser arrived on the scene sliding sideways past Jeremy, lights and siren wailing, and smoke coming from the brakes locking up, that finally gave Jeremy the hint that something might be awry up ahead.

Lombardo leaped from his cruiser and in seeing what appeared to be quite the battle, he decided to let Ninja, who was going absolutely nuts foaming at the mouth and chewing the cruiser to pieces, out from the car to do his stuff on the two who seemingly appeared to have Don down on the ground.

Jeremy was still struggling to get his seat back in the upright position, so he could begin to get out of his cruiser.

Convinced that Ninja would protect Don and make mincemeat of the two drunks, Lombardo opened the door to Don's cruiser, and Ninja jumped out like a cheetah. Never hesitating, the dog immediately turned around and bit Lombardo right on the ass. Ninja, in his over-excited state, had decided to attack the nearest target, which was Officer Lombardo's rear end.

When Jeremy was finally able to do his version of the worm dance and got out of the cruiser, he ran past Lombardo, who was desperately trying to get Ninja's teeth out of his bum and screaming in pain, and he pulled Skinny Minnie off Don's back. All the while Lombardo continued to be busy screaming and trying to pry a seventy-seven-pound thrashing and growling bear trap off his ass.

With the woman finally off him and arrested, Don was finally able to finish cuffing up the drunk fellow while yelling the command for Ninja to let go of Lombardo's butt cheek.

All three officers eventually arrived back at the station after making their deposits at the county jail. Don, looking quite tired and very muddy and dirty. Jeremy, who was still relatively clean as he hadn't really done much, and Lombardo, who was limping and had a big chunk of pants missing along with some skin from his butt cheek.

Ah, the good old days. ♦

CHAPTER 3

MY TURN

I was a couple of years into being a dispatcher and beginning to get more of an interest in the action on the road rather than just sitting in the dispatch chair, so I decided to put myself through the Maine Criminal Justice Academy's reserve officer training program. The academy had a full twelve-week training program for prospective full-time police officers, which later by the time I went through had evolved into an eighteen-week program. They also had the lesser forty-hour in-service program for those only seeking part-time police work, which in later years would turn into a 380-hour program. The primary difference in the training was that part-timers weren't allowed to handle major crimes, only minor ones, and really when it comes right down to it, could only perform basic traffic duties and associated traffic crimes. Part-timers in Maine could only work a total of 1,500 hours per year total, no matter how many local departments they were hired onto. Still, there was a demand for part-time staff. They could work full shifts, and they cost less overall and assisted in making up the gaps when departments were short-staffed.

To get into the reserve academy, an agency had to sponsor the prospective officer. My sponsor was obviously Hampden, and I paid for the schooling myself, which was standard practice. Agencies didn't feel like putting money into reserve officers, only full-time staff, even though they needed the benefit of the part-timers, too. The schooling was easy and had no physical requirements like the full academy had. Now, at the time I was in pretty good shape, but there were some fat slobs that managed to get their "green pin," a term for part-timers. As opposed to a "blue pin," a slang term for full-time officers in Maine that refers to the color of the graduation pin you get to wear on your uniform representing what level of training you have. A green pin is the bottom of the barrel in the grand scheme of academy training and of being an officer. Well, shortly thereafter I had my green pin and was ready to experience what was happening on the other end of the radio.

◆ ◆ ◆

Terry Lowe was the senior full-time officer in Hampden who had never been promoted and for good reason. He was certifiably insane, and I say that in a nice way. Actually, I liked the guy. He was a relatively short fellow in his late forties and had a bad attitude that came with a big ego, which we commonly referred to as "little-man syndrome." This is when you're shorter than five-foot-five but still act like you're six feet tall. He carried a six-shot wheel gun at a time when most officers were switching over to semi-autos. The department had four cruisers, two Ford LTDs, and one Volvo 240 with hard plastic headrests that were guaranteed to cause you a head injury and severe whiplash in the event of an accident. That car was primarily driven by the duty sergeant. Lastly, one older Dodge Diplomat P.O.S. that was assigned to Terry. The only cruiser to be *assigned* to an officer in Hampden.

The Dodge had the highest maintenance budget, not due to age but due to how Terry drove it. As a new part-time officer, I was warned never to ride with Terry, never! I thought at first that no one wanted to partner up with him because of his overall attitude and that he generally didn't like anyone. That is anyone, except me for some reason. I think it was because we had similar work ethics, and as a dispatcher, I watched out for all the officers on the road. I didn't just sit at the dispatch desk and watch late-night cable or fully fall asleep as some did. I made certain the officers heard from me fairly often to primarily check on their safety. I did the patrol checks. I'd make certain to radio the officers often just to make sure they responded back and were generally still alive and unharmed. The general rule was even if the officers weren't on a call, if we didn't hear from them after an hour, we performed three tries on the patrol check because, you know, they too might be sleeping in their cruisers as well. If we didn't get a response, we were to find them using any means possible including sending other duty officers to look or, if alone, calling out the duty sergeant to start looking. I did more than my share of patrol checks and more often than just once an hour. I also asked callers for more information than just the basic stuff and got my officers extra help when the situation called for it without them having to request it first. Terry appreciated that someone other than himself was watching out for his safety, even with his piss-poor attitude.

Terry also simply didn't like people riding with him, so when I asked if I could ride along one night, I was generally surprised when he said yes. Now, remember I'd been warned and had ignored the red flags being hurled at me beforehand. Everyone had told me not to ride with Terry. Not heeding the warnings, I found out why the hard way.

To begin with, I quickly found out why the high maintenance costs on the Dodge. Terry not only didn't drive the speed limit, but I also truly believe he was practicing for his next career as a NASCAR driver. Speed limit and safety of others were two phrases that Terry didn't bother to familiarize himself with. In fact, no matter what the speed limit signs said, Terry would add about fifty to it. Maybe he was dyslexic. Maybe for every twenty-five mile-per-hour zone sign, he saw fifty-two. Maybe fifty-five confused him, and he added the two together to make "110." Either way, he drove like a maniac.

Terry also didn't know the meaning of the phrases "town limits" or "jurisdiction" because I don't believe we patrolled Hampden at all that night. Terry lived several towns away in the small village of Dixmont and he liked to patrol between Hampden and Dixmont, which wasn't where we were supposed to be. He also liked to see how fast he could get to Dixmont, which was seventeen miles from the Hampden town line, and Terry could do it in about seven minutes. And we're not talking straight roads to get there. When he'd come up on a sharp turn, Terry would turn the headlights out and explain that he knew he was going so fast that he had a hard time keeping the car in his own lane, so he wanted to know if there was another car coming at him in the turns. So, he turned off his headlights to see if he could see their lights before he rounded the turn and hit them head-on. *Thank goodness for that explanation.* I'm sure there was logic in there somewhere, to Terry anyway.

Terry also said that if we did leave the roadway on one of the turns and wrecked the car, *and* if either of us were still alive to talk about it, we were to somehow get the cruiser up against the tallest tree in Hampden and make it look like the accident occurred within town limits, so if he was still alive, he wouldn't get fired for being out of town on duty. *Again, superior logic from a madman.* Like anything would be left of the car, or us, to get it back to town if that happened.

I had no way to express my disagreement with how he was driving due to the inability to speak at all from the zero-G force Terry was creating in the car at those top speeds. Not to mention I was clutching the dashboard so tightly that my fingertips were probably causing indentations like some cheap movie gag. He didn't have to worry about anyone complaining to the chief about his speed or patrolling outside of town due to the fact that he was going so fast, you couldn't read the name of the police department on the side of the car when he flew by. I was going to have permanent PTSD after this ride and probably would need long-term therapy.

The only time Terry slowed down was to stop a car for a traffic violation, including speeding. What a hypocrite. Issuing a ticket for someone doing ten over when we were well into double digits beyond the limit at any given moment was just wrong!

When Terry did finally mellow out, sort of, is when he headed for *his* spot. There was one road in town, the Monroe Road, where Terry liked to sit and wait for cars to come to him. It was a rural road nicknamed the "Lowe Zone" after Terry. The road was a few miles long coming out of town and continued into the next town of Winterport. Terry would find a place to tuck in and shut the car down, all lights off, and wait. If a car was speeding past or had a headlight out or whatnot, he'd stop it. There was no secrecy to it. If you were from the area, you knew about Terry and the "Lowe Zone."

Terry also didn't use a radar device, even though the cruiser was equipped with one. Terry used a tactic known as "speed estimating" whereas if you suspect a vehicle is traveling over the limit, you follow them for a distance, keeping a consistent space between the cruiser and the suspect vehicle, and watch your own speedometer to determine how fast the car in front of you is going. If Terry determined they were traveling above the limit, he'd stop them. *Again, hypocrite.*

So, there we sat in the Zone, in the dark, tucked just off the road so we could see both directions and waited for violators. I was just happy to not be traveling fast enough to break the sound barrier at this point, so I was enjoying the few brief moments of silence. After a few minutes and a few vehicles that were lucky enough to make safe passage through the Zone without incident, a vehicle came towards us with a headlight out and was obviously moving fairly fast.

Terry started the cruiser, and as soon as the vehicle passed by us, he pulled out. As usual, he slammed the gas pedal to the floor to catch up to the car, but he didn't turn any cruiser lights on, including the headlights. We were now traveling at high speed completely in the dark to catch up to them.

"Terry, turn your lights on."

"Not yet."

He quickly caught up to the speeding car and was way too close to their rear bumper, again without our emergency or any other lights on. The occupants in front of us were completely oblivious to the fact that in the darkness behind them, there was a police cruiser right on their hind end. Terry stayed glued to their backside and still had no lights on, traveling at the same high speeds they were.

"Terry, turn the lights on!"

"Not yet." An insane grin now on his face with only one hand on the wheel and the other down by the master switch on the control box in the center console that turns all the emergency equipment on at once, but still no lights yet. He looked over at me and uttered an evil giggle through an insane smirk. *Why didn't I heed the warnings?*

"Terry, turn the lights on!"

"Not yet," he sang in a high tone with a full sadistic smile on his face now. I was now totally convinced at this point that Terry was a full-blown lunatic.

Any closer and the two speeding vehicles would have mated, and still the driver nor the passengers in front of us, had any idea that we were behind them, and they certainly were unaware that an obviously escaped mental patient was driving this police car and about to give them the scare of their lives.

"Terry! Turn the goddam lights on!" I was truly terrified at this point for a number of reasons.

Suddenly, out of the darkness, Terry toggled the switch and activated every light on the cruiser. High beams, blues on the light bar, wig-wag strobes, flashing blues in the grill, and the wailing siren. The occupants in front of us must have all crapped themselves simultaneously when out of the darkness came the explosion of lights and sirens occurring behind them as the driver locked up his brakes and began to fishtail uncontrollably in the road, which caused Terry to have to perform a serpentine as well, braking and swerving in opposite directions to avoid crashing into their rear end. Both cars must have looked like a giant snake in the road with a bright, colorful tail. After several hundred yards of tire screeching, the two cars came to a stop in the middle of the road, one pointing left and the other pointing right. There was tire and brake smoke along with the road dust slowly rising from both vehicles and the wailing siren slowly whining down until all was quiet, except for the faint sound of the flickering blue lights.

I had no words and was just staring blankly, wide-eyed at Terry as he nonchalantly shifted the tired transmission into park, put his police hat on, reached for his flashlight, and exited the cruiser. He swaggered to the driver's window of his suspect to ask this poor schmuck, who was probably in the midst of a cardiac arrest, for his license, registration, and proof of insurance.

Now the best part. As the driver, whose hands were shaking uncontrollably, reaches over to get his registration from his glove compartment, he forgets that he has a loaded handgun inside of it. Not an uncommon occurrence, however, you should probably tell the officer before you reach into the glove box that there's a gun in there. The obvious problem was this guy was still in shock and simply forgot.

So, when Terry sees this guy's hand reach into the box next to the gun, he takes out his big wheel gun, sticks the barrel straight into this poor guy's ear, and yells, "FREEZE, OR I'LL BLOW YOUR HEAD OFF!" His voice was loud enough to be heard in the next county. It even made me jump in my seat. I can't imagine the effect on everyone in that car who just experienced an unidentified flying police cruiser scare the bejeezus out of them, and now the driver who's sporting a .45 caliber earring, courtesy of an insane cop with his hand on the trigger.

I almost immediately radioed for an ambulance because I knew by the end of the night someone was going to need one. And at this point, I'm thinking it might be Terry who'd be taken away in a straitjacket to the nearest rubber room. Luckily, the driver eased his shaking hand away from the glove box and Terry slowly removed the stainless-steel appendage from his ear.

Terry ultimately was able to get the guy's license and other information and he took the guy's gun. *Great, now this lunatic has two loaded guns.* He swaggered back to the cruiser, the same evil grin on his face and the same evil giggle as he got in and sat back in his seat. This lunatic was enjoying this way too much.

Handing me the driver's license, and just as calm as a cucumber, he asked, "You wanna check his license through dispatch?" *No, I want to lock you up using your own handcuffs and drive you back to the state mental hospital you escaped from and collect my reward!*

The license came back clean, active with no warrants. The gun was checked. Registered, not stolen. Terry wrote a ticket on the broken headlight and a warning for the speed. He swaggered back, issued the paperwork, and gave the still-shaking driver his gun back, this time unloaded with the magazine out. Good call on his part because this guy might just have been to the point of shooting Terry if I had to guess. Either that or he was just happy to be alive. I'm also quite certain they weren't planning on visiting Hampden again anytime soon. The driver took his paperwork and thanked the officer cautiously. Still in total fear for their lives, they drove away slowly.

Terry got back in the cruiser. We checked the time; our shift was over. We returned to the station. I got in my car, started it, rolled down the window, and thanked Terry cautiously. Still in fear for my life, I drove away toward home quickly.

I also never rode with Terry again.

There was once a photograph in the police station pinned to the wall that was taken as a joke one evening as we were booking in evidence. It was of me sitting in a beater car we'd impounded for one reason or another. I had a helmet on my head that I found in the car, smiling at the camera and giving a thumbs-up. The caption someone wrote on the photo read, "I survived the Lowe Zone." There was so much truth to that that most wouldn't understand.

I wonder if the photo still exists. ♦

CHAPTER 4

NOT QUITE READY

It was around 1993 that talks began about the consolidation of emergency dispatch centers into one centralized location within the county. I wasn't thrilled with the idea as about a year earlier I had become the dispatch supervisor for Hampden quite unexpectedly. In a tragic accident, we lost Rachel to a fire in her home, so for no reason other than I had done my job well, I was named the dispatch supervisor. And, here again, the idea of starting over and working for a communications center in another town wasn't on my agenda.

I also wasn't quite to the point where I felt I was ready to become a cop full-time, and to this day, I'm glad I made that decision. The truth was I was still too young and immature to be a good police officer. And I hate to say it, but there are very few in their early twenties who are mature enough to make the decisions that a police officer must make on a daily basis. To this day, I'm glad I waited, maybe not to the age that I did finally choose it as a career, but I believe at least until we're old enough to carry loaded weapons and use the common sense that others more mature than us have, and try to instill upon us. We should all wait until the appropriate time to enter into these types of careers.

However, as coincidence would have it, the Town of Hampden was looking to hire a Director of Public Welfare in the municipal office. Well there, I'd be able to deal with the same people that I'd been dealing with as a dispatcher, and I'd have the ability to continue as a part-time cop. And with that comes an opinion, so brace yourselves.

I don't like people who use the local public welfare system. There, I said it. Now if you're still reading, allow me to elaborate. I'll admit there are those who run on hard times or are having trouble getting ahead, and they need a form of temporary assistance to get by. These are the people who are completely willing and will work for their public assistance. Additionally, if given the opportunity, they'll accept a job and do their best at it. And then there are those who live off the welfare system. These types don't want to work, refuse to work, and feel that others should be working to take care of them. They wouldn't even know how to do a hard day's work if someone did it for them. They think the world owes them a favor and they spend their time praying on others and making excuses for themselves.

So, with this attitude in mind, I was perfect for the job! Now the local public assistance program, or General Assistance, is the last stop on the welfare train. This was where you ended up if every other avenue for other public and state assistance had run out. And there were strict guidelines if you bothered to follow them. Very few received assistance if both the client and towns were playing by the rules, even if they were eligible for the taxpayer dollars that directly funded this program.

Unfortunately, the previous person who held this title had been handing out vouchers like they were Halloween candy. I was hired with the understanding that I would work to get the program under control without denying clients for unjust reasons. So, other than the easy out, which was the fact that the income guidelines were beneath the actual poverty level and that denying clients because they earned too much money was fairly common, plus the fact that if they'd been fired from a job or denied any other public assistance meant they weren't eligible for the local program, I had to develop other avenues to get the budget under control. The problem was that most of these lazy jerks didn't *earn* any money to begin with. Most had the system down, they received monthly food stamps for their cigarettes and beer, free heating oil, free health coverage, free transportation, and free food. That's if they even lived on their own and not with their parents.

Believe it or not, the state finally had to put an actual cap on how many children of unwed mothers they'd pay for because these women would pop out a kid on a yearly basis just to get more cash from the state. No joke, people, this actually occurred quite regularly. Not to mention, couples would lie about their marital status and whether or not the useless boyfriends were living in the household because if so, they'd generally lose their eligibility or at least have it reduced. State medical programs were free for freeloaders while retirees still had to pay for their medical insurance. It was all a game, a game I didn't agree with, and a game I wasn't about to lose.

My nickname around the office was "Cleopatra, the Queen of Denial." One of my co-workers got a chuckle sticking me with this nickname because I basically denied everyone or found a reason to deny them soon after their application was completed. Very few saw vouchers, or at least vouchers that didn't come with strict rules that they wouldn't follow anyway.

At that time, the state was trying out a program called Workfare. This was basically a welfare-to-work program for the local-level assistance programs. The workfare program was optional for towns to institute or not, and most didn't for a number of reasons. Some because they simply didn't want the headache of another program to oversee. Some were worried about what would happen if the client injured themselves. Some claimed to have no work for them. Well, guess what, I was going to make these people work! I created the town's first workfare program. The idea was if you needed the assistance and were found eligible, you had to work off the hours for the municipality at a dollar-per-hour value for each hour worked. The value for each hour couldn't be below the state's minimum wage, and you could require them to work up to the value of their monthly allotment. Not only this, but you could also require anyone in the eligible household to perform the work, so the lazy boyfriends who'd send their girlfriends in to apply. Yup, I could make them do the work, too.

And here's the best part, these people rarely, if ever, showed up. Remember, these people generally applied for assistance because they didn't want to work. They wanted something for nothing. Now I was making them work. How dare I? And even better, the program was built to be work-first. They had to work off their allotment before receiving it. *Oh, my goodness, I'm a tyrant! I'm actually making people work for their paycheck!* It was too funny.

In my first year, I cut the welfare budget for the town by more than half. And to be fair, there were those again who needed the assistance and were totally willing to perform the work to earn it. We even had a guy who, at the conclusion of his workfare for the town, was hired full-time in maintenance. He had the skills and the determination, he was just down on his luck and earned a job from it. He even paid the town back for the monies we'd granted to him through the program. This was one of the rare success stories from the program.

And then there was this case…

I was gaining a reputation as a hard-ass from the Maine Department of Human Services. The state DHS set the guidelines for the local general assistance program and was the overseer, so whenever someone didn't like my decision on their case, they had the option of complaining to the state.

So, whenever I denied someone, I'd usually get a telephone call from the program's rep, which usually began with, "Whad'ya do now, Dave?" There were many calls.

Like the guy who was a known drug dealer living in town who came to apply for assistance, and I denied him for not reporting his "extra" income. Yeah, I got a call on that one. Or the girl who applied, and I discovered her live-in boyfriend had a warrant for his arrest. I assigned him workfare at the police department, and the dumb schmuck actually showed up. He ended up in pretty bracelets and a place to stay for the night. Yup, got a call on that one, too.

My usual response was, "Show me in the manual where I can't do that." I usually won the argument when they couldn't come up with a reason why I shouldn't do such things. Although I'm certain the rule book experienced a few revisions because of me.

But this next case made me famous in the field. For years after, I'd be well-known for this one in the world of public welfare.

I denied public assistance to a dead guy.

The young couple had lived in Hampden for some time and were gaining a reputation as welfare junkies. They had applied time and time again and were abusers of the system. They had even stooped to the level of claiming their young children were suffering from Attention Deficit Disorder in order to apply for disability on the children's behalf when in reality the children were simply nasty little brats being taught so by their parents. This was, and is, a pretty common theme for useless parents to claim their children have disabilities for two reasons. One was for the monthly disability checks that the parents failed at scoring for themselves but could get on behalf of their kids. Secondly, they could get ADHD drugs, like Ritalin, which was basically over-the-counter cocaine for their kids and either use it themselves or sell it on the streets for cash. I've seen it all too many times.

So as dumb luck would have it for this couple, they did score a disability check for one of the three kids in the household. Not only this, but the check was retroactive to the tune of about $10,000. Talk about winning the welfare lottery. So, immediately this was apparent when they moved into a better apartment, Rent-A-Center showed up with all new furniture and two new-used cars parked in their yard. After I found this out, there was no more local welfare from me, even though they did have the nerve to try right after they got their big check. *I've said many times that if criminals would just try as hard on a real job as they do in trying to break the law or work the system, they'd be very successful in life.*

A couple of months following this, the woman's brother was released from the state prison in Thomaston and moved in with the family. Now this guy, by all definitions, was a transient because he had no permanent home other than jail and technically transients were eligible for local welfare if they met the criteria.

Now this guy was released in the morning, and that first evening he was at his sister's apartment, he sits down at the dinner table, rests his elbows on the table, puts his head in his hands…and dies. Yes, right there at the table, he ceases to exist. The only, well, I say only problem was that nobody in the house noticed that he was dead, no joke. This dysfunctional family has dinner with the stiff, leaves him there, goes to bed, gets up the next morning, and has breakfast at the table with him again…and lunch! Around the time for the next dinner, a whole twenty-four hours after he croaks, someone starts to notice that Uncle Salty (*not his real name*) is tilting a little to the left and smells worse than normal. Finally, he tipped over into the evening bowl of potato stew.

When the police arrived, they asked the family how they didn't notice that this guy was dead? The brother-in-law responds, "Well, he was an asshole anyway, so we just thought he was ignoring us." This is a true story, folks. Have you ever heard the saying, "You can't make this stuff up?" Well, it's one-hundred percent true, you simply can't.

So, because this guy was fresh out of Tommy-Town, a slang term for the state prison in Thomaston, foul play was a consideration. The medical examiner loaded him up and took him to the state medical facility in Augusta for an autopsy. More to come on this in a bit.

The next day, the brother-in-law and his wife show up in my office asking for burial assistance on behalf of Mr. Dead Guy (*again, not his real name*). Well, the rules say, transient or not, if there's money in the family the application, which is made out on behalf of the deceased, is denied. And I was onto their game. I obviously recalled the disability settlement, and I denied the request immediately. At that point, I thought I was done with this case.

I was wrong.

As it turned out, the sister's mother had passed away a year prior and these two losers had failed to pay the local funeral home for the high-priced service the mother had received. The Hampden Funeral Home, operated by a gentleman named Gary, wasn't about to get *stiffed* again by this couple. Gary had not only refused to perform this funeral, but he had also called all the other local funeral homes within a hundred-mile radius and told them not to touch this dead guy as well. Several days passed without hearing anything on the matter when I got a call from my buddies at the Department of Human Services. It seemed the couple had decided to call the state and complain about my denial when they found that no one was going to perform the funeral that they were obviously unwilling to, and now had a reputation for not paying for.

"Why aren't you paying for the burial, Dave?"

"The stiff's unwilling to cooperate."

I could hear the heavy sigh on the other end of the phone. This was the usual immediate response. "I know I'm going to regret this question, but what do you mean by the *deceased* is unwilling to cooperate?"

"He refuses to sign the forms."

Another sigh, "You're not funny."

"He refused to come to my office. He wouldn't verbally answer my questions over the phone. He wouldn't shake my hand. He just kept staring into space through the entire interview, very rude."

"Again, not funny."

"How about the family who's applied on his behalf just received a lump-sum disability check for ten-thousand dollars?"

"That works."

The problem now being explained to me was that the stiff was starting to stink, now being a week dead, and the state medical examiner apparently needed the freezer space. The state rep explained that they may have to ask me nicely, a.k.a. force me, to pay for the burial where he was technically a transient and someone had to bury the guy. Not to mention the state had the ability to mandate that I do this through the program. The state enjoyed flexing its muscles in this way at times, and I knew it.

I spent the next two days trying desperately to give away a dead body. I called the university and asked if they needed a cadaver for whatever it was that they used cadavers for in their medical department. They asked how long the guy had been dead. When I told them a week, they turned me down. It seemed that a cadaver for the medical interns needs to be *fresh*, or it's of no use to them. I wasn't certain what the definition of "fresh" was, but I was fairly certain at this point that Febreze wasn't an option.

Less than forty-eight hours later I got a call back from the rep at the state advising me that their decision was to have the town pay for the disposal of the body. As unhappy as I was about this, I was in no position to try to fight this battle. The powers that be were issuing a decision that I couldn't argue with. I did, however, ask that the town be granted the authority to dispose of the remains in whatever humane way we saw fit. I didn't want there to be any chance that this family could come back on us and say we didn't *honor* the last wishes of the deceased or the family in any way. I also wanted it in writing and signed by someone important. Less than forty-five minutes later, I received a fax in my office, naming me specifically and stating that I could dispose of the remains in any humane way I saw fit. It was unfortunate that the word *humane* showed up on the form. So much for a late-night Burning Man ceremony at the town dump.

I telephoned Gary at the funeral home and asked him for a package deal, reassuring him that the town was picking up the tab. Gary offered me a bargain, responding, "I'll go pick up the body from the M.E.'s office and cremate him for seven-hundred." This was like a red coupon day at the crematorium.

"Deal," I responded.

Five days later and I had all but forgotten about the whole ordeal when Gary came walking into my office carrying a small cardboard box tightly wrapped in clear packing tape. He dropped the heavy little package on my desk. *"Thump."*

"What's that?" As if I didn't already surmise.

"That's your boy," Gary said with an all-too-happy grin on his face.

"Wait, what do you mean that's my boy? You said you'd…"

"…I said I'd pick him up and cremate him. I didn't say anything about burying him," Pointing at me like this was my fault. "He's your problem now."

Thanks, jerk.

Great, now I had a dead body, per se, sitting on my desk. What was I supposed to do with him? What would the public think? I couldn't turn him into a set of bookends, I'd need another dead guy for that. I could've wrapped him in gift paper and held onto him for the annual office Secret Santa Christmas gift swap, but everyone would've known it was from me. I couldn't give him away to the next customer who came in to register their car like some sort of door prize. Possibly I could've turned him into a doorstop, except that we had a Labrador Retriever in the office as a mascot, and it would've been bad if he gnawed open the box like it was a chew toy and got ashes everywhere. That might've gotten my name in the local papers, and not in a good way.

About an hour later, the town manager strolled by my desk and noticed the package. She pointed and asked, "What's in that?"

"A dead guy," I said without looking up, I just kept pretending to write notes on a piece of paper.

"Very funny." She almost made it past my desk when she stopped in her tracks. I glanced up and could see the look on her face change when she realized it. She backed up, now scowling, "Get it out of here!" *How disrespectful to the recently departed.*

I put the box in the passenger seat of my car and drove around a bit, giving the deceased one last ride around town and wondering how I was going to dispose of the remains. Local business dumpsters were looking pretty good right about then. I drove to the town's public works department and asked the foreman if he had any suggestions. Not for a moment did he question me or think I was joking, he knew me too well. He thought for a moment and then said that the year earlier when the stiff's mother had passed away, the town crew had dug the grave for the funeral at the town cemetery. He suggested we dig a hole above the mother and drop him in. So that's exactly what we did. No funeral, no fanfare, no marker. With a couple of shovels, we dug a shallow grave over the guy's mother, and in he went. And as far as I know, to this day, the family has never asked where the brother was buried.

Oh, wait, the best part. Several weeks later, I received notification of the autopsy results from the State Medical Examiner's office. I was informed the dearly departed had passed away from an aneurysm to the brain from a severely impacted wisdom tooth he was suffering from. He had sat down at that dinner table, held his head in pain from the toothache, and died.

So fresh out of prison for who knows what and his own mouth, as with many criminals, ultimately did him in. ♦

CHAPTER 5

AND THE REAL JOURNEY BEGINS

It was 1993, and I'd done as much as I felt I could for the town's local welfare program and its budget. I was starting to feel the need to move up the ladder that was leaned up against the private sector and I departed the town of Hampden for bigger and better things. All the while still remaining a part-time officer for various local police departments and doing a lot of volunteer firefighting as well. Spare time wasn't something that I knew the definition of.

I spent the next thirteen years working for various companies in either a supervisory or full administrative capacity, all boring and nothing that I really felt a passion for. Desk jobs just didn't seem to be my thing.

I also had gotten married and divorced during this time. There's not much to say about my first marriage other than it made me a dad to one child, a daughter. The marriage itself from day one was a mistake, and day two didn't get any better. After seven years, I wanted to shoot myself. In fact, the marriage was as mundane as the jobs I was holding, and my ex didn't care to work any more than the welfare clients I'd dealt with in Hampden, so it was as bad to be at home as it was to be at the office.

There were a few perks during this time period. With each new job came more responsibility, and everywhere I went, I quickly worked my way up and achieved status within the various organizations. My business background was getting stronger as well, and due to the types of organizations I'd work for, and my social work skills were strengthening, too. Again, the problem was that the so-called desk jobs bored me to death, and I was moving from company to company quickly, always tiring fast from what I considered thankless work. I had an adrenaline itch, and none of the private sector gigs were scratching it.

Along the journey, Dad had also changed careers. There came a point in the late 1980s when television sets had become maintenance-free, and really it was less expensive to simply buy a new television than it was to repair the old ones. Cathode ray tubes had given way to computer chips, and Dad discovered that he needed to find a new career. So naturally, he became a deputy sheriff for the Penobscot County Sheriff's Department which was located in Bangor. Dad began as a corrections officer at the county jail and later in his career became a bailiff, or officer who stands in court and protects the judge. He spent eighteen years as an officer, and on the day that he retired, my family threw a multi-purpose party. This was also the day that my full-time career in law enforcement was to begin and it, too, was being celebrated. Dad was very proud that day, I could tell. He had thoroughly enjoyed his latter career and was glad to see me finally entering into it.

♦ ♦ ♦

By the year 2000, I had divorced and re-married and was living in Dover-Foxcroft, a town forty miles north of Bangor, and I was doing a lot of part-time work for their police department. I was also working full-time as an administrator for an organization that worked with disabled adults. I was the manager of the program that places developmentally disabled adults in the workforce. I had started as a program manager whose responsibility was to get companies to buy into the idea of having physically and mentally challenged adults working for them. I had proven myself to be very successful at working with larger corporate companies rather than just the mom-and-pop stores and ultimately, they were calling me first to request people when they were experiencing staffing shortages. The success being that I didn't just "place" someone, I made certain the individual was suited and had the ability to perform the job with minimal or no supervision, something the other placement managers weren't doing. Most would just try to develop a site and then didn't care whether the client was suited for the job or not. They were just in it for the numbers and didn't care whether or not the employees worked out, which most didn't. I, on the other hand, had taken the extra time and gained the trust of the businesses that I was working with. This had earned me a spot at the top and ultimately a promotion to manager of the program.

The company I worked for was also big on post-secondary education and offered to pay for college courses. Oddly enough, they didn't care what you were taking for courses, they were simply pro-secondary education. When I asked if they minded if I majored in Criminal Justice, they didn't blink an eye. So, there I was, working primarily in social services and being paid to major in Criminal Justice, go figure. I was thirty-five- years old, working days and taking evening classes. Again, spare time was not in the vocabulary.

I had also, by virtue of working in the private sector for so many years and making my way up various ladders, gained experience in business administration, so my business resume was looking pretty good too. So, becoming a police officer was obviously the next step, right? *Wait, what?*

Yes, it was time to take the plunge into full-time law enforcement.

♦ ♦ ♦

Charles Dennison, the police chief in Dover-Foxcroft, was having trouble getting his newest officer of fewer than two years into the Maine State Criminal Justice Academy due to the fact that the lazy slob couldn't pass the physical entrance requirements. Charles had the same issue with the guy he hired before this one, so he was zero-for-two on the strikeout list with unfit candidates. The state academy would only allow two attempts to pass the entrance standards, after that your career ended, and this was expensive for small-town municipal police departments. Charles needed a candidate that could not only pass the educational requirements but also the physical requirements as well.

The academy was military style with strict entrance and exit standards. Laziness wasn't going to get you through. They were as equally focused on physical fitness as they were on the educational curriculum. The academy, at that time, had been recently extended from twelve to eighteen weeks of hell where you endured long days of rigorous physical, educational, and emotional demands, all designed to prepare you for the stress of being a police officer on the street. It's designed to prepare you physically and mentally to deal with high-stress situations, make you think fast on your feet, and keep you from getting seriously injured or killed. If you couldn't even pass the entrance physical standards, you weren't going to last the eighteen weeks, if even eighteen hours.

I had been working for Charles part-time and had been pulling my fair share of weight in shifts. Charles had been watching how I handled myself as a part-timer, and he felt I had the physical stamina to pass the tests and last through the academy, even though I was thirty-six years old now. He approached me one day and asked me to join his force full-time.

I said no. Let's face it, I had a good-paying job and tenure where I was working, why would I want to earn a cop's pay and put up with all the BS? And I'd be the low man on the totem pole, which also didn't exactly thrill me at the age I was.

A couple of weeks later, Charles approached me again. Again, he asked if I'd join the department as their newest full-time officer. Again, I said no. Even though I was working towards a degree in criminal justice, the idea of attending a military-style academy for eighteen weeks, especially at this age when most guys there are in their early twenties, didn't give me the warm fuzzies.

The third time was a charm. I think it was because Charles was begging at this point, and watching a grown man beg was pathetic. I thought about it, I'd be closer to home than the hour-long commute I had to Bangor each day at that time. I was in good physical shape, and I'd be doing something that I enjoy rather than sitting behind a desk. So, I agreed to begin my new career as a full-time police officer for the Dover-Foxcroft Police Department.

The department had an overnight person already who had no intention of giving up his shift, and this was also a plus because I didn't want to do overnights. The Town of Dover-Foxcroft is a small village with a population on average of 4,200 residents that had only one small combination store and gas station that remained open twenty-four hours a day. Other than that, everything else closed around midnight, so from about 2:00 A.M. on there was nothing happening and too much chance of me falling asleep in the cruiser. I was going to be assigned to the second shift, which was from 3:00 to 11:00 p.m., along with the evening sergeant on duty. This would be a busier shift and more chances to stay awake.

But first I needed to graduate from the Maine Criminal Justice Academy.

◆ ◆ ◆

As I'd mentioned earlier, originally the academy was a twelve-week program until around the turn of the century when it became an eighteen-week program. The curriculum is fairly rigorous in that cadets perform at least eight to ten hours each day of classroom instruction with occasional evening classes. Beginning very early each day are the physical and mental pieces to the program. Not to mention there's a whole secrecy behind the academy. You see, all those who graduate don't want others who come after them to know what they're in for. This was an unwritten credo amongst academy graduates. This was especially true for the dreaded and infamous "fight scenario" that comes around week seventeen. This is when you're required to muster everything you've learned from the sixteen weeks prior, and there's some sort of physical engagement that cadets must participate in, endure, and overcome. The fight was as secretive as the academy itself, and the thought of what it might entail scared the hell out of me and all the cadets. You see, if a cadet refuses to engage or loses the "fight," he or she fails the academy and doesn't graduate. And the worst part is you don't know when your turn is coming. You don't know who your opponent, or opponents, will be, what their limitations are, or how badly you were going to get your own ass whooped as a result. You also didn't know how the fight was scored or what the parameters were for passing. It was all very nerve-wracking to think about and the anticipation, along with the daily stress of the academy itself, was fairly overwhelming and mentally exhausting. And it's meant to be that way on purpose to prepare you to become the best police officer you can be. The academy prepares you to handle stress, exhaustion, anger, and physical encounters.

The grounds of the academy are fairly impressive. Built in 1828, it was once a school for boys as a precursor to college. It's nicknamed the "castle" due to its brick construction. It entirely resembles an actual castle, and the fact it sits on top of a hill adds to the atmosphere. The grounds are made up of several buildings that house the academy's tactical center, billets, classrooms, meeting rooms, kitchen, cafeteria, and office spaces.

Eighteen weeks minus the weekends. The academy's board of trustees didn't want to heat or air condition the behemoth of a building seven days a week, so cadets were allowed to go home on weekends but had to be back promptly every Monday morning. Two times a year the academy hosts the Basic Law Enforcement Training Program or BLETP (Ble-pee) for short.

Chiefy Charles had personally driven me to the pre-requisite physical agility testing. It was held at the academy several weeks prior to the start of the full academy in the fall. I was given the choice and had picked a fall academy over a summer one, thinking that it would be easier to perform the rigorous physical aspects in cold weather rather than in the hot summer weather.

There were two ways to pass the physical requirements of the academy. Pass at what is called the fortieth percentile or at the fiftieth percentile, meaning depending on your age and gender, you were required to perform so many push-ups, so many sit-ups, and pass a two-and-one-half mile run under certain time limits. If you simply passed right on the money, or at the fortieth percentile, you were in, however, by the end of the academy, you had to retake the testing and pass at the greater percentile in order to graduate. If you simply blew it out of the water during the prerequisite, you didn't have to take the exit physical exams. I was determined to go in at the higher percentile and not add any additional worries to myself. I was going to be in for enough already without that hanging over my head for eighteen weeks. Running was the worst for me. My credo had always been no need to run if someone wasn't chasing me. Push-ups and sit-ups were never an issue, however, running wasn't in my vocabulary. Everyone kept telling me, "It's all in your mind." *The hell it is, it's all in my stamina and legs.* At any rate, I practiced and practiced up until it was time to attend the academy. I'd run daily, and knowing that the academy sat on top of a hill, I made sure that at least half of my daily run was uphill. I was ready for this.

On the day Charles and I headed to the academy for the pre-entrance exams, we had also picked up a candidate from the police department one town over who also had to pass their entrance exam. On the ride to the academy, the other younger candidate mentioned that he hadn't had breakfast and minded if we pulled into a fast food joint on the way. *Wait, are you kidding? You're going to the academy to pass physical entrance requirements and you want to fill your gut with a greasy cheeseburger?* Both Charles and I tried to talk cadet Numb Nuts (*not his real name*) out of filling his growling tummy in an effort for him to have some chance of passing the examinations. Our pathetic pleas fell on deaf ears. Not that we cared, this guy didn't work for our department. Unfortunately, this is, at times, the attitude of young would-be cadets to allow their egos to get in the way. Some simply think they're invincible. So, we pulled into the local fast food joint on the way to the academy, and the young lad proceeded to pound down a sausage, egg, and cheese muffin, hash browns, and a Coke. I strategically chose to have absolutely nothing, and we proceeded to the academy some forty miles away. Plenty of time for his guts to begin the digestion process.

The academy's gymnasium, also known as the tactical center, was full of prospective cadets from around the state. We were paired up with academy staff who were to count and clock us through the physical process and record the results. Charles, having been through this at least twice with failed candidates as of late, was like an expectant father in a hospital waiting room, waiting to see if the birth of his new cadet goes well.

Push-ups were first. For my age group, within the allotted time of one minute, I had to do twenty-seven, military style. I banged out far more than I was required, along with most of the prospects, while there were some others who struggled to meet quota. As for cadet Numb Nuts, he groaned through three, failing the first part of the testing right out of the gate. Sit-ups were next. Thirty-six was the mark for my age in one minute. Again, I and many others met or surpassed what was required while others like Numb Nuts struggled. For this test, he was able to complete only two. *Wish you hadn't had that breakfast now, don't you?* Then came the mile-and-a-half run. I won't lie, many other younger and fitter cadet candidates did much better than me, but I did finish under my time of twelve minutes and twenty-five seconds. I felt like dog crap crossing the finish line and thought I might possibly require an ambulance, but I made it. Charles had finally given birth to an academy candidate. He was on his phone immediately to his other staff, joyfully letting them know I had passed the entrance requirements and was in the academy. And I had passed at the fiftieth percentile! No need to worry about this part again at least. Numb Nuts hadn't even attempted the run, now having retreated to the academy parking lot, hiding behind our car sobbing and puking. His chief was going to be proud.

I was now prepared for the eighteen weeks that were ahead of me. Or so I thought.

◆ ◆ ◆

The Maine Criminal Justice Academy, day one, in general, is fairly interesting and highly stressful for all of the cadets, and for me, it was no different. You're required to show up with a week's worth of Dickies-brand work uniforms, a set of sweats, five pairs of underwear and socks, personal toiletries, dress boots, new sneakers, duty belt, and gear, along with law books and other classroom materials all crammed into two large duffle bags. Of course, I didn't read the memo correctly and thought it said to show up in sweats and be prepared for immediate physical therapy, or PT. I was wrong, and this was my first lesson in paying attention. There I was standing in a hallway waiting to be let into the classroom with everyone else in their dress blue Dickies, and me in my sweats. To this day, I don't know how I managed to sneak back to my car and get changed before they let us in, but I did without being caught. Once inside, they ushered us into the stadium-style classroom and the director of the academy gave you his warm, fuzzy speech about how happy he is that you've decided to attend *his* academy and how much you'll learn over the next eighteen weeks. All the while, the cadres are preparing the tactical center.

The cadres, usually six of them, are primarily volunteers from the state police who give their time for two consecutive academies, or one full year, to help train the cadets. Now I say volunteer for the assignment, however, there are those officers who are assigned to the academy as if we're some sort of punishment and a few weren't overly happy to be there. These are the worst because they're as miserable to be at the academy as you are. We had one of those in my academy. I don't know what this officer had done to get sent to the academy, however, she made it her goal to make it as miserable as possible for the rest of us.

The cadres are paid by their sponsoring departments as if they were working the road during their year, and they're required to take it seriously. And I had to give them credit, the cadres were required to get up before the cadets each morning, go to bed after the cadets each night, and all the while they're required to look like they just walked out of a showroom. They are the drill sergeants of the academy and they're tasked with thinking up crap all day long to mess with the cadet's heads and make their lives miserable and stressful. On the road, they could be the nicest and most polite and professional officers, but at the academy, their job was to create as much stress on us as possible to see who doesn't have what it takes and quits. I ended up having a lot of respect for the cadres after I got over my initial hatred of them.

So, while the Director's cuddly speech was going on in the classroom, the cadre staff were preparing the tactical center. As I mentioned earlier, this is a huge gymnasium with an elevated quarter-mile running track that skirts the outer edge of a gym. There are garage-style doors at one end, so that police cars can be brought into the gym to simulate traffic stops for training, and there are storage rooms, a kitchen, and a weight room to use for simulations. The walls were painted to resemble a village or neighborhood for scenarios. It was very impressive. At the hallway entrance into the gym the cadres had covered large glass windows so the cadets couldn't see inside the tactical center before entering through the gymnasium doors.

Once the Director's speech was over, we were handed a form and told to report to the tac center. The form, known as a DD180, was what you signed once you'd had enough and wanted to go home. It was the "quitters form" that generally ended your career. You were required to keep this form on you at all times, and when you'd had enough, you were to take it from your pocket, sign it, and give it to a cadre. From that point forward, you were a civilian again, free to leave the academy and explain to your chief why you couldn't work for their department anymore. I vowed that form wasn't coming out of my pocket for any reason for eighteen weeks other than to wash my filthy clothes on the weekends.

After the speech, we proceeded to the tac center where, unbeknownst to us, the cadres were waiting on the other side of the doors. There were lined up three to each side and one additional cadre standing above the doorway on the running track so that you couldn't see him until you entered the gymnasium. The job of all of the cadre staff was to scream at you and cause intensity and stress as soon as you came through the doors, and that's exactly what they did.

So, there we were, going through the tac center doors and the game and academy was on! The cadres on the floor were in our faces, yelling at us to get into a formation that we hadn't been given yet, just simply get into a "formation!" The one cadre up on the track was yelling the same, and at the same time, screaming for everyone not to look up at him. Oh my, if you looked up at him, your day was going to get worse, much worse. Eyes forward and down at all times! The dysfunctional group of cadets formed into four or five lines, simply anything that resembled a formation, and one unlucky cadet became the first of many "class leaders" much to their unwillingness. Each week the cadres choose a class leader. This poor, unlucky soul is usually a younger cadet that doesn't seem to have their stuff together, and the idea is that by being in charge it teaches, or rather forces, this individual to learn some leadership and team-building skills. However, this first-class leader who was as green as the rest of us was a mess, and to this day many years later I'm glad it wasn't me. This guy didn't have any better idea of what formation to get us into any more than the rest of the group did. However, he was trying his best to get us to line up while cadre staff screamed at him from all sides, belittling him to nearly tears.

After we got into our "formation" I quickly discovered why the academy had us put our initials on each piece of clothing with a permanent marker before reporting for the first day, right down to each white pair of socks and underwear. I just thought it was so my roommates wouldn't mistakenly put on my pair of tighty-whities, but no, that wasn't the reason. After getting into one of the lines and trying my best not to do anything that would draw attention to myself and get me screamed at by the cadres, I glanced over to one side of the tac center. There, dumped into one huge pile, was everyone's gear. Every item we all came with was mixed into a heap, including our now empty duffle bags. Suddenly the cadre up on the track yelled out, "Everyone, retrieve your personal items, you have five minutes! And they better be yours! DO IT NOW!"

In a mad dash, all the cadets were pawing through the pile, trying to find every item they had brought by trying to find the initials they were supposed to have written on them. And of course, there were two or three cadets that hadn't read the memo and had no markings on their stuff at all. This was the very first test of teamwork with the idea that not only do you find your stuff, but you also help the other cadets find theirs. So, there we all were like seagulls in the parking lot of McDonald's when someone threw their last few fries onto the pavement. We scrambled to find our stuff while the cadre staff hovered over, screaming at us to get our gear back into our duffels and get back into formation. I grabbed what I could find and got back in line with my two huge duffle bags in front of me on the floor. One by one, everyone got back into the same, sad formation, hoping what they had in their gear bags belonged to them. And then one by one, the cadres came around and dumped out every gear bag in front of each cadet while we stood at attention, eyes forward, panting heavily and trembling.

The next thing I knew I heard, "Wilson! Why are you looking up at me?!" *Oh, crap.* I had glanced up at the track. How could you not with this fool screaming at us? I'm hearing a voice from above, and it certainly wasn't God, however at that moment, it may well have been the big man himself.

Instantly, I had cadres on both sides of me with the brims of their Stetsons touching my sideburns on both sides, and they were yelling loudly, "What do you think you're doing looking up like that?! Didn't he say not to look up at him?! You want to go home, don't you!? You want to pull that form out of your pocket and sign it, don't you!? Go ahead, make your day and mine better, sign the form, and go back home to your mommy!"

"Sir, no, sir!" And that's how you spoke to the cadre. Either sir or ma'am, "Sir, yes, sir," or "Ma'am, no, ma'am." And you better make sure you don't say sir to a ma'am by mistake and believe me, it's easier than you might think when they're all screaming at you at once.

"You're not signing yet?! Well, that means you're planning on staying! Now drop down and give me twenty!" And there I was, like many others in the room, on the floor doing military-style push-ups. The first of many that I'd do over the next eighteen weeks, not by choice.

Now back on my feet, we were being screamed at again by the voice above us, "I want to see in your left hand your five pairs of work shirts. I want to see in your right hand your five pairs of work pants. I want to see them held high over your head! DO IT NOW!" So, we all dug through our piles and held up five pairs of shirts in one hand and five pairs of pants in the other, holding them high above our heads. If you didn't do it fast enough, you had personal attention that you really didn't want.

After what seemed to be hours, when actually it was only minutes with all of us holding our clothes over our heads, the command came to put them in the duffle bags. "Now I want to see in your right hand your five pairs of white socks! In your left hand, I want to see your five pairs of underwear! Do it now!"

Oh, God, please let me have grabbed my own underwear from the pile. If not, at least make what I took to be men's underwear, or my life is over!

Luckily over my head were *my* five pairs of tighty-whities and five pairs of socks. The next thing I knew, I realized one of my fellow cadets, Cory Smithers, must have botched this part badly because he was running around the formation with his, or someone's, underwear in his hands over his head and yelling, "I will not be an idiot again! I will not be an idiot again...!"

And so, the "bag drill" as it was affectionately named, went on for what seemed like hours. Meticulously we were told to grab each and every item we'd brought with us, hold them over our heads, and finally into the duffle bags. All the time with cadres screaming at us and more push-ups than I could ever begin to count.

Next came the first two-and-a-half-mile run. We lost our first cadet during the run. The first quitter. One down and many more to go. Once we returned from the run, we were given our billet assignments where we again found our belongings in a heap in the hallway of the billets and were given very little time to gather them up and put everything away before we were to report to the classroom to be taught how to make our bunks. We'd receive a demonstration of exactly how tight the hospital corners were to be each and every time we were to make our beds. I will never forget as long as I live how to make a forty-five-degree hospital corner with a paper-thin, heavily starched sheet.

The first chow followed where we ate very little and very quickly, all the time being yelled at by the cadre staff for whatever it was we were doing wrong. Not using our utensils correctly, too much bug juice in our cups, whatever. Following chow, we returned to our billets to receive our first lesson on teamwork in having every room made to mirror the others. Once again all of our belongings were back out in the hallway in another big heap. Once again, we put the billets back together and made our first bunks before heading back to the classroom for an inspection, which we obviously all failed. Still sweaty from the run and the overall stress of the day, our once clean work uniforms were dirty, sweaty, and sticking to our bodies, which all smelled a bit foul. Our shirts were half tucked in, and certainly not to any academy standards, black ties were not tucked into our shirts between the second and third buttons as instructed, and our pants were not bloused into our boots. More push-ups. Back to the billets for our next lesson on teamwork with the billets tossed again, along with the mattresses this time all out in the hallways. I'm certain the hospital corners were a bit crooked and not quite as we were taught to make them.

Finally, night came around 9:00 p.m., and we were nestled into our bunks, sweaty and exhausted. Most of us had spent so much time trying to get our bed sheets tight enough to bounce quarters from that we didn't want to mess them up by sleeping between the sheets. Several cadets attempted to sleep on top of their sheets, however, cadres would perform rounds, several of them, checking each room to make certain we were sleeping between the sheets. If you were lucky enough to not move during the night, you might only have to fix the top sheet because as I was soon to find out in days to come the only way to keep the sheets tight was to literally crawl under the bunks and pull the sheets between the slim and pitiful mattress and the bed springs and find a way to jam them into a spring to hold them in place.

Finally, after our brains began to calm down and the adrenalin washed away somewhere around 10:00 p.m., the first night's sleep came in the form of total exhaustion and simply passing out. At 10:05 p.m., the first fire drill sounded. Alarms began going off and cadre screaming that we were all going too slow getting into our already filthy sweats and running out onto the parade deck, shivering, and wanting to be back in our uncomfortable bunks. The class leader was taking the brunt of our ineptness and inability to move fast enough to get into a formation so that he could account for each cadet whose names he didn't even know yet on a roster that he didn't have yet. This would be the first of several fire drills that first night.

The first morning arrived in the form of reveille at 05:00 only to find that during the night we'd lost another cadet. Not even his roommate realized when he'd gathered up all his gear, snuck out quietly, and left quickly. Another career down the toilet.

This second day, as many more to follow, would be mostly the same. You'd get up, make your bunk, take a dump, take barely a shower, cut yourself shaving too quickly, get dressed to inspection standards, get your books to the classroom from the billets, and get to the chow hall for the first of three daily inspections. All this had to be done in twenty minutes, and keep in mind the billet building wasn't connected to either the classroom or chow hall. On top of this, every cadet was assigned to specific morning detail assignments, which changed weekly.

There were several "details" assigned to groups of cadets each week. One was chow hall detail where you helped prepare every meal, served the cadres, cleaned up, and set up the mess hall again for the next meal. Hoping that during all this you might get two seconds to eat your own meal, but the reality was if you had chow detail, which I fell victim to several times, you starved that week.

Flag detail took place after morning chow. This is when every cadet assembled on the parade deck and the flag detail would march out with the American Flag, Maine State Flag, and the Academy Flag, and there would be a formal flag-raising ceremony. This detail would also have to post the colors, the American and Maine flags, in the classroom just before morning classes and during the Pledge of Allegiance. This detail entailed a lot of marching in formation and memorizing cadences and speeches that were yelled out during the posting of colors. I was terrible at marching. I have "duck foot" on my left foot, and it made it almost impossible to march in unison with others. I was always out of step, and for this reason, this detail was the most difficult for me and the one I dreaded the most. I think I had it nine times.

The billet detail was basically the bathroom cleaning detail and the classroom detail, which meant cleaning up everything else around the academy. Details had to be done on a daily schedule that didn't interrupt classroom time. In fact, the classroom educational piece was the only time that cadres weren't allowed to mess with the cadets. It was a learning academy as much as it was a physical academy. They were, however, certainly waiting for you in the hallways when classes were over.

And then there was the constant chatter about the rumored and dreaded "fight scenario" that I spoke about earlier. The make it or break it moment of your academy, and you heard mention of it many times. All throughout the academy, you're taught to tactically defend yourself, and it's instilled in you that as an officer if you must engage in a physical hand-to-hand battle, you must win to stay alive. The daily PT was tough and meant to teach you offensive and defensive moves that will keep you alive and take down your foe to the point of effecting an arrest. However, rigorous training or not, just the mere thought that the fight scenario that was coming at some point kept everyone on their toes and taught you to expect the least expected at all times.

I had chow hall detail my first week and I quickly learned that of all the details, this was probably the worst and most time-consuming. You had about twenty minutes before chow time to get the hall set up, do meal prep alongside the academy cook, set up the cadre tables, and wait on cadre staff while trying to get a bite in yourself. The problem was that chow had a routine as well. The cadres sat at a head table overlooking the rest of the cadets. They would allow about fifteen minutes to cram your food down before they started messing with you. They'd call out a name in which you were to drop what you were eating and stand at attention. Then they'd ask you some dumb question from the academy's handbook that you were expected to memorize before attending the academy. You may have to recite, verbatim, a statutory law or the Officer's Oath, or you might be asked to simply spell a word correctly. If you failed, you were required to remain standing at attention, and the next poor cadet was called upon to stand, and so on until some dumb schmuck got the answer correct, and all who failed before them were chastised for not having a brain.

The corner of the chow hall was affectionately referred to by one cadre as the "library." Cadres would send cadets who answered incorrectly to the library to perform push-ups. By the end of chow, the corner of the room would be full of cadets, all on their faces doing push-ups right after eating. The library was always full, and every cadet in the library was on the verge of puking.

When a cadre's cup was empty, someone from the chow detail would be expected to jump to attention and fill it, so no matter what, your attention was always on the cadre table if you had the chow detail. You were also expected, and taught, that when approaching a cadre at their table you approached from the rear, right shoulder side. You were to march to the table, all the while performing proper turns, about faces, all that stuff.

You then had to ask permission, such as, "Sir, may I fill your cup, sir?" *Sir, another cupcake for your fat ass, sir?* No, I never said this. However, there was one time that I completely lost my mind and approached the table from the front. Not thinking at all, I found myself addressing the cadre head-on and not from the rear. I quickly realized my mistake and marched to the rear, right shoulder of the cadre, and leaned in to make the proper request.

The cadre whom I addressed turned to me and simply said to me in a low voice, "Wilson, what the hell did you just do?"

"Sir, I don't know, sir." I spent the rest of chow in the library that day.

One of the cadres had this thing for his name being mispronounced by the cadets, and it was easy to do. His last name was McFaden (Mac-Fadd-Den), and it was easy to mispronounce as McFāden (Mac-Fade-Den). This appeared to piss him off greatly. Either that or this was part of his game to use to punish the cadets. One fine mealtime a cadet mispronounced his name and immediately the other cadres knew what was coming next. McFaden was seated at the end of the head table. As soon as it was said, the rest of the cadre staff each picked up their chow trays and held them above the table. McFaden proceeded to yell at the cadet for being an idiot and flung his own tray, making it surf the entire length of the head table underneath all the other cadre before taking flight and slamming, food and all, against the library wall, splashing perfectly good mystery meatloaf and powdered mashed potatoes and gravy everywhere. Of course, I was on chow detail that week and had the task of cleaning it all up while the other cadet that 'effed' up his name did push-ups in the library for the duration of the meal.

But I digress, we're still only on day number two. So, on the second day, we'd be introduced to the next bit of fun that would haunt us for the next several weeks. One of the cadres nicknamed it "pain compliance." This usually came in the evenings right before rack. We'd be brought as a group to the classroom where we'd be subject to rigorous workouts, more so than during the regular daily physical therapy which typically consisted of sit-ups, push-ups, or some other form of painful, physical stress on our bodies. The second night we had quite the introduction to this.

It seemed that earlier in the evening the flag detail had been sent out to the parade deck after a brief snow squall. They were shoveling off the deck as instructed to do by the cadre. Now the cadre had a sneaky skill of being able to see and hear the cadets no matter where they were throughout the academy without being detected. And, at times, the cadets had little supervision other than the detail squad leader, but you knew the cadre were always close by watching. So, when the parade deck was being shoveled, there was a cadre hiding somewhere close enough to hear that one cadet by the name of Brian Higgins was humming a tune to himself while shoveling the snow. Now, Brian was a good cadet and an overall good guy, but he was also the type of person who stood out in a crowd and at times could be considered the comedian in the room. Two very bad traits for a young cadet at the Maine Criminal Justice Academy.

On the evening of the second day, the cadets were called to the classroom. We were all instructed to get in the "washboard" position. Now, if you don't know what a washboard is, here is what I want you to do. Lay on the floor flat on your back, extend your legs and head off the floor, and place your arms straight down at your sides, off the floor, and hold in that position. No, you can't hold your legs up with your hands, your hands must remain empty, and you must keep your arms, legs, and head off the floor. Go on, put the book down and try it. You've just experienced the intense pain of a washboard. *They suck!*

Now that all the cadets were down in position and ready to begin, we heard the next command, "Cadet Higgins!"

"Sir, yes, sir!" A voice from somewhere on the floor.

"On your feet!" Higgins knew immediately this wasn't going to be good, but he didn't know just how bad it was about to get for him.

"Sir, yes, sir!" as Higgins sprang to his feet and to attention.

"What was that song you were humming on the parade deck earlier today!?"

"Sir?"

"Are you deaf, Higgins?! What was the song you were singing to yourself on the parade deck while you were shoveling?!"

"Sir…I…."

"Dammit, Higgins, what song were you singing!?"

"Sir, 'Free Falling,' sir." *Oh, man, this wasn't good, and it was about to get worse.*

"Everyone stay where you are doing your washboards! Not you, Higgins! You will stand at attention and sing the entire song for your classmates while they perform their pain compliance! Start singing!”

So, there was Higgins, crackling voice singing the first verse to “Free Falling” by Tom Petty while the rest of us were on the floor groaning to the pain of washboards. After the first verse and chorus, Higgins stopped singing.

“Higgins! Who told you to stop singing?!”

“Sir, I can’t remember the rest of the song, sir!” The groaning on the floor grew louder.

“Well, that’s too bad, Higgins, because all these cadets will remain in this position until your memory improves!”

“But, sir, what if I can’t remember it at all, sir?” Higgins was shaking now and almost in tears.

“Then sing the first verse again until you’re instructed to stop!”

So, like a broken record, Higgins continued to sing the first verse in his strained voice over and over until most of us were ready to pass out from the pain. And again, what was only a few minutes of listening to Higgins’s terrible, repetitive singing voice felt like an eternity to those of us on the floor.

To this day, I can’t stand that song. I’m also positive that Brian Higgins doesn’t care for it anymore either. There was also no more singing on the parade deck, or anywhere else, for the remainder of the academy.

♦ ♦ ♦

The daily inspections were a pain. At least three times a day we were to line up, and a cadre would look us over, making sure we appeared to look our best even though we were all pretty much a mess. Our shirts had to be ironed on the creases, bloused into our pants, and the “gig line” had to be straight at all times. The gig line means that the line of buttons on your shirt had to be in line with your crotch buttons and zipper on your pants. Any millimeter off and you received a “gig” which was a term for something you did or were doing wrong. Getting a gig meant you had to spend any free time you had in the evenings typing a report in the computer lab on what you’d done wrong. *Yes, I said computer lab, we didn’t have laptops back then.* The theory was to get the officer familiar with creating detailed daily reports. Evenings were spent with cadets typing reports on their gig lines being off, shirts being untucked, boots not shiny enough, hair out of place…whatever reason you received the gigs for throughout the day. And there was no limit to the number of gigs you could receive daily, it simply depended on how many things you got caught doing wrong on that particular day. I believe the record, held by Cadet Marin, was eighteen in one day.

One day I was in the chow line during the lunch inspection, which is where inspections mostly took place, in the chow hall line. The chow hall had two dining rooms, one for the cadets only and one for all the other students and teachers of the academy. Each day the academy was full of other seasoned law officers, game wardens, corrections and dispatch officers, and instructors who were attending the academy for other post-secondary training and instruction. Cadets were required to line up in the chow hall for all to see, and once they made it through their inspection line, they could retrieve their trays and head into the cadet dining room, which is off-limits to all others. It was quite the spectacle and again serves a purpose that others are always watching what an officer is doing out in the public eye. We were told we lived our lives in a "fishbowl" and that everyone watched what we were doing from all sides at all times.

We were also taught not to pay any attention to everyone else that was staring at us and, no matter what, to always look better and act more professionally than everyone else in the room. These were important lessons. Our inspections were in front of every other visitor in the dining hall for a reason.

So, I had it together that day, or so I thought. I had everything cleaned, pressed, and tucked in. I even had an extra minute or two in the morning shower to actually have soap and water on my body to make myself smell a little better, which was rare. Morning showers usually consisted of jumping in, and jumping out because you had to make time for the shave and other toilet-related necessities. About five to seven minutes each morning was all the time you had to squeeze it out and shave it off.

It was my turn at the front of the inspection line, and McFaden was looking me over hard. Looking straight ahead as we always did, I watched in my peripheral the brim of his Stetson go up and down as he checked me over. I just knew he wasn't going to find a thing to gig me on this day. He looked up and down, over and around, and finally looked me square in the eyes with a scowl on his face. I had all I could do to hold back a smirk. After what seemed like the longest, meanest stare I'd ever received, and not wanting to lose this battle, he then looked down at my chest again and his eyes stopped there. Puzzled, I couldn't help but look down as well. He lifted the pocket flap on my work shirt, and there on the underside of the flap was a tiny, microscopic thread stuck to the Velcro. This damn thing was nearly invisible, but it was there. McFaden lowered the flap slowly, we both looked back at each other, and he leaned into me as an evil smile crossed his lips. He then whispered those dreaded words to me, "Gig."

My evening was ruined again by having to type a full report on that stupid little thread.

◆ ◆ ◆

So, the days and weeks went on. For me, overall, it was fairly uneventful. There was something to be said about being the third oldest cadet in the class.

The cadre for the most part left the older ones alone, believing that the younger and more immature cadets required more focus. For the younger cadets, they thought of the academy as a form of torture. To us older guys, we knew what it really was, a game. The game was to simply make it through the academy without quitting from the stress. The harder you fought the cadre, the harder they made it on you, and we knew enough not to let it get to us and just play the game. I made it through without ever making class leader and I was squad leader only once. I learned just how much of a game it was one day. By coincidence, it was also the day I learned that I was no different than the cadre by anything other than a title.

I had injured myself in PT by tearing my hamstring to the point of having no choice but to report it to the cadre. Limping terribly, I mustered the courage to go knock on the cadre door. The cadre shared their own "suite" inside the billet, their own little apartments for the duration of their stay.

If you had to speak to a cadre, and there was none to be found, you had to approach their door, bang on it hard, and yell out as loud as you could, "Permission to come aboard!?" You did this very sparingly, only for the direst of needs, and the usual response was a loud and resounding, "Negative!" If it was truly important, you had to knock again and repeat the request.

I was allowed into their rooms and shouldn't have been surprised to find that the cadres' rooms were much nicer than ours and personalized. This, for lack of better terms, was their "home" for nearly a year, and these were in fact, real people. I was greeted by McFaden and once inside, the "uniform" came off, and we were both equals. Both of us were law enforcement officers, one no better than the other, and we spoke freely. McFaden allowed, and even insisted, that I call my family and my personal physician to advise of the injury. He also made certain that I was remaining at the academy. There was no way I was going home from this, however, it was arranged for me to return home for the day to be seen by my own doctor and make certain I'd have the physical ability to continue. It was all very relaxed and attentive. Once the arrangements were complete and it was time for me to exit the suite and return to my classmates, McFaden stopped me at the door.

"Wilson, once outside this door, you know it's game on, right?"

I smiled at my fellow officer and replied quietly, "Sir, yes, sir," and left the room. And the academy was on once again.

◆ ◆ ◆

It was somewhere around week six that the cadre stopped tossing our rooms. One cadet came up with the idea of drawing a diagram of how the rooms should look, right down to where you placed your pencil on each desk. Once he handed out the diagram, everyone's room looked identical, and no more hallway surprises from that point on. This was teamwork, and that's what the academy taught and expected. So, a small victory. What sucked was that each week we were required to change rooms. Monday's room assignments weren't announced until Friday, just before we were allowed to go home. This resulted in a mad scramble each Friday to get the rooms in order for Monday morning. And believe me, the cadre staff wanted just as much to go home to their families on Friday as the cadets did, so when it was time to leave, you better not be the only one holding up the wagon train getting your new room set up.

Weekends were spent washing the weeks' worth of dirty clothes, ironing and folding them appropriately to take back on Monday morning. You also studied hard. Memorizing criminal and traffic laws was integral. The craziest acronyms were thought up to help you memorize information for the written tests that we were subject to on a weekly, if not daily, basis.

During my academy, I would end up bonding primarily with the two other older cadets. The second oldest was a guy with the last name Winslow. Miles Winslow was only a year older than me, and the academy staff kept confusing the two of us, which was fairly amusing since I was Caucasian and Winslow was an African American. We were literally black and white, but the cadre continually kept calling us by the other one's name. This became quite the joke among Winslow and me and provided us with brief moments of humor throughout the training. It was so ridiculous that at one point we were walking the halls together, as cadets are never allowed to move about alone, always at least in pairs. I had pulled the hamstring during PT about a week earlier and had an obvious limp. We walked by the director of the academy, who looked squarely at Winslow and inquired, "Wilson, how's the leg feeling?"

Without missing a beat, Winslow replied, "Feels much better today, sir!" It was such a joke between us that we were genuinely worried that during graduation ceremonies our names would be announced incorrectly. We did make light of it though. On April Fool's Day, we were well into the latter part of the training, and the mood was a bit lighter between the cadets and cadres. All except for the cadre whose presence was apparently her punishment, she was still just as moody and mean as ever. Winslow and I switched up our name tags that morning and vowed to make it through all three daily inspections without the cadre staff noticing. Two cadres were on duty that day, the Wicked Witch (*not her real name*) and an older cadre by the name of Colonel Jenkins, who was from a Sheriff's Department in Southern Maine. The "colonel" as he was known by cadre and nicknamed due to his rank at his respective department. However, he was affectionately known by the cadet staff as Grandpa, much unbeknownst to him or the other cadre staff. Cadre Jenkins had a hard time being tough on the cadets, however, he did have a military background so, when need be, he could step up his attitude and play the game. We all had respect for *Gramps* and generally, we enjoyed it when he was on duty. This day he was on with the Wicked Witch, and that was our cadre staff for the day.

Winslow and I made it through the three daily inspections, two of which were conducted directly by the witch. She looked us over and handed out our gigs for other infractions, but never noticed that I had on Winslow's nameplate, and he had mine. All throughout the day we encountered the cadre staff. Our uniform tags continuously went entirely unnoticed, most likely because by this point, we'd both been called by each other's names so often that no one really knew who we were anyway.

Near the end of the evening, after a tedious day, Winslow and I were standing in our billet hallway. Grandpa Jenkins was nearby. The Wicked Witch was patrolling, and we came to attention and stood with our backs to the walls as she passed by us without her broomstick, but with a scowl on her face. After she passed by, I couldn't help myself and I called out, "Ma'am?"

She turned back around, obviously annoyed, and fast enough that she'd nearly caused herself whiplash, and she barked, "What do you want, cadet?!" She didn't dare try to call me by name, knowing she might screw it up.

Winslow and I each pointed to the nametags pinned to our shirts, hoping that she actually knew what our real names were without looking. The Witch came in close, her pointy nose nearly touching our chests as she gazed at both nametags. This was probably the end of the night for both of us, but it was to be well worth it. She looked back and forth several times as if she was watching a tennis match, the scowl on her face worsening until she finally looked up at us and screeched, "Have those been like that all day?!"

"Ma'am, yes, ma'am!" We both blurted out.

The Witch said nothing for a few moments. Over her shoulder, I could see Grampa waiting for her response and ready to help scrape Winslow and me off the walls and potentially call an ambulance for both of us. He knew once the Witch was done with the verbal beatings we were about to take, not to mention our pending physical punishments, we'd both need medical assistance. The Witch continued to look back and forth at the tags, hoping magically they'd switch back on their own, while new and permanent age lines appeared on her forehead. She was speechless at the thought she had failed to perform her duties during the daily inspections.

After a few tense moments, the Witch, still staring at the nametags, uttered in a low tone that progressively got louder, "Shit….shit…SHIT!" She then turned and shuffled away down the hall, simply uttering the same word over and over as her voice echoed throughout the halls, "Shit…shit…shit!"

Winslow and I stood there, stunned at the fact that we were still alive. We couldn't help but let smiles cross our faces in front of Cadre Jenkins. Our smiles faded as he approached us with a scowl on his face.

"Cadets!"

We both came back to immediate attention, "Sir, yes, sir!"

A moment went by as he sternly looked us over and then a smirk broke out on his face as he leaned into us and spoke ever-so-softly, "You just ruined her entire evening. Good job." He turned and walked away from us, but I could hear the chuckle from Gramps as he continued down the billet hallway.

Apparently, he didn't care for the Witch either.

◆ ◆ ◆

There were some other light moments during the academy. Inevitably someone's sponsoring agency would do something to make their cadet's time at the academy as difficult and embarrassing as possible.

My chief did it to me during the Chief's Inspection. This was a day, about mid-way through the program, that each cadet's chief would visit the academy and perform an inspection of their officer and watch a pathetic demonstration of marching and cadences.

My chief was notorious for bartering, or simply scamming himself a piece of equipment or garment wherever he went. If it was free or he had something to trade, like a department patch, he'd take advantage and he was always prepared to make a deal.

The day was sunny and unusually warm for mid-winter. We were all inspection-ready and in formation outside on the parade deck. We'd spent the prior days practicing several marching drills for when the chiefs arrived and we were prepared, following the inspection, to put on a display. The cadet squadron was formed into several rows with room for each chief to walk through and approach every cadet, inspect them, and move on, taking extra time when the chief arrived to inspect his or her own officer.

We were given instructions by the cadre that this was to be treated as any other inspection. Stand at attention, eyes forward at all times, and not address the chiefs in any way, except to say, "Thank you, sir or ma'am," if they spoke first and gave us a compliment. No other talking allowed.

At first, I didn't think my chief had made it this day as I could see the sea of chiefs off to the side and mine wasn't there. I was thinking to myself, "*The dipstick forgot what day it is.*" It didn't surprise or even disappoint me, Charles was always forgetting something. What I didn't know was that he, in fact, was at the academy and was just busy schmoozing with the academy director, seeing what he could scrounge, and taking his sweet time getting to the formation.

The inspections began, and finally, I saw my chief scurrying across the parade deck to get in the rear of the line behind all the other chiefs. Not surprising was that all the other chiefs were in their dress uniforms looking sharp while my chief had on his usual jeans, polo shirt, and police jacket in an attempt to make himself look official. Charles had stopped wearing a uniform on a daily basis years prior, and today was going to be no exception.

One by one the chiefs went by, stopping to check me over as they passed. I stayed at attention staring straight ahead and acknowledged any compliments as instructed. Cadre staff followed the chiefs right behind, making certain that no cadet made the mistake of smiling at their chief, winking at them, talking, or otherwise acknowledging their leaders in any fashion.

The parade of chiefs passed by. Then came my chief. Charles stopped in front of me, straight-faced, and inspected me as he was expected to, pretending to be all professional in his jeans. Charles had a hard time doing anything official, so I knew he was doing it just for show.

All of a sudden, Charles smirked and opened one side of his jacket just enough for me to see what was inside. Underneath was a polo shirt, with the academy's insignia, all bunched up like he'd just stolen it, which most likely he had. A wink accompanied his smirk. *What a prick.* I couldn't help the smile that came across my face and a chuckle that I desperately tried to hold back. Of course, Cadre McFaden had to be standing right behind Charles when this occurred, and I knew right then and there that I was done for. McFaden didn't do anything other than give me a scowl as he and Charles continued past. However, later on that evening, I discovered just how many push-ups it took to make me nearly pass out.

◆ ◆ ◆

During the academy, it was nearly a tradition for someone to receive the dreaded stuffed animal.

Several weeks into the training Cadet Radio, affectionately named after the character from the movie *Super Troopers* due to the fact that he was overweight, slightly arrogant, and looked just like the movie character, received a package that was opened by the academy staff in advance. It was during chow that he heard his nickname called, and he sprang to attention, spitting food from his mouth and nearly knocking his tray over as he gave the traditional yell, "Sir, yes, sir!"

"Radio, it seems you received a package today!" We all knew what was coming, we'd all been waiting to see who'd get it, and equally hoping it was none of us. The cadre then produced from a box a large, pink, stuffed pig. "It seems your department feels it amusing to send you this item!"

"Sir, yes, sir!" You could tell from the worried look on Radio's face and his low, fading voice that he didn't appreciate his department's gift.

Holding the pig up and staring at it intently, Cadre McFaden stated, "Well then must be that this is an integral piece of equipment that we have here! This must be a piece of equipment that your department depends on! They were good enough to supply you with this! As so, you will carry it with you daily for the remainder of your training with us!"

Oh, thank God my department didn't do this to me.

"Come get this equipment, Cadet Radio!" Radio marched to the cadre's table and accepted his new piece of standard equipment, a big fuzzy pink pig. "Radio! You will have this with you everywhere you go from this point on! Do you understand?! Are we tracking here?!"

"Sir, yes, sir," Radio's voice had little confidence in it as he marched to the cadre's table and accepted his new pink cuddly pig that for the next several weeks was never to leave his side.

This occurred during every academy class. Someone would receive a stuffed animal that they were then to carry throughout the remainder of the training. No one knew whose department was going to do this, and no cadet wanted it to be theirs. Getting through the daily grind and stress of the academy was bad enough. Getting through it carrying a stuffed animal was far worse than it sounds. Every training officer ridiculed you, and the pig managed to get in Radio's way no matter what the task was. And, the pig was like a flag, never to hit the ground or it was punishment for the cadet.

♦ ♦ ♦

One of the senior cadre staff who was permanently assigned to the academy was Sergeant Portman. At one time, he'd served on the State Police Demolition Team, and he knew all there was to know about demolitions and explosives. Not to mention he really enjoyed blowing things up. In his more senior years, he'd accepted an assignment as one of the cadet training directors for the academy. He was tough but fair, and we all liked him. He enjoyed telling stories about his days with the demolition team and he really knew all there was to know about explosives.

During a training session, about mid-way through, we were taken to the academy's firearms training center and outdoor shooting range. Prior to our arrival, Sgt. Portman had wired the entire length of the firing range with primer cord. In a demonstration for the cadets, he touched off the explosives in a massive exhibition, blowing up dust and sand from the range from one end to the other, showering us to show us the effects and power of explosives.

One week prior to graduation, Sgt. Portman had set up a plastic barrel on the range that he'd buried in the ground with only the top exposed. Before being bussed to the range, we were told to each bring one extra pair of work uniforms, one shirt, and one pair of pants. One by one the sarge marched us past the barrel and told us to put the extra set of clothes inside, which we all did. When it was Radio's turn, which Sgt. Portman purposely had him at the end of the line of cadets, he told him to put the pink pig on top of all the clothes.

What we didn't know at the time was that the sarge had wired the bottom of the barrel with explosives. Once all the garments were inside with the big pink pig on top, we were marched to a safe location and told to watch the barrel. Sgt. Portman then proceeded to blow up the barrel and its contents, sending shredded clothing all over the firing range. The blast sent the pig several hundred feet into the air. The poor little pig looked like he'd been launched into space and didn't make it. It came back down in pieces and hit the ground smoldering. A loud cheer erupted from the crowd of cadets. It was probably the first time since before day one that all the cadets smiled at the same time and were allowed to have a bit of fun.

And from that point on, Radio wasn't required to carry the pig anymore.

♦

CHAPTER 6

THE FIGHT SCENARIO AND GRADUATION

Week seventeen was "simulations week." This is when volunteer officers from around the state visit the academy and are stationed around the Town of Vassalboro at various locations to role-play situations that the cadets were to respond to as if they were actual police calls. Domestic situations, burglaries, thefts, neighbor disputes, and so on. Two cadets per call with one taking the lead. Each cadet is critiqued on how they handled each call.

We responded in actual police vehicles that were hand-me-downs from the state police and were pure junk, used primarily during Emergency Vehicle Operations, or EVOC. The week when the cadets are at a local abandoned airstrip and are operating the vehicles at all kinds of speeds through mazes and serpentines to simulate various responses and weather conditions. The cars were simply equipped with a two-way radio and nothing else. Cadets, in twos, were sent out to patrol the streets and responded to "calls" when their radio numbers were dispatched from the academy. The cadres were not in the vehicles with us. For the first time in sixteen weeks, we were on our own to prove we'd paid some attention to what we'd been taught without having our shadows constantly looking over our shoulders or yelling at us. Cars weren't dispatched to the same scene at once, and we were instructed not to meet up with other cadet vehicles, obviously in an effort to make certain you didn't compare notes or notify others of what types of calls we all were responding to and what to expect.

Winslow and I were assigned to a car together. We were having a good time with the ability to be alone, away from the academy grounds, and talk freely without being handed a gig for doing so. We were even laughing and joking a bit between calls. By this time in the academy, we were wearing full duty gear on a daily basis, gun belts, cuffs, inert mace (water in a spray can), and a fake, red, plastic semi-auto handgun in our holsters. We also wore bullet-proof vests under our shirts, which added weight and sweat to our already tired and smelly bodies.

Winslow was driving the car. We'd responded to a number of calls already, which were fairly routine. Both Winslow and I had the advantage of having worked the road prior to coming to the academy, which meant we'd both had road experience as officers, so responding to mock calls wasn't a huge deal for us. Many young cadets don't have the experience of working as an officer beforehand, and for the larger departments, they aren't allowed on the road without the academy under their belts.

It was a warm spring day. Winslow and I drove past a large, old cemetery, simply waiting to hear our call sign again over the radio. Winslow glanced over at the old granite markers and casually said, "I wonder how far back those stones go."

"All the way to the rear of the cemetery," I quipped. The joke wasn't even funny, but we both broke out in uncontrollable laughter like a balloon bursting from too much air pressure. The stress of the previous sixteen weeks that had weighed heavily on us seemed to wash away for a few moments.

And then we were interrupted, *"Academy to Vassalboro six,"* the radio squawked. *"Respond to the Maine Criminal Justice Academy for the report of a disorderly."*

Winslow and I looked at each other and we both knew immediately this was the fight scenario. My heart immediately started pounding. This was it, this would make or break my career right here. This was what had been on my mind, and every other cadet's mind, for sixteen weeks, not knowing when it would be coming. *This was going to suck.*

The purpose of the fight scenario is as much about confidence as it is about winning and always going home safe and alive. An officer can't be afraid of confrontation, and you can never lose. You can't always depend on deadly force, nor is it always called for. This was a time before Tasers, so non-lethal force was limited to pepper spray and batons, which you didn't always have the ability to use depending on how your opponent reacted to words. You must have the confidence that if you're required to engage in hand-to-hand combat, you will, and you will be successful. You will win, or you just might lose your life by only "trying."

We arrived at the academy outside of the tac center. A cadre was standing near the doors. Winslow and I approached the door as the cadre stuck his hand out, held Winslow back, and looked at me. "Just you, Wilson." *Awe, shit, what a time for them to get our names correct.*

I entered the tac center alone, sweating from more than just the vest. Inside the door was one of the physical training, or PT, instructors. Tunnel vision and adrenaline, which are both very real, took over and all I saw and was focused on was this one PT instructor. He directed me to the track stairwell, "Run, officer! Run to your call! Once around the track!"

Up the stairs I went to the running track. In full gear and vest, I started the quarter-mile run. My pulse pounded and sweat poured off me. Tunnel vision continued, and I only saw the track directly in front of me, nothing else. I still had no idea what was on the gymnasium floor below me.

"Run faster! You've got a call to get to! Run!" My heart was pounding out of my chest as I heard these words being hurled at me from below. I completed my run, once around the track, progressively getting slower as I went. I wasn't breathing now, I was panting. I came down off the track to the gymnasium floor to the same instructor waiting for me. He pointed behind himself and said, "There's your call, get over there!"

For the first time, I saw the other PT instructors, all standing around a set of thick wrestling mats on the floor. There were several instructors around the square, and I jogged with an exhausted limp over to one of them. Gasping for air, I said, "I'm Officer Wilson, what's the nature of your call, sir?"

The instructor just shook his head at me. "Not me, bud, you're here for him." He pointed behind himself, and there standing in the center of the mats was the largest, most muscular police officer I had ever seen. He made three of me easily. He was wearing a red man suit that was just screaming for relief because it barely fit his gargantuan body. He looked like an oversized quarterback wearing pads that were two sizes, too small. He had a look on his face that would have scared an old woman to death, and it was directed at me. Still gasping for air and sweat dripping off me, I cautiously approached him, standing as straight as I could and with confidence, my face coming to about his chest. I looked up, still panting, "What seems to be the problem?"

"I am going to fuck you up!" He spoke loudly and direct as he poked me in the chest with his huge pointer finger, nearly knocking me over.

"Yes, you are!" I couldn't come up with anything else to say. My mind was racing with the fact that this was the *fight* about to begin, and I needed to somehow win. I had to use all the training I'd been taught. I knew I wasn't going to hurt this guy, there was no possible way that I could. I also knew this was going to hurt me no matter what I did. I needed to use the moves taught to me and hope that something would work. If this guy gets me to the ground and pins me, I'm technically dead and I lose the fight, and fail the academy.

The standard words came out of my mouth, "Sir, you're under arrest for disorderly…." The red man picked me up like a football and tossed me to the edge of the mat. I quickly figured out that not all the instructors around the mat were here to critique me, they were here to keep me in play.

I didn't go down to my knees, luckily, and I quickly ran right back up to this behemoth. I took out my *inert* mace and sprayed him. This was allowed, and the "suspect" was to act briefly as if it had an effect. He played the game long enough for me to try to get a move on him. I was able to get him in a half-nelson before he tossed me again. *"Just don't go all the way down, don't let him get me down on my back."* My mind was racing, *"If he manages to pin me down, the fight's over,"* is all I kept thinking over and over.

I tried a few more technical moves, and each time he shook me off like a bug and tossed me around on the mats. Each time he threw me to the instructors, they'd shove me back to the center of the mats. *Give me a break, boys, I'm trying the best I can.* I realized that I was tiring fast. At our best, even with the adrenaline flowing, we're taught that we're good for about thirty seconds in an all-out fight. If you haven't overpowered your opponent after that amount of time in a hand-to-hand fight, the adrenalin will reduce, stress and exhaustion will take over, and your chances of success begin to decrease rapidly.

I was beginning to panic, I was well over a minute into this fight, well past the mark, and this guy was still coming on strong and not even breaking a sweat. I'm having a hard time staying on my feet, and he's toying with me like a cat with a mouse. I was about to lose the fight and fail the academy if I didn't think of something fast.

Red Man (*not his real name*) and I squared off again, face to chest. I decided this was it, either I do something now, or he's going to toss me over the instructor's heads and onto the gymnasium floor. Without putting a great deal of thought into it, I reached up, grabbed both of his shoulders tightly, reared my right leg back, and swung my knee right straight into his groin. I knew the red-man suit wasn't covering his balls very well, so I was hoping the padding there was thin, and for once I was correct in that assumption. I looked into his eyes, which widened with the shock of the kick and his shoulders drooped just a bit. I could tell this had hurt him. Before he could react, I swung my leg back and gave him an even harder one to his goodies. His reaction was real, this time his eyes squinted, and I heard *"Ooomph!"* blurt out of him. He wasn't faking, and I knew it. Still, with my hands tight on his shoulders, I swung my leg back once again and landed another knee hard to his groin. *"Ungh!"*

It was about the fifth time my knee connected with its target that I heard the groans from everyone around the mat who were watching this and felt the sympathy pains, along with the loud scream from Mr. Red Man himself. He went down to his knees, and I didn't let up. This time, with his crotch nearer the floor, I was able to connect with my shiny steel-toe boot to his gonads. His painful scream was accompanied by cursing this time, and this one had done him in. He tipped over sideways with tears in his eyes and went face-first into the mat. I managed one more boot to his balls before he was down completely, just to make sure he wasn't getting back up.

With him face down on the mat and his hands clutching his crotch, I managed to jump onto his back and quickly got my cuffs out. I yanked his arms back, and the cuffs barely fit onto his massive wrists. With one click on each wrist, he was down and cuffed. I had won the fight! I may not have done it the way the instructors wanted me to, but I had won just the same! I was never so happy, or exhausted at the same time.

I stood up and expected massive cheers from the audience while I did the Rocky Balboa victory dance. I did not receive this. Instead, I saw the head instructor nod to one of the other PT instructors who had been standing alongside the mat. This was his cue to join in and try to take me down. *Wait a minute, another one? C'mon, I did my job!* The instructor jumped onto the mat and joined the mock scene, pretending to be Mr. Red Man's buddy, and squared off with me. *No way! This isn't happening! I did my part already! And I'm tired!* I immediately leaped towards him with everything I had left in me, which wasn't much, and landed with my hands squarely on his shoulders, and I swung my leg back. This one wasn't wearing a padded suit, and I was going to make certain it hurt!

"STOP!" The command from the head instructor echoed. Lucky for this guy, too, because he was about to lose a testicle that day! The instructor had just saved him from becoming a permanent soprano in his church choir. The fight scenario was over.

I was directed to a table where I was to sit with the lead instructor and be told whether or not I had passed the test. The adrenaline had completely washed away, and I was feeling the effects of the fight. I limped over to the table, breathing heavily, sweating buckets, completely drained, and sat face-to-face with the instructor. My chest was heaving as I tried to get my breathing under control. He took his time looking me over. Finally, with a scowl on his face and one eyebrow raised, he let out a big sigh and remarked, "Kicked him in the balls quite a few times, didn't you?"

"It worked, didn't it?" I replied, still panting heavily.

Several moments went by with our eyes locked. After another huge sigh from him and without any change in the expression on his face, I heard the words I'd been waiting seventeen weeks to hear. "You passed."

I could barely contain myself, but I didn't show it. "Sir, thank you, sir," was all I could muster. I stood up and proudly limped out of the tac center and nearly collapsed once through the doors. This couldn't have been a good sign for Winslow, who was due to come in next, but it was all I had left.

I would be equally as proud of Winslow when I learned that he actually had training as a street fighter and had taken down his opponent in only ten seconds when he threw him over his head and onto the mat hard, pinning and cuffing him nearly instantly.

I also found out that throughout the day most of the PT instructors had donned the red man suit several times and had taken turns in the fight scenarios with various cadets. My opponent, however, only had the ability to take on one person this particular day, primarily due to his aching nuts.

◆ ◆ ◆

Very few moments in my life have I ever actually felt proud of myself and felt a sense of accomplishment from personal achievement. The birth of my daughter, my second marriage, having money left in the bank after all the bills were paid…

…And graduation day at the Maine Criminal Justice Academy.

I still get mushy thinking about this day. All of the cadets lined up outside the tac center's garage doors, all wearing their department's dress uniforms. The cadres are all wearing their best as well. A flag brigade from the Maine State Police heading it all up, and a bagpipe brigade, led coincidentally enough by the cadre whom we first encountered during the bag drill who'd been looking down and screaming at us from the running track on day one.

Inside the tac center were hundreds of chairs full of our family, friends, co-workers, and chiefs. On the stage were the academy director, other academy officials, and representatives from the State of Maine. At one end of the stage was a tack board with our department badges and blue graduation pins, waiting for our chiefs to pin on our uniforms as we marched to the stage once our names were called out, one-by-one.

The time had come. The bagpipes began, and the signal for us to begin marching in place. Commands came from the cadre, and the doors flew open. A standing ovation began as we marched into the tactical center for the last time. The feeling of accomplishment washed over me as I marched in line with my fellow graduating officers. I had made it. I had survived 126 days of training at the military-style Maine Criminal Justice Academy. I had achieved what many others before me had, and many hadn't had the ability to achieve.

I passed by my chief, seated next to my dad. By this time Dad had retired from the same profession of law enforcement and he was going to accompany Charles to the stage to stand with me as my badge was pinned on my chest. My wife and other family were seated in the aisle as well. The ovation from the audience didn't stop until we were all standing at attention at our seats in the front row. With the command to sit from the Director of the Academy, all went silent. After the obligatory speeches from the director, cadre, and other guests, we were called to march up by the stage. One by one our names were called, and one by one the cadets marched up on the stage and our chiefs came from the audience. One by one the badges and blue pins were attached to our uniforms, signifying we were now full-time academy graduates. Charles assisted my dad to the stage. Dad, who normally used a walker by now, refused it as he stood tall with Charles and made his way to the stage, and watched proudly as Charles pinned his department badge to my uniform, and cheers came from my wife in the audience. Charles saluted me, and I returned the gesture. The eighteen weeks were over, and as I look back, and to this day, I realize it was all worth the blood, sweat, and tears. I would never be the same person again. And I was damn proud of it. ♦

CHAPTER 7

HERE WE GO

Full-time law enforcement. I knew early on that I wanted to focus on illegal drugs as a specialty. Not necessarily prevention but rather the enforcement end of things. I knew that I wanted to be trained as a Drug Recognition Expert, a person who specializes in cases of people driving while under the influence, or DUI, of drugs other than just alcohol. Every full-time officer receives training in DUIs involving alcohol. However, the training for DUI drugs was specialized and intense. There were very few officers who had this training and even fewer who could teach it, and that was my ultimate goal, to be an instructor for the academy. It wouldn't be an easy road, with hundreds of hours of training ahead of me and many prerequisite educational and training requirements. I also knew that if given the chance during my career, I wanted to go undercover as an agent for the Maine Drug Enforcement Agency, the state's version of the Federal DEA.

Okay, it's time for another opinion, and a strong one at that. The strongest one I have as a law enforcement officer with extensive training in drugs, drug symptomology, and drug addiction. I simply can't tolerate people choosing to take illegal drugs. And yes, I said, "choose." I realize this may be an unpopular statement for some. I also realize many don't have the training and experience, and it's very easy to be naïve, especially when society and popular beliefs are force-fed to the public. No one forced the user to start using, and as a society as long as we're going to keep treating it like some big game of *The Boy Who Cried Wolf*, and continue to coddle the users, we're all in big trouble, especially the user.

It's not an "epidemic" as sort. Drugs have been around for hundreds of years. People today are treating it like it's new and just became bad; it's been bad for a long, long time. There is no medical cure for addiction and there never will be. This, to me, is the excuse of the moment and a great way for the medical profession to receive more money if they claim that this "disease" requires research for a cure. It's also a way for the medical profession to save face after the pill explosion that occurred about a decade ago, which caused much of the problem.

The cure for the addiction is simple, the user must stop taking the drugs. That's it people, no other miracles or mysteries surrounding it. Now, I'm certainly not saying it's easy once your body has reached the level of tolerance, and the user *must have* the drug simply to feel 'normal'. That's what it is, and the medical community knows it. The user's body, over time, must have the drug to simply function. The body needs to be taught how to return to normal by removing the drug either slowly or all at once, and allowing the user's body and system to detoxify. And let me be clear, everyone with the training that I've had over the years and experience that you'll learn more about knows this to be absolutely true. Unfortunately, mostly for political reasons, it's too easy to *agree* with those who want you to think otherwise, or use public pressure to agree with them.

I'm actually offended that anyone would label drug use a medical condition or call the user "diseased" like they're all suffering from some sort of mental illness, or they have a virus creeping through their bodies. What a stigma to attach to someone who's already having difficulty with an addiction to drugs. To me, it's insulting.

I've dealt with many users over the years, and I'll tell you that in my conversations with people who were addicted to drugs, I've discovered some things in common with those who have truly kicked the habit. One; they needed to go through the sickness of being off the drug. Some have felt like they were going to, and wanted to, die, and they don't ever want to feel that way again, so they've stayed away from the drugs. Two; they got away. And I mean physically moved away from their *friends* who hounded them to buy more, or offered them the drugs in the first place. These are the "cures," not a pill prescribed by a physician. As I said, there's no magical or medical cure for drug addiction, and blaming everyone other than the user doesn't help that individual at all. It only gives them an excuse.

I've also had several people tell me that it required being in jail, in a small cell with no other outside influences, to kick the habit. I'm all for treatment programs that offer support if the user wants it. That's the other thing; if the user doesn't want to get clean, they won't. You can't force rehabilitation on someone who isn't willing to get clean in the first place, and you can't always prescribe more drugs to help someone kick a drug habit. So don't get me started on things like methadone, Suboxone, or Narcan. These aren't cures. They're meant to assist the user to suppress withdrawal symptoms or reverse the effects and, only if used correctly. They're not meant to be long-term medical solutions.

Rehabilitation comes from two places, my friends, the heart, and the brain. You have to *want* to kick drugs and you have to be smart enough. And, by that, I mean strong-willed enough to get clean. These are the two ingredients, and much respect for those who do get clean, and the treatment plans they utilized, if any, to help them do so.

These losers that claim to want to get clean, or worse yet, *claim they're clean,* are one of the lowest forms of worm slime on the earth. They want you to believe they're willing to clean up if you help them, and this "help" usually takes the form of asking for money to purchase more drugs. And then they're *so sorry* when they get caught again. Folks, they never tried to get clean in the first place. And, news flash, methadone is an opiate! Duh, let's take an opiate to kick an opiate habit. *Oh, please don't get me going on Methadone clinics!*

And yes, we should blame the dealers obviously. We should punish them to the fullest extent and never allow them to walk our streets again. But along with this, we should also be punishing repeat offenders that use drugs. This idea that if we offer rehab programs, *a.k.a. forced rehab*, repeatedly over and over, then the user just might get better? Not so. I'm on the three-strike bandwagon. If you've been given the chance to clean up more than three times, I've got a nice long-term jail cell for you to spend a lot of time in to think about what you're doing. I don't want these people around me or my family, and stop coddling them by blaming society. If I go out and steal something, do we blame the store that has the item on its shelves? If I burn a building down, do we blame the company that created the match or the lighter? And holy crap, do we still blame the victims of sexual assault and not the perpetrator in the case of rape!? Hell, no we don't, so stop coddling hardcore drug users, and let's make them responsible for their actions!

There, that opinion is now out in the open. Let's continue, shall we?

♦ ♦ ♦

So, back to the start of my new career. Now there I was, the newest full-time officer for the Dover-Foxcroft Police Department, and still relatively green. I now had an entirely new set of responsibilities that came with a full certification as opposed to only the part-time training.

Dover-Foxcroft was a fairly quiet town. Of the more serious routine calls were the domestic disputes, which can get ugly. Burglaries were also popular, and many DUIs. Dover-Foxcroft, along with many other northern Maine communities, were former mill towns and somewhat depressed with high unemployment rates and not much for industry, or local jobs. Most of the mills had closed in the 1970s and 80s, and many of those who did have jobs had to commute out of the area to work. Local bars and intoxicated drivers were abundant. I gained a great deal of experience in administering the standard DUI field tests and became fairly comfortable with DUI traffic stops, which along with any other traffic stops can be unpredictable and dangerous. Traffic stops were routine when you weren't required to respond to other types of calls.

♦ ♦ ♦

As far as the traffic stops are concerned, I did have some interesting ones over the years. For instance, there was the guy I stopped for speeding who had his radar detector mounted to the dashboard when those things were still popular. While I was walking up to his vehicle, I could hear it beeping and I knew it had done its job to let the guy know I was nearby. Too bad he hadn't paid attention to it. I couldn't help but immediately ask him how his radar detector was working out for him, even before asking for his license and registration. He was obviously annoyed with his own stupidity, and his response was sarcastic, "Great." By the end of the stop, I didn't have the heart to give the guy a citation. By the time I'd finished writing his warning and walked back to his car to hand it to him, he'd taken the radar down, torn the wires out of the dashboard, and handed it all to me. "Here, I don't want it anymore." That was pretty amusing.

I had a system on which to base my decision on whether or not to issue a traffic citation. I would take into consideration how fast they were traveling or the severity of the violation. Their overall demeanor, the number of previous violations on their record, and most importantly, how creative their excuse was for violating the traffic laws in the first place played a part.

I had stopped a guy once for speeding. He was doing ten, maybe fifteen over the limit. I approached his car and leaned into his window. The guy immediately slapped his dashboard and said, "It's running out of gas!" He wasn't angry when he said it, and it struck me as amusing in the moment.

My response was, "And this makes it go faster?" We both laughed, and I let him go with a warning.

You'd always get the standard answers, "I'm late for this," or, "I'm late for that." Or, "Tires aren't the right size." I always loved that excuse. It really did depend a lot on their attitude. Those who were polite and admitted to the violation rarely received citations from me. Those that took an immediate attitude, like I was the person causing them to speed or whatnot? Yeah, those ones didn't make out so well. I always found it amusing when it was my fault that they were committing a violation and got caught. Like if I hadn't been sitting on the side of the road waiting for them, they wouldn't have been going that fast? *No, jerkoff, you just wouldn't have gotten caught.*

I stopped a pickup truck for speeding one fine day. The driver was going over the speed limit coming into town. Driving the vehicle was a young man, and cuddled up against him was his equally young girlfriend. I walked up to the truck with the full intention of issuing a warning. That is until the girlfriend decided to open her mouth and speak.

The man was polite, and when I introduced myself and asked for his information, he provided it. His girlfriend, on the other hand, who was busy fixing her makeup in the rearview mirror, felt the need to turn to me and say in a most egotistical tone, "You're making me late!"

"Oh, really?" I said in an equally sarcastic voice with one eyebrow raised. The look on her face told me that she was convinced that she was ten times more important than the rest of the population in the world, and I decided to give her the attention she most certainly deserved. I made it a point to spend the next twenty minutes going over the pickup truck with a virtual magnifying glass. It wasn't difficult to find three inspection violations to go along with the speeding infraction, and I spent just as much time writing out the booklet of tickets. I felt I was teaching this young man an important lesson. All the while they were waiting for me to finish writing the citations, being careful to check my spelling on each and every ticket, and enjoying the air conditioning in my cruiser, he had to deal with his girlfriend's piss-poor attitude in a nice cramped, and overheated pickup truck.

I walked back up to the vehicle and handed the young lad all four tickets, explained each carefully and fully, and told him to sign on the dotted lines and to make sure he pressed hard, each ticket had four copies. As I tore his copy of the summonses from the book and handed them to him, I smiled and said, "And you can thank your girlfriend for these." I then turned and walked back to my cruiser.

I think it's important to have fun at work and be polite to others.

It was mid-winter in Dover, and I was on a Saturday day shift. There was a fair pack of snow on the ground, but it was sunny and warm. Well, warm for a Maine winter's day, which means it was around ten degrees outside.

I received a call to respond to River Street, which is exactly what the name implies, it's the road that runs parallel to the Piscataquis River. A fairly large, fast-moving body of water and this particular house was located nearest to a dam next to an old mill site.

It seemed this young girl of six years of age wanted to go sledding in her own backyard that day. She was dressed warmly and had a nice pink sled that was sure to do the job. The problem was the backyard. It seemed that the backyard sloped towards the river and lasted for only about forty feet from the back door of her house before it dropped off a sharp embankment and down a twenty-foot drop right next to the river's edge. Additionally, there was no fence to prevent her from going over. The little girl had slid right off the edge. Now, you can't blame the young girl, she just wanted to go sledding.

But you can blame the idiot parents who let the kid go sledding in the backyard like she was Evil Knievel trying to jump over the Grand Canyon, and for not putting a fence up to stop her.

Now flowing water doesn't tend to freeze, so the only hard ice was just along the river's edge. Luckily for the girl, she went straight down instead of sailing into the swift-moving river and she landed, in her sled, on the narrow edge of ice along the bank.

I arrived and peered over the edge to see a young, frightened little girl looking back up at me. Her sled was pointed straight towards the water, and I knew if she moved, her plastic sled might very well slip right into the river with her still in it.

I yelled down and asked if she was alright, and in her tiny voice she said, "Yes, I'm alright. Are you coming down?"

"Yes, but not the same way you did." I told her not to move and called for the fire department to respond with a rope and, just in case, an ambulance. Although I was sincerely hoping we wouldn't need that.

By now a few neighbors had arrived to see what the commotion was all about, and I asked them to keep an eye on her. I needed to get down to her and I knew I couldn't go over the edge from where I was. I started to trudge along the edge of the drop until I could find a place to safely get down to the riverbank without breaking my neck. I had to cross several backyards downriver to find a spot where I felt I could safely get to the water's edge and work my way back to her. I climbed, or rather mostly slid down. I wanted to get back to this kid quickly before she went past me in her tiny, plastic, makeshift sailboat. And I can't say that once I was down and crawling along the narrow ice bar that my weight didn't make the ice crack, and even more dangerous under my feet as I made my way back toward the little girl. It certainly did.

There wasn't more than a foot or two of ice width, and thin ice at that. Beyond that was deep, fast-moving open river water. By the time I literally crawled on the edge back to her, the fire department had arrived on the bank's edge above us. I stood up and found some footing as best I could and picked the little girl up out of her sled. Any wrong move now and we were both going into the river together.

The fire department lowered a rope down to us, and I managed to tie it around her until I was certain she wouldn't slip out of it. "You're going up without me, okay?" I said to her.

"What about my sled?" *Great, I'm about to do my best impression of a river otter and she's worried about the sled.*

"I'll get your sled back to you, don't worry." I smiled at her. She smiled back.

The firemen hoisted the little girl up. However, there was no way I was going up the same way; she weighed a lot less than me. Plus, with my luck, these guys would get me halfway up just to drop me back in the river, laughing, watching, and waving bye-bye as I made my way towards the ocean some several hundred miles away. As soon as she was safely at the top, I grabbed the sled and started to make my way back to the spot I had come down to the river, thinking maybe if I went into the river now, I could use the sled to do some surfing and make the evening news. Once I was back at the point where I had come down the bank, the firefighters were there to toss me a rope and help me back up to safety.

The girl's parents were grateful for the combined efforts to help save their daughter from drowning. I still wanted to punch both of them for letting the kid go sledding in the backyard in the first place. *Take your children to a park or something!*

Years later I was in a grocery store somewhere else in Maine and was approached by a lady and her teenage daughter. The lady asked me if I knew who they were, which I didn't. It turned out to be the little girl that had gone over the cliff years before and her mother. They'd recognized me, and I was flattered they had. I was also pleased to know she was still safe and had given up her dangerous pastime of cliff diving on little pink sleds. Once again, they thanked me for the effort years ago and it felt good to know that they remembered the officer that helped them out that day.

◆ ◆ ◆

As I had mentioned earlier, fairly soon after becoming a full-time officer I expressed to my chief the desire to become a Drug Recognition Expert, or DRE. Again, any officer could perform a DUI that involved just alcohol, but very few had the training to process a DUI that involved drugs or a combination of alcohol and drugs, which is what we were seeing more and more on the streets, especially with synthetic drugs like methamphetamine being easily produced and still relatively new at the time.

The training was intense and required a good deal of commitment. An officer had to be accepted into the training program and had to prove to the academy they weren't doing it simply to boost their resume. You were required to apply, and be accepted into the course, be interviewed by the academy, and be accepted as a student. Between the time the schooling was completed, and the certification process was complete, which included a number of practice field drug evaluations in the presence of an instructor and a final exam that typically lasted several hours, it could be as much as six months or better before you were certified a full Drug Recognition Expert.

The information the instructors provided during the training was overwhelming, and the learning was ongoing far beyond graduating from the course, with there being literally thousands of legal and illegal drugs and many more being produced synthetically every day. The training taught you how to recognize the signs and symptomology of the drugs and drug categories, and delved heavily into the effects of drugs on the human body, tolerance, and dependence. Hence my strong opinions on drugs and users of drugs. I actually do know what I'm talking about sometimes.

The steps to processing a DRE are strict and straightforward. First, the officer who makes the traffic stop must determine that the suspect is operating a vehicle while under the influence of drugs, not just having simply taken drugs. The drug(s) must be impairing their ability to drive safely, the same as they would if it were strictly an alcohol-related offense. Once the officer makes the arrest, they contact the DRE to perform a series of physical and psychophysical tests on the suspect to determine what types of drugs they've taken, and whether the effects have impaired their ability to drive a motor vehicle.

By the way, alcohol, by definition, is a drug. A lot of people don't recognize that. It's categorized as a central nervous system depressant. In fact, any substance that causes a change in the body's physiology or psychology is a drug. Nicotine, caffeine, codeine, all drugs. Not every drug cause impairment, that's the key when determining a DRE-related offense.

The classroom piece was very intense with a pre-academy followed by the full DRE school. Every day we were tested on that day's knowledge, with no chance or time for studying until it came to the final exam. By then you had better know your stuff and have retained the classroom information because again, the final exam may come months after the classroom piece has ended and you've performed all of your required field examinations.

So, all in all, there were, and are, very few of us DREs out there. And I wasn't just satisfied with becoming a DRE, which I have to say once I achieved this, I became quite desirable and employable by other agencies. I wanted to become a DRE Instructor for the academy, which meant much more time and effort. In all, it took me seven years of prerequisite training to become an instructor in DRE, which also along the way afforded me the training in instructing other courses that dealt with impaired driving.

I also was among the elite few who became a state-certified instructor through the academy. However, my method of instruction training was somewhat unorthodox and something the academy hadn't experienced before, and I dare say not again since.

In the certification training, known as the Methods of Instruction Course, or MOI, towards the course conclusion one of your final assignments is to teach a brief course on a topic of your choice in front of your peers and academy staff who critique and grade your ability to present to an audience. Most students choose a topic that deals with the law and law enforcement. Why wouldn't they? They're students of the criminal justice academy and are being certified to teach criminal justice topics, and they're cops, so it makes sense, right? So, I say that most teach a criminal justice-related topic. Most, except for me.

Actually, during the course, you teach in front of your peers three times. I must admit, I was getting pretty bored with teaching and listening to classes about how to conduct traffic stops and how to fill out accident reports. Bored to the point I wanted to hurl if one more student told us which direction to point your cruiser's front tires when you make a traffic stop. *By the way, the answer is you point them out toward traffic and park your cruiser part way in the road. That way if some dumb rubbernecker hits your cruiser while you're standing at the window of the stopped car, your cruiser will go out into traffic and not slam into either you or the car you have stopped.* See, don't you want to hurl too after learning that? And, I had to listen to it over and over again for weeks.

For my final presentation which I was to be critiqued and graded on, I made the decision not to talk about anything that had to do with law enforcement. So, you might ask, what did I teach a class about? Social work? No. Firefighting? No. Airline catering or truck driving? No.

I decided to give a class on the history of the southern rock band, Lynyrd Skynyrd. *No, I'm not kidding.* It wasn't because I was obsessed with their music. They simply were a band that I enjoyed listening to and I admired their story, from the early years when they were formed, to the tragic airplane accident of 1977, to the resilient members who brought the band back ten years later and the success, to ultimately the additional members who'd passed since the crash. I had everyone in the class listening intently to this lesson, literally. Whether they enjoyed their music or even knew who this band was to begin with didn't matter to me. I was informative, animated, detailed, and taught the history of the band like it was a topic they were to be graded on later by written test. While I was teaching the class, I watched the sea of faces, and no one was falling asleep. In fact, they were even asking questions during the course, and ultimately, I ran past the allotted time that I was given to make the presentation. When I was finished, I received an ovation.

After class, my peers approached me with more questions about the band, and when it was time to meet with the three academy staff that were to critique my performance and grade me, they all shook my hand and told me I had conveyed the information like I was telling a bedtime story rather than instructing it for learning purposes and that it had a greater effect on the students. I received the highest grade, and the academy staff asked if they could keep a copy of my presentation outline for reference in future classes.

So ultimately, I must credit Lynyrd Skynyrd for helping me achieve my certification in teaching and with my Drug Recognition Expert Instructor certification. And seven years after beginning, I finally had attained the goal I'd set out to achieve. Not to mention that I had also, along the way, been deemed an Expert Witness in drug testimony in the courts and the district attorney was contacting me for my opinion on all the drug cases that came across his desk. I was also the only DRE in Piscataquis County and remained with that un-prestigious title for many years afterward. Most DREs are in the more populated, southern part of the state, and where I was in rural northern Maine, they were fairly scarce, and I was in high demand.

I would become very busy as a Drug Recognition Expert in the years to come. ♦

CHAPTER 8

THE FRIENDLY SKIES

It was 2011, and I'd arrested a guy for DUI who had caused a pretty serious accident. He had struck a pickup truck head-on that had a man and his young daughter in it. Luckily, the little girl was buckled into a safety seat, which is probably what saved her because her father flew head-first through the windshield. Luckily, he too survived.

The suspect had also, shortly after this, committed a federal crime of some sort like stealing checks from mailboxes or something. Nothing too serious but enough that when he was convicted, he was sentenced to a federal prison out-of-state. When it came time to arraign him in Maine on my DUI charges, he was required to be picked up and brought back from the federal penitentiary. At that time there were no "con-air" flights coming into Bangor, so our district attorney's office offered to pay my expenses to fly to North Carolina to pick this guy up. I was to take one other officer of my choosing to assist, so naturally my chief, Charles, offered himself for the free, all-expense paid round trip. Not that I could refuse, but he was my first choice as well. The gig was fairly simple, fly down the day before, grab a nice meal and hotel on the county's tab, pick the guy up the next day, and fly back home. Sounded easy.

It wasn't.

Believe it or not, I had never flown before, so I was nervous to begin with. As it turns out, I love flying! The feeling of being off the ground and above the clouds was incredible, and I've flown hundreds of times since. The day was clear when we departed for the Raleigh-Durham Airport. The only bad part, which will become important later, was that this was just post-9/11 and fairly soon after commercial flights were allowed in the air again, so the national "terror alerts" were still in effect, color-coded for significance. The alert was yellow this day, fairly low and safe.

We landed at the Raleigh-Durham Airport right after a light snowfall, which turned out to be the first snow North Carolina had seen in a couple of years. There was barely a quarter inch of snow on the ground, but it still brought the city that rarely sees snowfall to a standstill as opposed to Maine wherein at any given time during our harsh winters we can have one to three feet of snow on the ground and its business as usual.

The lady at the car rental center didn't want to rent us anything smaller than an SUV that had four-wheel drive, and they didn't have one. We tried to explain to her that we were from Maine, and a quarter-inch of snow was shorts and flip-flop weather to us. Finally, she agreed to rent us the largest sedan that she had, a white Chrysler luxury model with Texas license plates. *Really?*

So, we headed out in our pimp-mobile and located our hotel. It was nice enough and paid for. Later that evening when it was time to eat dinner Charles got the idea that we should find a strip club. Yes, a strip club, or at least someplace with cute, big-boobed women for Charles to stare at while he enjoyed a meal and cocktails. This didn't surprise me, Charles was an old whore-dog, which he was fully aware of and never denied.

Charles had also recently purchased a mobile GPS, which were just becoming popular in 2011, and he'd brought it with him. He didn't know how to use it, but he brought it anyway. He'd said it would help find the federal facility, which was in the extremely small town of Butner. In reality, I knew he'd brought it just so he could find a strip joint. He thought if he simply entered the location "strip club" he'd find one. He was wrong.

Now the Raleigh-Durham area, like many cities, has various ethnic-based neighborhoods. And don't get me wrong, mentioning this doesn't make me a racist. As I mentioned earlier, I'm about the furthest thing from a racist and I believe we're all equals. There's no skin color, only how we individually act and treat one another.

In fact, to get off-topic for a moment, one of my good friends who worked for the local ambulance service and has responded to many mutual calls with me over the years is a gentleman named Magid Shahin (*yes, his real name*). He's the nicest, gentlest, and funniest guy I've ever known, and we share laughs every time we see each other, reminiscing about calls we've responded to together. When we do get together, as soon as we see each other, we start laughing before words are spoken which always leads us to reminiscing. And yes, he has a cultural background from another country and has a slight accent. The best part about Magid is his ability to make fun of himself, a trait we all could benefit from. He's the kind of guy who walks up to people on the street and asks where he can get a green card. He strongly resembled Saddam Hussein, and he's the type of guy who'd ask someone if they minded if he dug a spider hole on their property. Again, I truly believe we all could benefit from his sense of humor and retain our ability to poke fun at ourselves. We'd all live longer with less drama in our lives. So don't get upset when I talk about ethnicity, I'm not attempting to be hateful. *No hate mail, please. I won't answer it anyway.*

Now back to our story.

The GPS first sent us to an abandoned strip mall. This didn't work for Charles. It wasn't quite the definition of "strip" that he was seeking. Next, it sent us into the Latino neighborhood to a restaurant that had the word "strip" in the name. We received a good deal of looks as we passed through, and I quickly told Charles to get us out of there. Finally, the GPS sent us into a neighborhood that appeared fairly low-income. The little talking box directed us to a vacant, dilapidated building that apparently hadn't been a business for quite some time. It could have been a strip joint at one time I suppose, there was no way of telling now.

"Jesus, Charles, we're two naïve white guys from Maine driving around this neighborhood in North Carolina in a luxury sedan with Texas plates on it. Someone's going to call the cops for just the way we look! Either that or they're just going to shoot us. Can we please get the hell out of here?!" Luckily Charles agreed, and we found our way to another neighborhood. He still wasn't done looking for boobs, but he finally figured out his expensive new GPS wasn't going to do the job. As we were about to pass by a fire station, Charles spotted one of the firefighters washing down the trucks in the parking area. Oh, yes, did I mention that now several hours later it was around eighty degrees out and the snow was gone about fifteen minutes after it fell that morning? Charles pulled into the fire station and up to the guy scrubbing the trucks and rolled down his window. "Hey, buddy, where can we find a Hooter's around here?" *Oh, Christ. Nice, Charles, you just made us sound even more stupid than we look.*

The guy smiled and belted out in his southern drawl, "Y'all want to go to Hooter's?!" *Oh, great, he's one of you, Charles. This is so embarrassing.* "Sure, I can give y'all directions ta Hooters!"

With the directions in hand, or rather in his head, we discovered the local Hooter's. The food was good, hot wings and beer. The scenery wasn't bad either; Charles had to make sure we got photos with all the young, well-endowed waitresses. And I didn't have to worry about where Charles's GPS was going to take us next for the remainder of the evening.

The following morning, we struck out for Butner, North Carolina. Now I have to say, there's nothing in Butner. Nothing but this huge federal prison complex in the middle of nowhere. The entire site consists of several ominous-looking buildings with very high security, even for a low-risk federal prison. We drove up to the main gate after getting so lost driving around the grounds that an unmarked security vehicle began following us. We were met outside by two large guards carrying equally large semi-automatic AR-15 assault rifles. They greeted us like we were going to commit a prison break. They were, however, just as amused by our northeastern Mainiac accents as we were with their deep southern ones. After explaining we weren't drug dealers looking to bust El Chapo out of their prison, they escorted us inside and through several locked, secure areas until we were in the correct wing of the facility. Charles handed the guard in charge the paperwork showing we were to escort one of their prisoners back to Maine and he, in turn, sent two guards to retrieve the guy for us.

The prisoner, Quirky McButterfingers (*not his real name*), showed up in wrist and ankle shackles with two heavily armed guards on either side of him. The way they had him chained up and were escorting him made you think he was one of America's worst offenders and a serious escape risk.

His initial statement to us, "Boy, am I glad to see you two, let's go back to Maine," was met with a loud, thunderous, "Shut up!" from one of the guards.

They wouldn't take the shackles off this guy until Charles promised to at least put handcuffs back on him for the transport out of there. They were surprised that we didn't bring an entire set of shackles with us. *That would look good on a commercial flight, the two of us bringing Hannibal Lechter on board. What's on the flight menu?* Charles cuffed up Quirky, and we were on our way to the airport.

What I expected to be a nice, quiet flight back to Maine quickly became apparent it wasn't to be. Immediately this guy wouldn't shut up. On the entire ride to the airport, this bonehead talked and talked like we were his best friends. And, I should say, he complained and complained about the conditions in the federal prison, which I completely didn't care to hear. I could care less how an inmate feels, their conditions are good enough for them. Most of the time too good. *Just shut up and do your time!* This guy just wouldn't stop squawking, and I didn't feel like flying several hours back to Maine with a Chatty Kathy. I had had enough when he finally asked, "Do you think they'll have peanuts on the flight? They better have peanuts!" I knew by now Charles had enough of this guy's mouth as well.

When we got to the airport and turned the car into the rental agency, we took Quirky from the vehicle and off to the side of the building, out of sight from the public. We decided to handcuff him in the front only, so he'd be more comfortable than having his hands cuffed in the rear, but it still looked bad. We were about to get on a commercial airline just after 9/11 with a guy in handcuffs. This was a time when people were terrified of flying, and security was at its highest in the country. However, I did manage to think of a way to use this to my advantage, which I'll explain in a moment.

"We can't take him on the flight looking like this," I said to Charles. "Even if we sit in the back of the plane out of sight, people are still going to wonder."

Charles thought for a moment, then he dug into his overnight bag and pulled out a T-shirt. He wrapped the shirt around Quirky's wrists, hiding the handcuffs, and then put a light jacket over his shoulders. It looked natural enough, or at least that it might just not make everyone nervous. This is when I seized an opportunity, which wasn't exactly politically correct, but I didn't want to hear this idiot's mouth the entire trip.

I leaned into him and quietly said, "If you open your mouth one time during the flight, *just one time*, I'm going to take that T-shirt off those cuffs, stand back, point at you, and yell out to everyone that you were responsible and see what happens. *Got it?!*"

"Yes, sir," he quietly and timidly replied. I could see out of the corner of my eye that Charles was smirking.

We made our way into the terminal, not without some funny looks. As best we could, we tried, but still couldn't entirely hide the fact that we were boarding a commercial flight with a prisoner. We spoke to security and informed them of the circumstances. They spoke to the flight crew who opted to put us in the very rear seats of the plane. We put Quirky between us in the three-seat row, and we were air bound for Bangor.

About an hour into the flight, Charles was reading a book, and I was watching the news on the inflight television. Quirky was happy enough as the stewardess did bring peanuts and a soda. All was quiet, but not for long.

Suddenly, the news announced that the terror alert had just gone to orange. I wasn't immediately concerned because, in the day's prior, the terror alerts had run the spectrum of colors depending on which politician had opened their mouth that day and said something stupid to put the country in an uproar. Then came the announcement from the cockpit that we didn't want to hear, "Ladies and gentlemen, we're being diverted temporarily to Liberty Airport in New Jersey. This is precautionary only, and we should be back airborne shortly after arrival."

Awe, shit!

Charles and I looked at each other with disgust. This just made the trip even longer. We landed on the tarmac in Jersey and that's where we sat. The airport was already packed with grounded and diverted flights by this time, and no one was being allowed off the plane. Every half hour for the next two hours, the airline staff would walk through the plane and reassure us it wouldn't be much longer and would hand out more bottled water, which just made us all have to pee more often, including Quirky who was far beyond being quiet anymore. And who can blame him? Charles and I were getting pretty agitated, too, and the more time went by the bleaker the outlook of this flight getting off the ground again that day.

Finally, about three hours later and well after dark, the final announcement came. The flight was grounded for the night, and they'd be pulling up to a terminal to have us disembark. We got off the plane into a terminal full of hundreds, if not thousands of others who were in the same boat as we were. No more flights were going out that night. We were stuck at the Jersey airport at least until morning.

"What are we supposed to do?" I asked Charles.

"Looks like we're bunking down here for the night and getting a flight in the morning," Charles replied, pointing to the floor.

"Oh, great. And just what are we supposed to do with Al Capone here?" Pointing at Quirky, "Cuff him to a kiosk? I'm not sleeping here. Wait here."

I left Charles with the prisoner and quickly located a security guard and explained our situation. He was more than accommodating. He told me to wait where we were, and a few minutes later, a Jersey Port Authority officer showed up. "Come with me, gentlemen," was all he said.

The officer escorted us down to the outside of the terminal where he had a cruiser parked. We piled in, and he lit the blue lights up, hit the siren, and we took off across the tarmac at high speed. This was like a movie, and I was enjoying every minute of it. We were weaving in and out of all the planes on the ground all the way to the other side of the airport and onto the streets of New Jersey. We ended up at the Jersey Port Authority station itself in record time, or should I say the usual time for the Jersey cops.

We were escorted to a holding area where several cells were lined up. The officer locked up Quirky and said his supervisor would be down to talk to us in a while. He then asked us if we wanted to see the memorial. We didn't know what he was speaking of, however, we politely accepted and followed him. The Port Authority had recently completed an in-house memorial to the public safety officers they'd lost at the Twin Towers on 9/11. The memorial was breathtaking, and even though neither Charles nor I had ever met any of the men and women pictured, we were brought to tears instantly. These were our brothers and sisters in blue and included fire and EMS who were lost in the tragedy as well. Neither of us had any words to offer, we just took it all in. The lump in my throat wouldn't have allowed words anyway, and tears threatened to stream down my face.

We should never, ever forget.

Afterward, we returned to the holding area and were met by the shift supervisor, who was more than willing to allow us to stay the night. The only condition was that one of us had to stay up and be responsible for our prisoner. Charles and I would take turns throughout the night getting some shuteye on a nearby couch. The officers at the Port Authority offered to get us each a meal from a local takeout and wouldn't accept any payment in return. This was better than any alternative considering our situation, and we weren't sleeping in the airport terminal and eating out of vending machines. The next morning, the terror alert returned to yellow, and we were driven back over to the terminal. The situation at the airport, however, was worse than we could have imagined. We knew that others would be looking to get on new flights out, but we had no idea. There were literally thousands of people in the terminal, all lined up in a massive crowd trying to get tickets to flights out of the city. Our wait in line was going to be hours, and that was if three seats on any flight to Bangor still existed once we got up to the attendants.

The officer who brought us back looked at me and asked, "Do you have your badge on you?"

"Sure, I do," I replied.

"Flash it."

I was puzzled, "My badge says Dover-Foxcroft, Maine."

"Flash it," he repeated.

Now I don't know if it was out of respect for authority, or simply fear, or a little of both, but when I took out my badge and held it up, it was like Moses had parted the seas. The throngs of people all stepped aside, and I walked straight up to the gate, not being stopped nor questioned by any of the hundreds of people who were in line ahead of me. It was the most amazing thing I'd ever seen. I approached the attendant's station, thanking everyone as I passed by them. At the ticket counter, I was provided three tickets to Bangor on the next flight out, no questions asked.

Luckily, there were no further issues and we arrived in Bangor safely and in time for Quirky to be arraigned on my charges. Charles and I would end up flying back to North Carolina three more times to pick up and drop off this guy before he was convicted on all charges. After that, the prisoner transports were contracted out to the feds, and no more crooks on commercial flights, and no more trips to Hooters in North Carolina. ♦

A MID-BOOK SHORT STORY

I was on the stand in the courtroom testifying in a DUI case as a result of an arrest I'd made one evening several months prior. My prosecutor had begun my testimony by asking me to physically demonstrate the Walk and Turn Test. This a standard roadside field sobriety test that asks the suspect to walk a straight line, heel-to-toe, nine steps out, and nine steps back without losing their balance and other indicators of intoxication. It wasn't uncommon for a prosecutor to ask the arresting officer to physically demonstrate field sobriety tests to a jury so that it helps them understand the process.

Now, I've always said that a defense attorney, whether hired or court-ordered and paid with our tax dollars, knows in advance when their client is guilty. If they feel so, at that point, they have no choice but to attempt to ruin the credibility of the prosecution witnesses, specifically the arresting officer. Defense attorneys will truly try anything to make us look bad to a jury, and I never knew what to expect of them.

When the prosecutor was finished with me, the defense rebutted. Mind you, the court-appointed attorney was barely educated, severely overweight, poorly dressed, and his greasy, stringy long hair looked as if he'd dunked his head in a bucket of lard that morning. He looked like the illegitimate love child of magician Penn Gillette. And he proceeded to attempt a magic trick that I had not seen before.

"Officer Wilson, you have demonstrated the standardized way in which to perform the Walk and Turn test to this good jury. Now, would you please stand up and demonstrate how my client performed the test on the night you arrested him?"

To this day, I'm not entirely certain why this bonehead asked me to do this. Possibly simply to make me look silly in demonstrating how poorly balanced his client had been, and then challenge how well I was imitating his client, I'm still not certain. I'd never had a defense lawyer try this trick before.

"No, sir, I can't," I said with a straight face, trying hard to control the anger that the question itself had invoked in me.

Impressed with himself in thinking he'd caught me, the magician waddled towards the jury box, smirked, and said in a louder, more direct, and sarcastic tone while pretending to act surprised, "But why then, Officer Wilson, with all your *experience* and *training*, can you not demonstrate how my client performed this test?!"

Not changing my expression at all, and responding in the most serious tone I could muster, "Because I'm simply not as drunk right now as your client was on the night I arrested him."

The magician's smirk turned downward, the jurors broke out in laughter, my prosecutor shook his head and gave me one of *those* looks…and I ultimately won my case. ♦

CHAPTER 9

THE STALKER AND THE BOO-BOO

Not all stories have, or should have, humor attached to them. The latter half of this chapter might. However, the first part of this chapter is the most personal segment that I'll offer. This segment deals with stalking and the victims of stalking, which I once was. No kidding, I had a stalker, and there's not much to joke about when this occurs. However, because it's a personal experience, if I do happen to add a bit of humor it's because once again humor is a coping mechanism and helps keep us from going crazy.

It was around 2003 when the young lady came into the Dover- Foxcroft Police Department and explained to the chief that she was taking a course in journalism or some crap at the Dover Higher Education Center and wanted to know if she could interview an officer for an assignment. She explained that she had been to the Sheriff's Department as well and had been given permission there to interview a deputy and now she wanted to interview a local police officer.

The young lady was maybe in her early to mid-twenties, and that's all the description I'll provide. No other descriptors are necessary as far as what she looked like. There are no physical similarities between stalkers, nothing that immediately stands out to say, "Hey, avoid this person, they're going to stalk you."

The chief offered me as her test subject as I was the officer on duty, and he wanted to show his willingness to work with the local higher education center. Again, there was nothing in her initial presentation that led the chief or me to believe this young lady wasn't legitimate.

I sat down with Miss Crazypants (*not her real name*), and she explained the course she was taking, her topic, and the assignment. It all sounded reasonable, which many good sociopaths have the ability to accomplish and present as the real deal. She proceeded to ask a series of questions, the standard stuff you'd expect. How long had I been a police officer? What made me want to be a police officer? Simple questions and I provided simple answers. At some point during the interview, however, the questions became a bit more personal. Was I married? How long I'd been married? How did my wife feel about me being an officer? At first, these were a bit off-topic, but you could initially believe that there was a tie-in for these. Then the questions became even more personal when it came to my relationship with my wife and the questions seemed to stray completely from the topic, and I quickly became uncomfortable and ended the interview. I attempted not to be rude, still believing this student was performing research for an assignment, I simply told her that time was short, and I had other things to do, and the meeting ended. Once she left, I took the opportunity to sarcastically thank the chief for offering me up on a platter to the weird student and thought no more of it.

A few days later, I met up with Deputy Peter Duncan of the Piscataquis Sheriff's Department who was working the same shift that I was that particular day. We met just to chit-chat during a quiet time, and during the conversation, Peter mentioned to me this weird young lady who'd interviewed him a few days earlier. He mentioned it because of the personal questions she'd asked him during the interview and how afterward it had bothered him. We quickly determined that we'd both been interviewed by the same student, and the questions were eerily familiar with both Peter and I being married, and the inquiries were more about our personal lives than law enforcement. Still, we both blew it off for the most part and simply thought the student was particularly bad in her interview techniques and probably wouldn't receive a positive grade on her assignment as a result.

It wasn't long after that my shift, and as part of our regular rotation, was in the evening slot for a couple of weeks. This is when the strange calls began. Almost like clockwork, every couple of nights I'd get called to the report of suspicious activity, and upon arrival, I'd find that the complainant was none other than the student who'd interviewed me. She'd call in reporting someone "following her" or she attempted to report "suspicious" activity that she'd noticed. The odd thing was that she didn't live in Dover-Foxcroft, so all of her calls were tied to the town. For example, she reported a car was following her in Dover, or she'd be shopping in Dover and thought someone was following her around the store. At times the calls would have nothing to do with her and they were more as if she was acting like some out-of-place "neighborhood watch" and reporting suspicious activity on someone else's behalf. All of the calls were unfounded and over time became more frequent.

The other thing that became noticeable almost immediately is that she'd only call in when I was working the shift, not on any other shift or when any other officer had the ability to respond.

Several weeks after the onset, I had another opportunity to speak with Deputy Duncan who'd mentioned to me that he was experiencing similar occurrences. Whenever he was on the evening shift, he'd be called to respond to the student, and as his poor luck would have it, she did live in the county and under his jurisdiction. As a result, her calls could be more home-related with all having to do with "suspicious" activity that she was complaining about. Also similar was that not all of her calls were related directly to her, but again the "neighborhood watch" type calls of activity. And again, all unfounded and only when Deputy Duncan could respond.

Deputy Duncan and I decided to keep track of the calls in the weeks that followed. What we were able to determine was what we'd expected, that the student would call in the activity when only Deputy Duncan or I were on duty and only when we could respond to the calls, as if she were monitoring the radio traffic on a portable scanner. We found that primarily the calls would be received in the evening and were more frequent on the weekends. As coincidence would have it, we also discovered that he and I primarily worked opposite each other. When Duncan was on evenings with the S.O., I would primarily be scheduled during the day shift in Dover, so the calls wouldn't overlap or be more than one per shift when either of us was working. If Duncan was working an evening shift, he'd get the call from her to respond at or near her residence. When I was on, I'd be called to respond to her somewhere in Dover-Foxcroft.

The calls themselves, at first, were nothing spectacular. Again, they'd be for something "suspicious." One of us would show up, find nothing going on, and leave. However, they were becoming more frequent over time and did have a pattern, which other than the fact they were an annoyance and taking up our time, they were beginning to become troublesome.

It also wasn't as if this woman was our only "frequent flyer." Every town has its constant complainers. Someone who calls in complaints for either attention or otherwise. It's like the person who constantly calls for an ambulance to take them to the hospital frequently because they have a mysterious ailment that turns out to be nothing. These people do this for various reasons. Most are for the attention and some just so they can see other people and have someone to talk to or take care of them. However, our situation was quickly becoming creepy and cause for concern.

Duncan and I continued to monitor her calls and frequency, and we both complained to our respective departments, who chalked the calls up to another nutjob seeking attention. But then things took a dark turn.

It was later in the evening in early winter, and I received a call to respond to a car that had struck a deer on Route 15 heading out of town. Car-deer accidents are very frequent between October and January each year, and it wasn't out of the ordinary to receive at least one per shift. These types of accidents cause a lot of damage to vehicles but rarely cause physical injury to anyone, except the deer which almost always resulted in having to put down the animal on site if it wasn't dead already from the impact to eliminate its suffering.

I arrived at the scene and found that the caller was my frequent flyer. She was sitting on the side of the road with her four-way hazard lights flashing. As usual, I became immediately annoyed to find I'd had to respond to yet another call with her. I approached the vehicle to find her sobbing in her front seat and I asked what had occurred. She stated she was traveling home, and a deer had jumped out in front of her, the standard explanation for a car-deer accident, however, again something didn't jibe.

It had snowed lightly enough to cause a coating on the roadway. She said the accident occurred right where her vehicle was now sitting on the side of the road. I observed no damage at all to her vehicle where she'd said the deer impacted it. But, more than this, there was no sign of a deer. No hair, no blood, no deer lying in the roadway. Not even any tracks in the fresh snow where it had come from the woods and supposedly impacted her car or had run away after the accident. The accident simply hadn't occurred.

After months of frequent calls from this woman, I finally snapped and had a meltdown of sorts on her. This was also the first call that didn't involve something "suspicious" that couldn't be explained away, and I took the opportunity, in no uncertain terms and in a stern manner, to explain the consequences of making a false report to the police. Up until this point she had been careful in that any call she'd made to law enforcement thus far, even unfounded, could possibly have had merit but now it was clear that no accident had taken place, and I'd had enough. Her BS calls were taking Deputy Duncan and me away from important issues and other crimes that needed our attention, and I was determined that it would end this evening. Or so I thought.

I was wrong.

It wasn't long after this incident that I was on the day shift with the chief when little Miss Crazypants walked into the department sporting a black eye. By this time, the chief and I had enough conversations about this young lady that he was beginning to listen to me when I spoke about how unsettling this had become. We both took the opportunity to interview her, and I don't doubt for a moment that her timing was planned so that she'd have another witness in the form of the chief to believe her next story whereas I had confronted her only a few days prior.

She detailed a domestic violence incident between herself and her "boyfriend" whom she'd named "Eric," in which he had assaulted her after suspecting that she'd been cheating on him. We listened to her story as we would any other complaint of this nature. However, I had my concerns immediately beginning with the supposed boyfriend which up to now we hadn't heard about nor ever seen her with, and we'd been responding to her bogus calls for a few months by this time. She had a name for the boyfriend, however no one that we immediately recognized as anyone we'd dealt with, and the boyfriend supposedly didn't live with her, which was convenient in that this would be the reason that Deputy Duncan had never encountered him on any response to calls at her residence either. In fact, she described this as a "long-distance" relationship in that he didn't live in Piscataquis County at all. That was convenient.

Then came the magic question, Chiefy asked her what had sparked the violence and who her boyfriend had suspected her of having an affair with. She responded that her boyfriend suspected she was having a relationship with a local "cop." I immediately felt ill along with immense anger in hearing her answer. I also, if I hadn't already suspected, knew that this woman was a true sociopath and was on her way to believing, or trying to make Charles believe, that she was actually having a relationship with either Duncan or myself. Just which poor bastard it was going to be was yet to be known. When asked, she also refused, for now, to name the "officer" in question.

As the report continued, and as both Charles and I suspected, she didn't want to press charges against her *boyfriend* out of "fear" that he'd retaliate. She was taking advantage of all the known fears that a true victim of domestic violence displayed and using them to her advantage to hide the truth. The truth, which both Charles and I were aware of, was that she'd injured herself. And, that she was seeking not only the attention, but also attempting to make herself believable and prove that this was a real situation whereas she'd been caught making false reports, and she was upping the ante big time with this newest claim. We immediately reported this to Deputy Duncan and the Sheriff. Duncan and I were permitted to work together to end this situation and investigate her newest "claims" of domestic violence to get the evidence we'd need to prove it false. We also were, from that point forward, not to respond to calls from the nutjob alone. Even if there were no other officers scheduled on duty with us, we were to use mutual aid from another department to respond to her bogus complaints.

The immediate problem was tracking down the "boyfriend," if he even actually existed. We ran the name she'd provided locally and came up with nothing, no one of this name existed in our area. The name was also suspiciously common, so in a search, we found hundreds of people around the state with the same name, so where to start?

We caught our break a couple of weeks later. Before this, her "relationship" had become her new "complaint" to us. She was now using her issues with her illusive boyfriend as a reason to have Duncan and I respond to her calls once again. The boyfriend would "show up" at her home or work, making threats, and then mysteriously disappear before our arrival. And as it turned out, she did, in fact, take classes and worked at the Higher

Education Center in Dover-Foxcroft in the evenings. Coincidentally, alone, so now it was easy for her to have us respond to her workplace and have no witnesses to back up her story.

The break came in a call to my department one evening. She reported that her boyfriend had left a threatening note on her car's windshield. As luck would have it for me, Duncan was also working the evening shift at the sheriff's department, so I asked him to respond with me. We arrived at her workplace, and she pointed out a note written on a small piece of notepad paper that was tucked under her windshield wiper. The note read that her boyfriend was aware of her "affair" and threatened not only to harm her but also the "officer" she was seeing. The note had a distinctive, simple tone to it, but it was the signature that caught my attention. It ended with, "Signed your boyfriend, Eric."

This was immediately found to be odd. Why did her significant other feel the need to not only remind her that he was her boyfriend but also what his name was? Didn't she already know these two facts? Plus, why use the word "signed?" We know he's signing it, so why the need to remind us that he'd signed it, or even who he is? Who else is going to leave a note like this on her windshield?

The other interesting thing that stood out was the handwriting. It appeared to be deliberately messy, so as to not match our immediate suspect's handwriting, the girl herself. There was no doubt we suspected she'd written the note herself as another excuse to have us respond to her calls and increase the attention she was gaining from the fictitious boyfriend's recent behavior. And, if she had any brains at all, she knew we were suspicious and had deliberately attempted to disguise her handwriting.

We took the report and left. On a hunch, we also took the opportunity to return the following day when she wasn't working to speak to her supervisor. Not only did we think it would be important that they know that they had a scorned boyfriend leaving threatening notes at her place of work, but I wanted to look for something else. I gained permission to look around her work area and the office in general. In a storage closet, I found a notepad matching the paper the note had been written on. Even more interesting was that the notepad was part of a stock and not sold individually or in retail, it had to be ordered in bulk. As suspected, the note had been written from within her office on paper that was only obtainable in bulk, and it happened to be in this very supply closet that we were looking in.

We were close now but not quite enough yet. Duncan and I were determined to figure out if there was any actual person named "Eric" so and so in her life. We'd exhausted quite a few resources to determine if the full name she'd provided was an actual person, and every trail had come to a dead end. We did have enough of her history that, on another hunch, I was able to locate her high school yearbook and we indeed found a classmate of hers with the exact name she'd provided. Due to her age, we knew the contact would be at least ten years old, but we had to take a chance and eliminate every possible angle. With a bit more digging, we located a telephone number for the "Eric" in the yearbook who now lived out of state, and I placed a call to him. After explaining who we were to a very confused person, I asked him if he knew our suspect.

"That crazy thing?! Yes, I *knew* her. She's nuts!" This was his first response and the one we were seeking. Eric went on to explain that our suspect had fixated on him and stalked him all through high school to the point he'd had to report her to the faculty. He said that he'd never been her boyfriend, but not as far as she'd been concerned. As he continued to explain his situation with her in school it became overwhelmingly familiar to Duncan and me, and the circumstances with her. Right down to the fact that even with Eric, she'd created a fictitious "boyfriend" and the self-harm to attempt to cause jealousy and attention for herself.

As we continued to listen to Eric tell the story, it was as if we were watching an episode of crime TV on a cable investigation network, only we were the victims of the episode. It was sad in a way, however, we now had all the evidence we needed to bring an end to our case of stalking before it became any worse.

Ultimately, she was charged with filing a false report, and through a plea deal that included mandatory therapy sessions, the stalking charges would subsequently be dropped. She was ordered to pay back to the two law enforcement agencies the equivalent in cost of manhours that she'd caused with all the false complaints she'd reported over a total of ten months.

And this finally put an end to the stalker.

♦ ♦ ♦

So, strange things happen. In anything we do, there is the potential for good results as well as bad. There are logical decisions and some that could have used a bit more thought. We're all human. Well, most of us anyway.

Some stories are worth telling and some are better left untold, it's difficult at times to determine which is which. And then there's that whole "gag order" thing that comes into play from time to time, but the time limit has expired on this next segment, so I'm going to tell this next story anyway.

I'm a true believer in a cop's intuition. Some of you may have heard of this, some not, but most of you probably have an idea of what true intuition is and its actual meaning. That little warning bell that goes off in our heads alerting us when something isn't right. That rush of adrenalin when the little voices on your shoulder are telling you that all isn't as it should be and to pay more attention. And I don't believe in intuition just because I think I possess it or because I've been told I do. I think it's something that comes with experience and training that many dedicated police officers have, even if they don't realize it. I believe it's something that's self-taught over time, and most of the younger officers don't yet have it. It takes a few years of experience under your belt before it kicks in, but when it does, it's a good tool to have and certainly may save your life. A few stories to come will show examples of how my intuition worked for me, including this one.

It was a rainy day in June, and I was on the day shift, late afternoon. An arrest warrant had been sent over from the dispatch center for a guy who was supposedly living in an apartment in town. Every so often, we were provided a list of arrest warrants for people who were supposed to be living locally, however, most lists were fairly inaccurate, and many had old and inaccurate addresses. Most criminals don't stay put in one place very long, so the address they had when they committed their crimes wasn't necessarily correct when warrants of arrest were issued. Plus, wanted criminals aren't quick to report their change of address to those who need to know for some strange reason.

The lieutenant was on duty that day, Albert Baker. We had a warrant for a guy in town, and he wanted me to go with him to make the arrest. I didn't ask immediately what the warrant was for, although I probably should have, but I assumed Baker had that info and if it were important enough, he'd let me know. *By the way, never assume.*

I'll call the "wanted" guy Donald Castroni, which obviously wasn't his real name, but in the grand scheme of things he was nothing anyway, so let's not give him any credit.

What we knew was that his most recent address was apartment number 4 over the local pizza joint on Main Street downtown. The LT and I proceeded downtown to pick him up if he was even still living there. The apartments were on the second floor of the business with a front and rear stairwell that led up to a long, narrow hallway with two apartments on either side, numbered one through four. The problem was that none of the apartment numbers were displayed on the doors, so good luck to us in figuring out which one it was. The hallway was tight, only about four feet wide. The apartment doors were solid, except for one which had a window with the shade drawn most of the way down.

We stopped at one door that we believed belonged to Castroni. We stood on either side of the door, and Baker knocked. No one immediately came to the door, however, I could hear people talking in the apartment across from this one and could see movement through the cracks in the shade. I waved to Baker, letting him know that I thought Castroni might be in this other apartment. Before I could knock on the other door, it opened, and our suspect stepped out into the hallway. He gave us a nervous look and didn't stop as he slid between us to his apartment door. He opened his apartment door as the LT was attempting to explain why we were there.

It was at this point that intuition kicked in and I had "the feeling." I knew this wasn't going to go well at all. It was the scowl and semi-confused look on this dude's face, no words from him, and his continuous motion without stopping that told me this guy already knew why we were here and that he wasn't going to go back to jail easily.

We followed him inside his apartment with Baker still giving the obligatory speech, "We're police officers and we need to speak with you…"

The apartment was tiny. Inside the door was a barely twelve-by-twelve-foot room that served as the kitchen/dining area. Another same size room adjacent was the living room with an opening between the two rooms about the size of a large doorway. Just off the room we'd entered was a small bathroom and a tiny bedroom. I wasn't able to see what tiny rooms were off the living room area, but it couldn't have been much. The small spaces were filled with various furnishings, there was very little room to move around with this guy's personal junk in our way.

Castroni was also a large man. Not necessarily muscular but just physically large, almost to the point of obesity but also tall to go along with it. He made at least two of me.

He was still looking at us nervously when Lt. Baker got to the important part of the speech, "We have a warrant for your arrest."

And the fight was on.

Castroni said loudly, "I'm not going back to jail!" and he backed away from us. I grabbed onto his left arm while Baker took hold of his right. Castroni began to fight and swung me around, trying to get me to let go of his arm. He ended up thrusting me into the side of his refrigerator. The impact of my body slamming up against it knocked the fridge over enough to block the doorway to the bedroom. I wasn't about to let go as he continued to try to shake me off. Baker still had hold of his right arm and was having just as much difficulty as I was trying to get this guy under control, or at least to the floor to get him cuffed up, but the issue was space. We were wrecking the kitchen with our bodies as we tangled with this guy. This was a time before the taser, and our only other option was pepper spray, which in a small space like this apartment if we'd unloaded a can on this guy, we were surely all to feel the effects, so hand-to-hand was all we had at the moment.

Castroni continued to fight and flail and finally managed to get his right arm free from Baker, and I saw his hand disappear down towards his waist. When his hand came back up, he flipped open a butterfly knife that he apparently had in his pants pocket. He reached over his head with the weapon just as I yelled, "Knife!" and began to backpedal, letting go of his other arm to get out of his reach, and to reach down for my gun.

Unfortunately, Baker didn't see the knife in time to back up as quickly, but he did get his left arm up in a defensive motion just as Castroni brought the blade down across Baker's bicep. I was ducking backward to Baker's right side, so I watched the blade of the knife cut the air in front of my face, and if I hadn't started backing up when I did, I would have been cut from brow to cheek. Quick reflexes kept my nose on my face, but Baker wasn't so lucky.

There were only a few feet to back up, and I managed to get my gun out and put the sights straight on Castroni's chest before I found myself standing in the small opening between the kitchen and living room. Baker stumbled backward and ended up on my right side in the same space with his gun out as well.

We both began shouting the proverbial, "Drop the knife, or I'll shoot!" over and over in unison together. In these first few moments of adrenaline, Baker hadn't even realized yet that he'd been cut. Castroni had backed up against his kitchen counter with the knife raised above his head again and soon realized he was about to be full of holes if he moved towards us, or moved at all.

Almost immediately he lowered the knife to his other wrist and held it as if he may cut himself and began yelling, "Kill, me, just kill me…I won't go back to jail…just kill me! KILL ME!" *Oh, great, now I can't shoot him! These walls are probably paper-thin, and the rest of the building can hear us. I can see the headlines now, "Man asks the police to shoot him, so they did."*

We continued to command Castroni to drop the knife, and he continued to hold it to his wrist. I held tight to my gun and kept the front sight square on his chest. If he so much as coughed in our direction, I was going to put two in his torso and one in his head. I was carrying my own .40 caliber semi-auto at the time, and I was certain that it would do the job if need be, not to mention that he did just cut my co-worker and at any moment he could change his mind again and lunge toward us. We were now in a full-blown standoff with this guy, and it was tight in there.

As it turned out, the apartment he'd come from belonged to his girlfriend, who was curious as to why her boyfriend was now yelling, "Kill me, kill me," from his apartment. The door to Castroni's apartment began to open. I was standing right beside it and kicked it back shut with my left foot, planting it against the door, telling the woman to stay outside in between yelling for Castroni to drop the knife. I didn't need her coming through the door right between us and Castroni. The worst-case scenario is that he grabs her in his desperation, puts the knife against her throat, and uses her as a hostage in an attempt to get us to back away. Yes, folks, criminals will use their girlfriends and even their own children as shields. I've seen it before.

What a sight this must have been. Me with my feet spread, holding a gun on this guy and using my left foot to keep the apartment door closed while the girl was banging on it from the hallway side, demanding to be let in. To my immediate right was Lt. Baker with his left shirt sleeve torn open and blood beginning to stain it while Castroni was holding a knife to his own wrist and begging for us to shoot him. Where was Norman Rockwell, I needed this picture to be painted for posterity.

I managed to get my left hand down and across to my right side where I kept my portable radio on my duty belt. I keyed the mike, and for the only time in my career, I called out the ten-code that let everyone else on that frequency know that something had gone terribly wrong and to send the cavalry fast, *"10-74."* This is the, *"I need help now and I don't care who you send,"* code for when things are very bad. And they were very bad at that moment.

The shouting stopped from both sides and now we were somewhat more calmly attempting to get Castroni to put the knife down. For the moment, he wasn't asking for us to kill him, or anything else for that matter. His girlfriend realized she wasn't getting through the door, and she'd shut up for a bit, too. Baker's adrenaline lowered enough for the pain to kick in and he now realized that he was cut. And in the brief moment of silence, for the first time, I realized that Baker and I were standing in the opening between the kitchen and living room, and all of a sudden, my academy training flashed back into my head.

The room behind us was just as small as the kitchen we'd been fighting in, and there was no other exit door than the one I had my boot up against. Training teaches us that even if a suspect is shot full of holes, the adrenalin will keep them going for fifteen to twenty feet if they decide to rush you before they drop. We're taught to have a space to retreat to while we're shooting, so the perp doesn't "tag" us with a knife, even though they may be mortally wounded. We currently didn't have an escape route behind us, and we both weren't getting out the apartment door safely. The truth was if he lunged and we ended up shooting him, he may still get one of us with that knife again before he drops.

The brief silence and my concentration was broken by the door lady banging on it again, "What's going on in there?!"

"A situation! Stay out!" I yelled to her, my foot still tight against the door she was trying to open. Castroni started repeating again that he wasn't going back to jail. At that point, I'm beginning to ponder just what he'd done to hate prison so much. I also had to reach down to my radio again and turn it down with dispatch trying desperately to get back in touch with me. *Sorry, I don't have time to chat right now.* I also didn't want Castroni to hear the radio traffic. He was under enough stress at the moment.

Lt. Baker leaned over to me. *Damn, I almost forgot he was here.* He said softly, "How bad is it?" *Oh, that's right, he's been stabbed, hasn't he?* I glanced over briefly and saw a bloody sleeve and red fluid dripping from the tear.

"I can't tell, I just know you're bleeding," I whispered. *Like I have time right now to perform an examination.* Obviously, this wasn't what Baker wanted to hear. He began trembling and his hands were shaking nearly uncontrollably.

"I have to leave," he said softly. *What?* Either that was a really good ventriloquist act by Castroni or Baker just said he has to leave. *Really? Do you have somewhere more important to be? What a coincidence, so do I, but I have to stay!* "I have to go," the LT said again, his voice crackling.

"What did he say?" Castroni inquired calmly.

"He says he has to go," I said almost sarcastically to Castroni.

"Why?" A surprised reaction from the perp. *Why do you care, dumbass? Are we all friends here now? You all of a sudden care? This is getting stupid.*

"Because you stabbed him," I said very straightforwardly. There was no sense in lying, and judging by the look on Castroni's face and the tone of his voice, up until this point I honestly didn't think he knew that he'd hurt anyone. I think his intention had only been to threaten us with the knife and get us away from him. The look was of total surprise, and if I was lucky, it would work long enough for me to get Baker out of the room.

"Okay," Castroni replied. *Oh, good, the guy with the knife is on board with an officer leaving the room. Go figure.*

I looked back over at Baker, who was now not only shaking violently but also turning pale. Now the next problem is how do I get him out of the room? He can't go behind me, there is no behind me, just another room without a door. He has to go in front of me, which poses its own issues seeing that in front of me is my gun pointed at Castroni who's holding the knife he'd stabbed the LT with in the first place.

"Okay, I'm going to let this officer out," I said softly, looking straight at Castroni's eyes for any reaction. He simply nodded. I called out to the woman, "Hey, lady, I'm opening the door. *You are not coming in*! An officer is coming out. Got it?!"

"Yes," came the response through the door.

Looking at Castroni, I said, "You ready?" Castroni nods again. *Great, now I'm asking the perp's permission.* I look over at Baker, "You ready?" He nods. *This is just ridiculous now.* I looked back at Castroni, "And you stay still right where you are, got it?!" He nodded again. I realized I was speaking like a schoolteacher to her first-grade children.

I raised the barrel of my gun and took my foot off the door just long enough for Baker to dart in front of me and out the door. I slammed my foot against the door again, closing it tightly. Okay, Baker was now safe, now it was just me and Castroni, my gun pointed back at him and his knife still tight against his wrist. My head tilted against my right arm, eyes right down the sights and onto his chest and my neck hurting terribly now. I knew backup was on its way but every second, and we still have only been a few minutes into this so far, seemed like an eternity. "You ready to leave yet, too?" I asked Castroni, again almost sarcastically.

"Can I have a cigarette?" was his response.

"I don't have any," I said.

"Neither do I," Castroni said with a sigh.

"I do," the door lady spoke in a casual voice from the other side of the wall. *Oh, for Chrissake!*

"Can she please give me one?" Castroni whined. I thought for a moment. Might as well. Might keep him calm, build some trust, and it certainly can't get much stranger than it has been so far. I let my foot ease off the door just a bit, and an arm extended inside with a cigarette in its hand. I reached over and took it and pushed the door shut again with my boot. I tossed it over and Castroni caught it in the hand whose wrist he had the knife against. If nothing else, we made a good circus act.

"Can I light it?" making a motion to a lighter on the counter next to him.

"Go ahead." As I glanced to see the lighter, I also noticed for the first time several kitchen knives that were lying on the counter just behind Castroni. I didn't get a good feeling knowing he was that close to even more potential weapons. He didn't seem to notice them as he put the cigarette in his mouth and grabbed the lighter to blaze it up. It was almost amusing watching him hold the cigarette in his left hand while he continued to hold the knife to his left wrist in his right hand. I wasn't about to make any assumptions as to his intentions with the knife though. That would have been a mistake that I wasn't willing to make. Rule number one as an officer, never get complacent. Rule number two, never assume anything. Rule number three, don't think about having to go to the bathroom, or you'll have to go to the bathroom.

I needed to start a conversation with Castroni in an attempt to keep him calm and start to build that trust, so we could end this mess. I had received some minimal training in hostage and standoff negotiations that included taking a blank piece of paper and on it creating two columns. In the first column, you have the "positives," the topics that the suspect doesn't mind talking about, and to help keep them calm. In the other column, you have the "negatives," or topics that agitate the suspect and you avoid talking about these things. I had to create the form in my mind and began a casual conversation with Castroni, all the while keeping my gun up and pointing at him, and every few sentences asking him to put down the knife and see where this all goes. He was willing to carry on a conversation with me, having earned some trust on the whole allowing Baker to leave the room and the cigarette thing.

Shortly into the conversation, a knock came at the door. "Dave, it's Jerry Robinson, can I come in?" It was the county sheriff along with other deputies waiting in the hallway.

I asked Castroni if he minded the sheriff coming into the room. I assured him that no one was going to try anything, it was just another officer coming in to take Baker's place and to talk with him. He was okay with this as long as no one else came in with the sheriff.

I took my boot away from the door, and the sheriff squeezed into the room cautiously and introduced himself to Castroni, obviously not getting too close and not extending his hand. Almost lightheartedly I explained the situation to the sheriff to keep the mood light. *Sheriff Jerry, this is shithead, shithead, this is Sheriff Jerry.* That sort of thing.

Castroni slowly began to ease his way backward towards the corner of the kitchen closer to the bathroom door. This put a couple more feet of distance between us but unfortunately, this also put him closer to the other kitchen knives on the counter, and we weren't talking butter knives, these were steak knives. I moved away from the door to face him better, cautiously, and the sheriff slid behind me and took up a position to my immediate right.

"Donald, do you mind if I remove those other knives?" I asked, motioning to the counter with my head. Castroni looked at the counter and realized what I was speaking of. There was probably a total of five or six steak knives within his arm's reach.

"Why?"

"I'd just feel more comfortable if they weren't there. Do you mind if I pick them up and hand them to the sheriff?"

"Okay." If nothing else, he was quite agreeable to everything. Everything that is except for putting down the knife that was in his hand and leaving with me.

Keeping my gun well within my control, I reached forward and took all the knives in my hand, stepped back, and handed them to the sheriff. This is how freaking small this room was and how close we were to each other. As I did this, Castroni backed up further and was now completely in the tiny bathroom just behind the doorway. I actually didn't mind this because unwillingly he was backing himself into a corner that had no way out, and he could only see me in front of him. Unless the sheriff tilted his body in towards me, Castroni couldn't see more than half of the sheriff, and he also didn't have a view of the rest of the kitchen or adjacent living room. In his current position, he also couldn't see the apartment door anymore. After handing off the knives, the sheriff silently opened the apartment door and allowed three more deputies to quietly enter the room without Castroni even knowing he'd done this or that they were now inside the apartment with us.

Castroni and I carried on a conversation with me keeping track of the 'positives' and 'negatives' in my tired brain. The sheriff chimed in only to back up anything I was saying and never attempted to take over the conversation. I began to attempt to convince Castroni to go to the hospital with me where he could receive crisis counseling rather than jail. I wasn't lying to him, I had the ability to do this whereas if he agreed to go with me to the hospital, he'd receive a psychological evaluation before being taken to a jail cell. I figured this might get him to put the knife down and leave with me peacefully, thinking he wasn't immediately going to prison. The sheriff continually backed up this idea each time I mentioned it. The other deputies in the room remained quiet and hidden, with their sidearms out, ready to assist only if needed.

About forty-five minutes into the ordeal my gun felt like it was weighing about a hundred pounds, and my arms were threatening to fall asleep, so it didn't bother me at all when Castroni asked if he could sit down on the toilet seat.

"You're in charge here, Donald." If he did park his butt on the toilet, it would put him further into the bathroom and behind a sink. In this position, if he had any inkling of charging me, he'd have to stand up and go around the sink. This heightened my comfort level and allowed me to place my gun in the "ready position" which allowed me to lower my tired arms and point the barrel at the floor, still ready to spring back up if needed.

The sheriff leaned in and chimed in at this point, "See, Donald, the officer has lowered his gun. We're all friends here. You can trust us, and we need to bring a peaceful resolution to this situation." The sheriff then leaned into me and whispered, "The Goddam tac team is on their way."

Awe, crap! The State Police tactical team.

The tactical team was the division of the Maine State Police that deals exclusively with hostage and standoff situations. They're your typical gung-ho, dogs on a leash, just waiting to be let out of their cage-type guys who aren't very stealthful. They were good, but they also worked very independently, and I knew these guys were going to charge in and take over when they arrived, and I really wanted this situation to end another way. I could also tell by the sarcastic tone of the sheriff when he told me that felt the same way. The sheriff's department didn't exactly play well with the state police. More on that a bit later.

I also knew these guys had to respond from various other parts of the state, so I had a little time left but not much. I ramped up my efforts with Castroni and focused solely on having him leave with me. I told him straight out that the tac team was on their way, and once they arrived, I wouldn't be allowed to stay and how important it was to take him to the hospital.

"These guys don't fool around, Donald. They'll come in and take you by force, and I don't want that."

The sheriff reiterated my words, "He's telling you the truth, Donald. If you leave with Officer Wilson, he'll take you to the hospital quietly and you won't be harmed."

It was apparent that Castroni was beginning to wear down and our words were having an effect on him. He was asking a lot of questions about the process of a hospital crisis evaluation, which meant that he was seriously considering it. He also knew his alternative was jail and he didn't want to be taken by force.

One of his positives was his family, so I stressed hard, "Think of your family, your family would want you to…*etcetera, etcetera*." I have to admit, I was just as tired as Castroni at that point; I was desperately trying to think up things to say to convince him to give up.

We were into this for well over an hour when I began hearing the tac team coming. As I said, stealth is not in their vocabulary. You could hear the speeding engines and sirens approaching. I began to plead with Castroni now. "Donald, we've got to go. Just you and me, bud, the two of us walking out together and we head to the hospital. We're running out of time. These guys don't fool around." The sheriff the whole time backed me up on every word.

Now, I was hoping that even though the tac team was on site, they'd have the good sense to have a bit of tact as the title hints. You know, take a few minutes to get themselves filled in on the situation and use some protocol. I'd been taught that in negotiation situations, a secondary negotiator listens to the primary negotiator for a bit to see what they're talking to the suspect about. See what's working and what's not working in the conversation, so if they have to switch out, they have some idea of what they should and shouldn't discuss with the suspect. I knew that information was getting in and out of the apartment, having seen a deputy come and go out of the corner of my eye that Castroni had been totally unaware of. I had it in my head that a negotiator would sneak into the room along with the other deputies that Castroni couldn't see and listen for at least a few minutes to what the conversation between Castroni and me was about before deciding to take over. I was hoping.

Once again in my career, I was wrong.

You could hear commotion on the streets below. Yelling, K-9 dogs barking, more sirens and engines. I was at the point of begging now, "Donald, please. Give me the knife and walk out of here with me!" The sheriff echoed the words with me, pleading for this guy to give up peacefully now.

Castroni could also hear the commotion outside on the street, and the expression on his face nearly turning to fear. Fear of what the tac team might do to him or where they'd take him. We could hear boots stomping up the stairs and knew the team was in the building. As soon as Castroni heard this, he stood up from the toilet. I kept my gun down but heightened my awareness, not certain of what he was about to do. Castroni then looked me straight in the face, turned the knife around in his hand, and holding the blade instead of the butt, he reached his arm out. *Holy crap, he was handing me the knife!* He was ready to go with us and avoid the confrontation with the tac team. This was about to be a win-win situation.

Castroni took one step forward, and I was about to do the same and take the knife from him when the barrel of an AR-15 semi-automatic assault rifle came over my left shoulder, pointing at Castroni. Holding the gun was a member of the tac team who simply said to me, "You can leave," in a stern, no-nonsense voice. I looked back at Castroni, who had quickly turned the knife back around and had the blade back on his wrist again. I looked up at the sheriff, who was now glaring at the tac team member, obviously disgusted by his presence. Before either myself or the sheriff could say anything, the tac member said just as sternly to us, "Leave, now!"

We backed out of the room along with the other deputies who had been inside with us throughout the ordeal. We were met outside the apartment door by other tac team members each directing us to leave the building. I'd be lying if I didn't say the frustration within me was welling up as I stormed down the hallway, down the stairs, and out onto the streets, which were now lined with officers of both my department, other deputies from the sheriff's office, and state police uniformed officers. Behind a line of caution tape that had been strung along the street and surrounding the entire downtown neighborhood were members of the media and the public. Inside the caution tape were police vehicles and the tac team's command vehicle, which resembled an oversized motorhome.

It was now evening, and the combination of lights of the media cameras and emergency lights on all the vehicles was bright and blinding, colorfully reflecting off the light rain that was falling from the sky. Oh, and Lt. Baker was back on the scene as well. He had gone to the hospital, and it turned out he had barely a boo-boo on his arm. In his defense though, he didn't realize at the time that a band-aid would have sufficed, and possibly he'd been able to remain in the room as my backup. Go figure. He was lucky though that the blade hadn't cut deeper.

I exited the apartment building with steam coming out of my ears from a combination of stress, exhaustion, and anger, which must have been obvious to my chief as he grabbed me and threw me through the doors of the pizza shop below the apartment to get me out of range of the media. *I may have been doing some loud swearing at the time, too. My memory's a bit fuzzy on this.* Charles reminded me that there were reporters outside and that no matter how upset and stressed I was, I needed to remain professional. The problem was that Charles hadn't been in that room for nearly two hours and was on the verge of success when the gorilla squad ruined it all in a matter of seconds. In retrospect it wasn't their fault, they were simply acting on the commands of someone in charge who didn't think the situation through before sending in their troops.

As I exited the pizza shop with better composure, all the deputies who'd been in the room with me approached and each shook my hand; they'd been witness to the negotiations and knew what the outcome should and would have been. I was handed a cup of coffee by Doug Stimson, the local probation officer who I worked with nearly daily as he had an office within our department. I looked at the scene that had unfolded around us. Within the bright flashing lights and through the rain, I could see tac team members on ledges and rooftops, hiding around corners and running around in and out of the apartment building like they had a purpose.

After the sheriff approached me and patted me on the back, he rounded up all his deputies and cleared the scene, disgusted at the actions of the state police, and he was literally done with the night as a whole. He had no intentions of assisting the tac team after the way they handled the situation in the apartment and forced us out when we were on the verge of a peaceful end to the standoff.

I went into the mobile command center, mostly to avoid the media who all wanted to get in an interview with me, and I wasn't in the mood and certainly wouldn't have presented well in the moment. Inside the mobile unit was the tac team commander, the guy in charge. He was talking to Castroni's girlfriend, attempting to get information that might help the negotiations. The funny thing was, even this guy wasn't asking me what I had done and said that nearly led to a conclusion. I found this amusing and maddening at the same time. Apparently, it was beneath the elite commander to ask advice from a lowly local cop. He was also careful not to speak to anyone who wasn't one of his officers and made certain no one else knew what their "plan" was. The truth was they didn't really have one.

It was about an hour later, and I was still in the mobile unit along with Charles and Probation Officer Stimson, still drinking coffee and basically being kept in the dark as to any progress, when the commander finally approached me. He reluctantly asked, while looking down at the floor and running his hands through his thinning hair, "So, ah, seems that Castroni's not speaking to my guy up there. In fact, he hasn't said a word since you left. Mind if I ask what you and he were talking about? Maybe we can get him to start talking and work with us."

At this very moment, two little versions of myself appeared on each of my shoulders. You know, one being the little angel and one being the little devil. The little angel on one shoulder whispered to me, *"Don't do it, Dave. Don't do it."* The little devil on my other shoulder yelled back, *"Just do it!"*

So, this is the part where I either say I acted as the bigger man and calmly, professionally explained to the little commander what I'd been talking to Castroni about, or this is the part where I say that the stress and anger were still prevalent within me, and I acted quite unprofessionally and told the little commander just where to stick his baton. I won't say which I did, however, the aftershock of my immediate response caused Stimson to spit his coffee out while Charles simply shook his head, although not surprised.

I turned to walk out of the mobile unit but not before I heard Stimson say sarcastically to the mighty commander while giggling and taking another sip of what was left of his coffee, "I guess you shouldn't have asked him that."

I feel the need to interject and explain that there's an important lesson to be learned here about working your way up the ladder of success, and how you handle important situations with tact that may help your career. But then again, up to that point, I had never aspired to be a member of the Maine State

Police.

It was nearly two hours later and now well into the night when I heard that negotiations had totally failed, and in fact, I had been told that Castroni had not uttered a word since I was ordered out of the apartment hours earlier. The tactical team had run out of options and was planning to pull the negotiator and every officer out of the apartment and send in a tear gas canister attached to a long pole through a tiny window in the bathroom in an effort to force Castroni out.

So that's what they did. Within minutes two troopers donning gas masks escorted a cuffed Castroni, tears and mucous pouring out of his eyes and nose from the gas, out of the building and placed him in the back seat of my cruiser. Seems they were willing to allow me to take him to the hospital for that evaluation after all. In reality, they didn't want him covered in gas and snot in their vehicles, and he needed to be deloused at the hospital, which is where he would have ended up if he'd left with me hours earlier.

Along with my chief, we transported Castroni to the hospital and into one of the ER rooms. We sat him down, cuffed him to the gurney, and waited for the hospital staff to come in to clean him up. While waiting Castroni looked up at me, barely able to open his eyes from the stinging gas and in obvious discomfort and pain. "Wish you'd done things differently?" I asked.

"Yeah, I wish I would have come out with you sooner," he responded.

So, the standoff ended, and Castroni was eventually taken to a jail cell and ultimately back to prison to serve out his sentence. He would also be charged with creating a police standoff, a criminal charge in the State of Maine. Additionally, he'd be charged with assault on an officer and resisting arrest, two charges that would ultimately be dropped in a plea bargain. Don't be disappointed, this was the norm in any criminal case in Maine. I don't agree with it, but I had no control over it, and neither did any other officer. There are always criminal charges that are used by the District Attorney as bargaining chips to get a suspect to plea to other charges, and it always starts with the offenses against police officers. It's not right, but it's the way it is.

As it turns out, Castroni's warrant was for sexual assault on a minor child, and this was most likely the reason he didn't want to go back to prison. As heinous as the crimes are of other prison inmates, many of them have children and child sex offenders often find themselves beaten severely and left for dead in the corner of a cell, if not worse. Go figure, a code of conduct among criminals. Castroni had probably been to prison and found the experience even less pleasant than most when they discovered his crime, and he didn't want to relive it again. *I happen to call things like that poetic justice.*

So as amusing as this chapter of the story may have been, and trust me, it was all true, this guy was, and I'm sure still is a total scumbag. Castroni caused a lot of trouble not only for his underlying crimes, but to me, the lieutenant, my department, the sheriff's department, and the state police in the exhaustive costs to have all these officers tied up for hours dealing with his unwillingness to go quietly. This is why suspects, and officers, get hurt or die during arrests. The unwillingness of people to submit to peaceful arrests. This is where it all begins and unfortunately sometimes tragically ends.

◆ ◆ ◆

The following day, Baker and I were in his office talking. He was obviously still distraught from the previous day's event. In conversation, he asked me, "What were you thinking about while we were in that room with Castroni?" I wasn't certain that I understood his question at first, especially since I was in the room far longer than he was with the suspect.

"What do you mean? What were you thinking?"

He replied, "I was thinking about dying, about my family, and what would happen to them if I wasn't around anymore…" *Okay, fair enough, I get where you're going with this.* He continued, "What was going through your mind?"

"You really wanna know?" Baker nodded to me in response to the question. "I was thinking, while my sights were square on his chest, I was thinking if I shoot this guy, how long will my administrative suspension be, and will I still get a paycheck during it? That's what I was thinking."

As luck would turn out, this incident did provide me with a small pot of gold at the end of the rainbow. By this time, I'd been on the Dover-Foxcroft Police Department a few years and had some experience under my belt that apparently hadn't gone unnoticed. That same day, I received a telephone call from Sheriff Robinson. He assured me that my performance during the entire ordeal was outstanding in his opinion, and he offered me a position as a deputy for his department. As much as I enjoyed and was thankful to Charles for the experience he'd provided me, I had thought about applying for the county, and my opportunity was now presenting itself on a silver platter. I was soon to be a Deputy Investigator for the Piscataquis County Sheriff's Department. ◆

CHAPTER 10

ONWARD AND UPWARD

It was late summer, early fall, and after most camp owners had closed up their cottages for the season. All except for those who'd be back in late fall for the annual deer hunt. I received a call from a camp owner in Bowerbank, a tiny village on the northern side of Sebec Lake. Bowerbank has only 116 residents, no stores, only a small-town office that's open for two hours each Saturday morning, a church, and a small volunteer fire station. In the summer, the population increases with the seasonal camp owners arriving. Sebec Lake itself is eleven miles long and has a number of small towns and villages along its shoreline.

The camp owner, Miles Nelson, told me that he had been in to check his place a week before and discovered a pickup truck parked in the roadway at the mouth of another short lane off his camp road. He said he didn't think anything of it at the time, believing it might be another camp owner who'd left the truck there and walked into their place for the day. He said today, a week later, when he'd returned to his camp to check it again the truck was still parked in the same spot blocking the roadway.

I told Mr. Nelson I'd be in to check on it and would meet him at his cottage. I hadn't thought much about the possible circumstances and didn't mind responding alone, which I did to calls quite often anyway. Mr. Nelson said he was on Fire Road 9. Now when roads in town are referred to as "fire roads" you know you're in a rural area. This gives a sequential direction of travel for the other fire departments to let them know where to bring the hot dogs and marshmallows when they're responding to help watch a camp burn down deep in the woods. There are no active hydrants in these rural locations, and by the time most other departments arrive, there's not much left to save. So, with only ten fire roads in Bowerbank, I knew this one was pretty far into the woods.

It took about forty-five minutes to arrive at Fire Road 9 and Mr. Nelson's camp. Just before his camp, which was about a mile in on a dirt road off the main town road, I did see the truck he was referring to. A few camps just before Mr. Nelson's, the road forked both east and west along the shoreline. The truck was parked in the roadway on the portion that forked west. The truck itself wasn't anything special, somewhat older and well-used but not total junk.

I called dispatch, and surprisingly enough I discovered that I had cell service where I was, and I gave them the license plate number of the suspect vehicle. Dispatch advised that the registered owner was from out of the area, had a warrant for his arrest, and had a lengthy criminal history. *Oh, great. Well, this just narrowed the possibilities.* So now I had to make a few assumptions. One being that this piece of human trash had come here to break into camps and his truck had broken down here, forcing him to abandon it and walk out. There was some random stuff in the bed of the truck that could have come from a camp or two and could possibly have been stolen. I just wasn't certain yet.

I continued and met with Mr. Nelson and relayed my suspicions to him. I assumed that since the truck had been parked in the road for at least a week, there probably wasn't much chance of the suspect still being in the area. But why leave the truck here if it wasn't stolen with the license plates on it? The plates matched the truck and could lead back to and identify its owner. Odd.

By the way...have we all heard the cliché about assuming stuff?

I told Mr. Nelson I'd take a walk and check the camps along the west shore and see if any appeared to have been broken into. He offered to walk along with me, and if he knew any of the camp owner's names, he'd provide them to me if we discovered a break.

We started down the west shore past the seemingly abandoned pickup truck. There were several camps along the road and at each one, we checked the doors to see if they were open or showed any signs of having been opened forcefully. Most were closed up tight, doors locked, and windows closed and covered. Typical for camps, locked tight and no way to see inside. I'm not sure if this keeps criminals out or invites them in. If you're hiding something, then generally you have something to take. After several camps, we did come upon one with an unlocked front door. There were no signs of entry, and I took it upon myself to go inside and look around. *Yes, without a warrant. I felt that if the camp had been broken into, the owners would mind me checking, so don't judge.*

Nothing was in disarray. No mess, it was a well-kept camp. I even came upon a rifle that wasn't very well hidden, a true sign that the camp hadn't been broken into. If a place has been broken into, the first items always missing are guns and alcohol. Some camp owners' figure that if someone is going to break in anyway, why make it tough enough for them to cause damage? I've even seen camps with signs hanging inside that say, "If you break into my camp, at least have the decency to leave it clean." *No joke.*

We finished checking the camps along the road and started making our way back. The mystery still remained, why was this truck here? The truck itself wasn't stolen, and this guy wasn't from the area. He certainly could've had the intention to burglarize the camps and simply broke down before he had the chance and hitched his way out without taking anything. And being wanted and all, he surely wasn't about to call the police for assistance.

"…Hi, uh, yeah…ah, my truck is broke down in the middle of East Podunk, could you come help me, but please don't ask my name or check my ID…What? No, no reason at all…"

Mr. Nelson and I made it back to the first camp that we'd checked, and I now noticed something different that made the hair on the back of my neck stand up. One of the side windows, which had been closed when we first checked the place, was now open just a bit. I knew right away this dirtbag was inside that camp. Not to mention, he probably knows there's a cop outside. He obviously heard us checking the doors earlier and probably had been watching us go by. I didn't let on to Mr. Nelson and continued past until the cottage was almost out of our site.

When I could just barely see the camp behind me, I stopped and told Mr. Nelson to go back to his camp, explaining what I had noticed about the window. Out of a sense of responsibility, Mr. Nelson asked if I wanted him to go back with me. As much as I wanted to say yes, I didn't want to put this guy in the middle of a potential battle. With the history of the wanted guy and his obvious hatred of law enforcement, I saw this ending up as a fight and I didn't want Mr. Nelson harmed. I politely thanked him and reluctantly told him I'd be alright. Mr. Nelson did what I asked and returned to his cottage.

It was too late to call for backup, it was too far away, and I didn't want to give the suspect time to make plans or get away. I had no idea if he was armed, dangerous, tweaking on drugs, or a combination of the three. I snuck back up to the camp cautiously and waited at the front door long enough that I didn't hear a lot of commotion inside. Finally, I knocked on the front door, and surprisingly enough, a man matching the description I had been provided answered and stepped outside onto the step, immediately closing the door behind him. This right away threw up two red flags. One, the fact he answered the door at all. He's wanted and hadn't made himself purposely known up to this point, so why answer the door now? And secondly, he stepped outside to me rather than allow me in or to see inside, so what's he hiding inside the cabin? Not to mention he stepped out with his hands showing, and I could see that he was apparently unarmed. He only had on a T-shirt and jean shorts, not many places to hide a weapon.

This guy was also far too friendly right out of the gate. Instead of coming out yelling and screaming, he was greeting me cordially. I asked for his name, (*which is not relevant for purposes of this chapter. Again, I don't want to give scumbags any recognition*) and he provided his correct name. This was both surprising and shocking. I advised him he had a warrant for his arrest, and he was too accepting of this fact. He said he knew that he was wanted, understood this, and was ready to go with me. He practically put the handcuffs on himself. *Something was very wrong here.*

This is where the intuition began to kick in. This guy's history showed that he enjoyed fighting with the police and resisting arrest, his record proved it. So why was he so willing to go to jail that day? I'm a lone cop in the middle of the woods, an easy target for him if he's in a fighting mood, with no backup. Well, the truth was, I wasn't about to argue with him.

I cuffed the guy up. Which, by the way, is something that I teach all new, fresh young cops. For goodness' sake, when you tell someone they're under arrest, put the damn cuffs on them quickly! There's a brief moment once you inform someone that they're under arrest when the surprise factor actually works to your advantage and there's a much better chance of compliance. Believe it or not, most criminals don't think you're going to arrest them, or they believe they can talk their way out of it. If you give them any time to think about it, or worse, let them ask questions or challenge the arrest, then the fight is usually on, and you both get all banged up getting them in handcuffs if they decide to resist. So, get the damn cuffs on! It's not like you're going to change your mind and not arrest them. It doesn't work that way! Get the cuffs on before both of you or more, get hurt! This is how people end up on the national news!

So, all cuffed up and he was ready to go. However, I was getting a bad feeling about the entire situation. "Is anyone else with you in the camp?"

"My girlfriend, but she'll be alright here alone for a while." He went on to say that he'd be able to come up with bail money after a couple of phone calls and would be back for her later today. He said she had his cell phone in case of an emergency, so no worries. *Yeah, right. I'm not totally buying this story.*

As I walked him to the cruiser, I carried on the conversation; something definitely was wrong here, but I needed to get this guy to jail before his attitude turned and he tried to bolt or something. As we walked past the truck, I casually asked him about it being in the middle of the road. He said the truck had broken down when they tried to leave earlier in the week and were waiting for a family member to come and help. He assured me that a close relative was on his way to help with repairs and get them on their way.

When we got to my cruiser, I did something I normally didn't do. I put the prisoner in the front passenger seat. I had a plexiglass barrier between the front and back seats and didn't like anyone sitting beside me. The rides to jail were at times lengthy and cuffed or not, the criminals could still cause damage. But I wasn't done talking to this guy, and he was certainly open to chatting. I wanted more information, truth or not.

On the ride to jail, I asked how he'd come to be at the camp. He stated that camp was a "family camp" and was his turn to use it. He said he and his girlfriend had arrived about a week prior, and the truck had broken down when they tried to head to town for supplies. He repeated his story that his relative was on their way to help fix the truck. He talked the entire ride to the jail about this, that, and the other. Very talkative this guy was, which is a sign of nervousness about something. It was also a sign of lying. *Yes, folks, criminals do lie. I realize that's hard to believe, but it's true.*

Something still wasn't right. This guy, who's telling me his life story, by reputation, hates the police. Those who dislike the police don't speak to the police, don't carry on cordial conversations with the police, and certainly don't give up to the police as easily as this guy had. They don't like jail or prison, and they don't volunteer any personal information, ever. Most of the time, if they speak at all, they offer their opinion on what to do with certain parts of our anatomy, which was usually anatomically impossible.

We arrived at the county lockup, and I took the opportunity to check his arrest warrant, which I discovered wasn't a local warrant. This meant that he wasn't simply going to make bail today. He was required to be transported back to the county where the warrant originated from, which would take at least a day to set up the transport and another day or longer to be seen by a judge. And with this guy's record, he knew this when he told me his girlfriend would be fine until his return.

Intuition kicked in completely now. *There's something wrong back at that cabin.* I checked into the ownership a bit further before heading back out. The owner's last name matched my suspect's, so it was a "family" camp, which didn't necessarily mean that he was allowed to be there, however, he apparently hadn't broken into a random camp. I had a strong feeling something was up with the girlfriend.

I drove back out to the cabin in the woods and knocked on the door, announcing myself as an officer. A young girl, probably in her twenties, cracked the door open just enough for me to see her and the room immediately behind her. She was disheveled, wearing dirty clothes and a hooded sweatshirt with the hood up, however, I could see bruising on her face. She looked like she hadn't had clean clothes or a shower in quite a while. The room behind her didn't look any better. It was messy, and dirty, and was apparent that the camp hadn't had maid service in a while.

I introduced myself and asked the girl her name and if she was alright.

She provided her first name, and I'll call her Jessica for the purposes of the story. She immediately asked where the man was that she'd been with, looking around and behind me as if he was going to suddenly appear. She was obviously frightened. I explained that I'd taken him to jail, and he wasn't going to be back. Then she asked where she was. *Oh, crap, this isn't good. She doesn't know where she is.* When I explained she was in Bowerbank, Maine, she asked where that was. *Also, not good.*

I asked Jessica where she had gotten the bruises, although it wasn't as if I didn't already know. I assured her again that her "boyfriend" wasn't there and couldn't harm her. After some hesitation, she said the man she'd been with had caused them. At this point, I knew I had at the very least, a battered woman who should not be left here alone and probably needed some type of medical attention. I didn't know yet how dark this was about to turn.

It took a bit of convincing to get Jessica to leave with me. This isn't uncommon for a person who's been the victim of domestic abuse either. They're afraid the abuser will be more violent later on when they discover that their victim didn't stay put and keep quiet. She finally agreed to go with me after I told her I wanted to take her to a hospital to have her bruises looked at. By this time, she admitted to more bruising under the hoodie and on other parts of her body.

We left, and the further we drove from the cabin, the more Jessica opened up to me. She wouldn't look at me, she stared out the passenger window as she spoke. Jessica said she knew the guy as a "friend" whom she'd met very recently. He'd told her they were going for a weekend camping trip to his family camp with other "friends," and she'd agreed. She wasn't from the area and thought they'd be gone for a day or two and would be meeting others when they arrived at the camp. She was from southern Maine, and she quickly discovered that she was being taken far outside of her comfort zone the further north they'd driven. She said when she protested, he became violent and began beating her with his fist as they drove. She had no idea where she'd been taken to and quickly discovered she was being taken and held against her will.

There was no cellular phone. The phone the guy had told me he'd left with her was a lie, so she had no way to call out. Jessica said that after the first sexual assault the very first night, she decided to stop bathing and continually wore dirty clothes in hopes that he'd be repulsed and leave her alone, at least sexually. She also stated she'd been drugged in the first few days and afterward became more cautious about eating or drinking anything that he was trying to give to her.

Jessica said in the first few days she was afraid to simply run away because she didn't know where she was and felt he knew the area and she wouldn't get far. He'd given her the impression that they were deep in the northern Maine woods where, "No one could hear her scream." She also said that after the first weekend, he'd told her they were going home and they did leave, only to discover that he'd once again lied, and they only made it to a "small town" and a store where he bought "more alcohol" and then turned to go back in the direction of the cabin. While briefly in town, he'd threatened her life and the lives of her family, so she didn't protest or try to get away when they visited the store. Jessica said she protested going back once they'd turned around, and he proceeded to beat her repeatedly on the return ride again.

As I drove with her toward the hospital, it became more apparent to me that I had a kidnapping and rape victim in my cruiser. Once I noticed I had cellular service, and while continuing to listen to her story, I placed a quick call to my chief deputy who was also our department sexual assault investigator, and told him to meet me at the hospital in Dover-Foxcroft.

Jessica continued to talk and said she had been told repeatedly that she couldn't get away and there was no one around to hear her or run to anyway. She said she believed this to an extent, not knowing the area and feeling she was very far into the woods of northern Maine.

In reality, Bowerbank is only ten miles from the nearest town of Dover-Foxcroft, however, I understood her mindset where she wasn't from the area and was being told over and over that she was deep in the woods. She was in fear for her life by this time and had nowhere to go.

Jessica said that about two-thirds into the first week, she felt she had an opportunity to try to escape. She had grabbed the truck keys, which he'd left on a counter while he was semi-passed out from alcohol and drugs, and she'd put them in her pocket and waited. She couldn't go right then because he had forced her to drink whenever he did, and she didn't feel she could get to the truck without him catching her if her drink had been spiked. She waited until she felt the time was right and ran out of the camp, jumped in the truck, and tried to drive away. Jessica said he ran after her, and at the point where the truck now sat in the road is where he caught up to her, reached into the truck, and threw it back into park. He pulled the keys out and tossed them into the woods where they'd been lost ever since. She said he dragged her back to the camp where she was beaten again for the escape attempt. She said after that she gave up trying and was in more despair with the only means of exiting the area now gone with the loss of the keys. Jessica said he did try to find the keys once or twice but couldn't find where he'd thrown them into the woods. She said at that point she felt hopeless, with both having no way of leaving and no phone.

Jessica said that in all she believed she'd been at the camp for about two weeks. Her story shocked me, and it took a while for me to realize the totality of what she'd gone through. I also thought to myself how smart of her to remain unbathed. It just may have helped to possibly ward off the repeated sexual assaults, but beyond this, it may have also provided crucial evidence that still existed on her body that the hospital staff might have the ability to collect.

We arrived at the hospital, and I turned the investigation over to my chief deputy and hospital staff. As she walked away towards a safe hospital room, I couldn't help but feel a sense of accomplishment for what I'd done by taking the extra time to follow my instincts. I also couldn't help to wonder what would've happened if I hadn't gone back to that camp. Would she have ultimately tried to walk away and find help? Would she have stayed, not knowing when he'd come back, but after her first attempt to leave, was she far too frightened to try again? And what about when he did finally make bail in two or three days or longer? Would he have made his way back? And if so, what would have been the ultimate end to her situation? Too many "what-ifs."

The suspect was charged with kidnapping, terrorizing, and sexual assault. The case never went to trial, and I hate to think about what the charges were dummied down to get him to plead guilty. I also don't know what ever happened to Jessica. All I can hope for is she went on to live a far safer and happier life.

I was given a commendation for my actions on that day. During the ceremony and in the newspapers, it talked about "officer intuition" and how sometimes we just have that feeling that something isn't right, and it's our responsibility to take the time to follow our gut feelings. As I mentioned, I don't think we all have this intuition, or at least we don't all take the time to pay attention to it or understand what it means or what it's trying to tell us.

I do know that some stories have no shred of humor in them, and there's nothing you can say or joke about to make them any better. This was one of them.

◆ ◆ ◆

It was the spring of 2009, and from late spring into the summer, I noticed a disturbing trend. The town of Dover-Foxcroft had been experiencing late-night burglaries and thefts. Cars and houses were being broken into, and mostly the thieves were seeking cash and prescription drugs. The investigations had revealed the vehicles were almost always found to be unlocked, as were the houses. More and more as time went on, more breaks were occurring, and I found Dover wasn't the only town being hit. As summer went on, I began to notice that other towns in my county seemed to be experiencing the same thing, car and residential burglaries were on the increase, and all similar in detail to the original Dover breaks. Now, the occasional burglary or theft wasn't out of the ordinary, but the numbers we were dealing with were. We had dozens of petty thefts taking place, and the locations were becoming more random.

I put a teletype out on the system asking other departments across the state if they were having burglaries with the similar Motive of Operandi, or M.O., that Dover and the surrounding towns were experiencing, unlocked cars and house burglaries with primarily cash and prescription drugs taken with a pattern of "neighborhood" burglaries. I received quite a few responses that other small towns did have the same issues taking place.

I decided to go back and take a closer look starting with the Dover cases. What I found was that they seemed to all have begun on the same street, and night after night, they "fanned" out to other areas of town further away from the apparent source before moving on to another town, first close to Dover and then again further away. In each town, it appeared the same M.O., with the thefts beginning on one side of town and ending on another, almost in a circular pattern that widened out the further it got from one source point in these towns, almost like a spiral.

In looking at the Dover's cases, I took a look in the area of the first street again where they seemed to have begun, and ultimately located a suspect. It was a guy I'd dealt with in the past on some minor stuff who, at the time of the first burglary, he'd been living with his mother on this particular street. As summer went along though, he'd picked up a girlfriend and was living in another town in her apartment. Coincidentally, he hadn't had a driver's license or car when he'd been living with his mother, however, his girlfriend did, and about the time he hooked up with her the burglaries started to fan out away from his mother's neighborhood and into other towns. I suspected this turd bird might be the guy, however, I had no solid proof yet. The burglar wasn't leaving anything else to go on. No prints, no sightings, no nothing. What I did have though was the usual volatile relationship between my suspect and his girlfriend, which always worked to our advantage in these situations. They seemed to have an on-again, off-again romance, and the off-again usually got pretty heated. When these situations occur, all bets are off. Girlfriends would turn their boyfriends into the police quickly when they were angry with them over something.

I received a call from the girlfriend who said she was tired of her boyfriend's drug use, and she hinted he may have committed some thefts to support his habit. She also said that the two lovebirds were having domestic problems again. Fingers Magee *(not his real name)* had assaulted her the night before, and she'd kicked him out of the apartment. I grabbed Charles from Dover PD where his was the first town hit, and he had a vested interest in solving the local theft ring, and we headed to her apartment in Brownville.

When we arrived, she answered the door and her face showed signs of the prior evening's argument. Charles and I talked to her for a bit, making certain she was alright and didn't need some sort of medical attention. She said she didn't, but you could tell that Mr. Fingers had pissed her off and good this time. Once we were certain that she was physically okay, we brought up the burglaries. Even though she denied knowing anything about the thefts directly and said she wasn't involved, she said Mr. Fingers had committed some burglaries and she allowed us to do a quick search of the apartment for any evidence of his involvement. She even signed a voluntary search form. She was obviously quite upset with this guy.

Now, a couple of things about people who commit crimes and think they can get away with it. One; they usually deny their involvement thinking that you're going to believe them. Two; they feel that they're so good at hiding their crimes that they don't mind you searching for evidence, believing there's nothing to hide. Three; as I said before, a woman scorned will roll over on her lover quickly if she's mad enough and wants to get him in trouble as some sort of punishment. Plus, they feel that if the story is good enough, they won't get in trouble themselves if they're involved in some way.

In performing a quick search of their hallway closet, I found a road atlas. You know, one of those large blue books with maps of the state in it that you kept in your car under the seat and grabbed when you thought you were lost. Do you remember? They were popular before mobile GPS units. Yeah, one of those. *And yes, I know, even mobile GPS units are outdated now!*

I opened the atlas up and noticed something peculiar. In the glossary, some of the names of the towns were highlighted in yellow and some of the highlights had lines drawn through the name. Further, when you looked up these towns on the various maps, some towns were circled, and others had circles with an 'X' drawn through them. I knew enough from my research into my case that the towns with lines and X's on them were towns that had experienced recent burglaries, including Dover-Foxcroft. When I asked the girl about the atlas, she was quick to say that it belonged to her boyfriend, Mr. Fingers, and she knew nothing about it. This opened the door for me to seize it as potential evidence. We also, with this in hand, performed a more thorough search of the apartment and seized a few random items that we believed may have been stolen, mostly jewelry. You see another thing about criminals is that even though they may have a primary focus when they're committing thefts, such as cash or drugs, they can't help but take nice shiny things that catch their eye as well or that they think their girlfriends might like. It didn't take long to match up some of the trinkets we'd seized to various burglaries around the state. It also didn't take long to connect the road atlas to the other evidence seized. I drafted an arrest warrant, and within days we arrested Mr. Fingers on charges of burglary and theft.

Mr. Fingers was charged with multiple, and I mean well over 200 burglaries across the state and was desperate to cut a deal. I'd arranged to have him transported to the Bangor Police Department where I'd reserved a meeting room that was wired for video recording. You know, one of those fancy, technological things we didn't have in the county. I also invited representatives from law enforcement in all of the towns that had outstanding burglary cases that may be connected to our suspect to join us for a sit-down with Mr. Fingers. I'd also spoken to my district attorney who agreed to cut Fingers a deal. If he copped to all the burglaries he'd committed and agreed to provide details, he'd be given a package deal, which would result in a lighter sentence than if he was tried separately in multiple counties for all the burglaries that we could ultimately tie him to. The key was that he had to agree to admit and provide details of all of his crimes to get the deal. The bad part was that under the agreement, any crimes we were unaware of that he confessed to would result in a "get out of jail free" card for him, barring something like murder or a sexual assault. In legal terms, this is referred to as a "proffer."

Now, the one thing I'll repeat about criminals in general, if half of them worked as hard at a real job as they do at committing crimes, they'd be quite successful in life. Mr. Fingers sat down with us like he'd been hired to make a presentation on a topic he'd earned a Master's degree. He proceeded to explain that he had, in fact, started his crime spree in Dover when he didn't have access to a vehicle and "circled out" from his mother's house at night, working his way further away each night until he finished the town while only targeting unlocked cars and vacant houses, at first anyway.

Once he hooked up with a girlfriend and a car, he started burglarizing other towns. He explained that he'd have his girlfriend drop him off on one side of town and told her to park on the other side. Throughout the night, he'd work his way toward her. And here's the astonishing part, Fingers could recall the makes, models, and colors of each car he broke into. Same with the houses, he could tell you the house color and sometimes even the house number. He knew which windows he crawled through, and which ones were locked or unlocked. He knew just what he'd taken from each and he could prove this by also telling us not only everything he took but also where he took it from, so we could match up each and every item to the exact location it was stolen from. It was quite amazing to listen to him describe it all Over 200 burglaries and he described each in intricate detail. And remember, his crimes occurred at night when it was dark out and difficult to see.

Unfortunately, though, Mr. Fingers had let his drug habit get the best of him. He admitted he was a pill junkie, and once he had access to wheels, he acted as a mule for the local cocaine dealer and would deliver the product in exchange for his preferred drug in payment, which was Oxycontin pills. He'd be sent to a town on a run, and while there, he'd take his opportunity to burglarize the neighborhoods. The one place he wouldn't hit though was the houses he was to deliver the cocaine, although he did say that during one mule run there was a party taking place, and took the opportunity to hit all the vehicles in the yard thinking there'd be money and drugs within them. He admitted this was fairly poor judgment on his part. Go figure.

Mr. Fingers mentioned that only a couple of times did the police come close to catching him, and in one town his girlfriend was questioned by police as to why she was just sitting in her vehicle late at night but nothing further. The cops didn't have anything on her, and she had a clean record. She came up with some excuse, and sitting in a vehicle alone wasn't a crime. Fingers did admit to becoming cockier as time went on and more daring by changing his rule about unoccupied residences when he began breaking into houses with the owners still home sleeping in their beds. He said he was lucky no one ever woke up and found him inside their house.

We all sat there listening like children being told a good bedtime story. We didn't need to ask questions, he was providing everything in detail. The interview went on for hours as he described all the things he'd stolen and where it was all taken from. Now the stupid part. *Well, it's all quite stupid, isn't it?* The one detail that blew us all away was that as sharp as his memory was, the one thing he couldn't remember were the names of each town he'd hit. Remember the atlas? His downfall was that he had to cross off each and every town he'd burglarized for fear that if not, he'd hit the town twice and was sure to find nothing to take, not to mention the increased chance of getting caught if he re-visited a town that he'd already burglarized. In the atlas, he'd highlight the towns he was to perform cocaine runs or simply wanted to burglarize, and he'd cross them out after a night of cleaning out the neighborhoods.

At the end of the interview, Mr. Fingers stood up and shook my hand. He told me he was impressed. He said he never intended to get caught (*they never do*) and he was impressed at my ability to catch such an intelligent mastermind, which it was obvious he felt he was. He expressed that he felt that my mind was as superior to his in my ability to catch him. *Gee, thanks, what a compliment.* In reality, it did involve some luck in finding the atlas in the first place and his stupidity for not being able to memorize the names of towns as well as he could remember every other detail.

In the end, many townships cleared multiple cases off their records. Mr. Fingers was sentenced, through the agreement, to eight years for all the burglaries, mostly to serve out at the Charleston Correctional Facility. I kept the road atlas even after the case was disposed of as a conversation piece. A few years later, when I became a criminal investigator for the state prison system *(more to come on that)*, I dusted the old book off, and in plain clothes one day was riding around the grounds of the Charleston facility with the warden. I knew that Mr. Fingers was working at one of the on-site work programs and I spotted Fingers strolling across the work yard and told the warden to pull up next to him. The warden did so, rolled down his window, and called Fingers over to the car. When Mr. Fingers spotted me in the passenger side, it was like an old friend that you hadn't seen in years. I had the atlas down by my side as he approached the driver's side of the car and began asking me what I'd been up to.

I smiled and said, "Not much, same old, catching criminals and all." He smiled and shook his head. I then remarked, "But I'm kinda lost, can you help me find my way?" Just as I raised up his old atlas and opened to a random page filled with circles and an 'X', Fingers peered in at it and recognized that it was his atlas. He cocked his head sideways, smiled, looked up at me, and simply said, "You're an asshole."

Again, sometimes you have to make it a point to have fun at work. ♦

CHAPTER 11

A KIDNAPPING AND 'X' MARKS THE SPOT

It was late summer, early fall, and after most camp owners had closed up their cottages for the season. All except for those who'd be back in late fall for the annual deer hunt. I received a call from a camp owner in Bowerbank, a tiny village on the northern side of Sebec Lake. Bowerbank has only 116 residents, no stores, only a small-town office that's open for two hours each Saturday morning, a church, and a small volunteer fire station. In the summer, the population increases with the seasonal camp owners arriving. Sebec Lake itself is eleven miles long and has a number of small towns and villages along its shoreline.

The camp owner, Miles Nelson, told me that he had been in to check his place a week before and discovered a pickup truck parked in the roadway at the mouth of another short lane off his camp road. He said he didn't think anything of it at the time, believing it might be another camp owner who'd left the truck there and walked into their place for the day. He said today, a week later, when he'd returned to his camp to check it again the truck was still parked in the same spot blocking the roadway.

I told Mr. Nelson I'd be in to check on it and would meet him at his cottage. I hadn't thought much about the possible circumstances and didn't mind responding alone, which I did to calls quite often anyway. Mr. Nelson said he was on Fire Road 9. Now when roads in town are referred to as "fire roads" you know you're in a rural area. This gives a sequential direction of travel for the other fire departments to let them know where to bring the hot dogs and marshmallows when they're responding to help watch a camp burn down deep in the woods. There are no active hydrants in these rural locations, and by the time most other departments arrive, there's not much left to save.

So, with only ten fire roads in Bowerbank, I knew this one was pretty far into the woods.

It took about forty-five minutes to arrive at Fire Road 9 and Mr. Nelson's camp. Just before his camp, which was about a mile in on a dirt road off the main town road, I did see the truck he was referring to. A few camps just before Mr. Nelson's, the road forked both east and west along the shoreline. The truck was parked in the roadway on the portion that forked west. The truck itself wasn't anything special, somewhat older and well-used but not total junk.

I called dispatch, and surprisingly enough I discovered that I had cell service where I was, and I gave them the license plate number of the suspect vehicle. Dispatch advised that the registered owner was from out of the area, had a warrant for his arrest, and had a lengthy criminal history. *Oh, great. Well, this just narrowed the possibilities.* So now I had to make a few assumptions. One being that this piece of human trash had come here to break into camps and his truck had broken down here, forcing him to abandon it and walk out. There was some random stuff in the bed of the truck that could have come from a camp or two and could possibly have been stolen. I just wasn't certain yet.

I continued and met with Mr. Nelson and relayed my suspicions to him. I assumed that since the truck had been parked in the road for at least a week, there probably wasn't much chance of the suspect still being in the area. But why leave the truck here if it wasn't stolen with the license plates on it? The plates matched the truck and could lead back to and identify its owner. Odd.

By the way…have we all heard the cliché about assuming stuff?

I told Mr. Nelson I'd take a walk and check the camps along the west shore and see if any appeared to have been broken into. He offered to walk along with me, and if he knew any of the camp owner's names, he'd provide them to me if we discovered a break.

We started down the west shore past the seemingly abandoned pickup truck. There were several camps along the road and at each one, we checked the doors to see if they were open or showed any signs of having been opened forcefully. Most were closed up tight, doors locked, and windows closed and covered. Typical for camps, locked tight and no way to see inside. I'm not sure if this keeps criminals out or invites them in. If you're hiding something, then generally you have something to take. After several camps, we did come upon one with an unlocked front door. There were no signs of entry, and I took it upon myself to go inside and look around. *Yes, without a warrant. I felt that if the camp had been broken into, the owners would mind me checking, so don't judge.* Nothing was in disarray. No mess, it was a well-kept camp. I even came upon a rifle that wasn't very well hidden, a true sign that the camp hadn't been broken into. If a place has been broken into, the first items always missing are guns and alcohol. Some camp owners' figure that if someone is going to break in anyway, why make it tough enough for them to cause damage? I've even seen camps with signs hanging inside that say, "If you break into my camp, at least have the decency to leave it clean." *No joke.*

We finished checking the camps along the road and started making our way back. The mystery still remained, why was this truck here? The truck itself wasn't stolen, and this guy wasn't from the area. He certainly could've had the intention to burglarize the camps and simply broke down before he had the chance and hitched his way out without taking anything. And being wanted and all, he surely wasn't about to call the police for assistance.

"…Hi, uh, yeah…ah, my truck is broke down in the middle of East Podunk, could you come help me, but please don't ask my name or check my ID…What? No, no reason at all…"

Mr. Nelson and I made it back to the first camp that we'd checked, and I now noticed something different that made the hair on the back of my neck stand up. One of the side windows, which had been closed when we first checked the place, was now open just a bit. I knew right away this dirtbag was inside that camp. Not to mention, he probably knows there's a cop outside. He obviously heard us checking the doors earlier and probably had been watching us go by. I didn't let on to Mr. Nelson and continued past until the cottage was almost out of our site.

When I could just barely see the camp behind me, I stopped and told Mr. Nelson to go back to his camp, explaining what I had noticed about the window. Out of a sense of responsibility, Mr. Nelson asked if I wanted him to go back with me. As much as I wanted to say yes, I didn't want to put this guy in the middle of a potential battle. With the history of the wanted guy and his obvious hatred of law enforcement, I saw this ending up as a fight and I didn't want Mr. Nelson harmed. I politely thanked him and reluctantly told him I'd be alright. Mr. Nelson did what I asked and returned to his cottage.

It was too late to call for backup, it was too far away, and I didn't want to give the suspect time to make plans or get away. I had no idea if he was armed, dangerous, tweaking on drugs, or a combination of the three. I snuck back up to the camp cautiously and waited at the front door long enough that I didn't hear a lot of commotion inside. Finally, I knocked on the front door, and surprisingly enough, a man matching the description I had been provided answered and stepped outside onto the step, immediately closing the door behind him. This right away threw up two red flags. One, the fact he answered the door at all. He's wanted and hadn't made himself purposely known up to this point, so why answer the door now? And secondly, he stepped outside to me rather than allow me in or to see inside, so what's he hiding inside the cabin? Not to mention he stepped out with his hands showing, and I could see that he was apparently unarmed. He only had on a T-shirt and jean shorts, not many places to hide a weapon.

This guy was also far too friendly right out of the gate. Instead of coming out yelling and screaming, he was greeting me cordially. I asked for his name, (*which is not relevant for purposes of this chapter. Again, I don't want to give scumbags any recognition*) and he provided his correct name. This was both surprising and shocking. I advised him he had a warrant for his arrest, and he was too accepting of this fact. He said he knew that he was wanted, understood this, and was ready to go with me. He practically put the handcuffs on himself. *Something was very wrong here.*

This is where the intuition began to kick in. This guy's history showed that he enjoyed fighting with the police and resisting arrest, his record proved it. So why was he so willing to go to jail that day? I'm a lone cop in the middle of the woods, an easy target for him if he's in a fighting mood, with no backup. Well, the truth was, I wasn't about to argue with him.

I cuffed the guy up. Which, by the way, is something that I teach all new, fresh young cops. For goodness' sake, when you tell someone they're under arrest, put the damn cuffs on them quickly! There's a brief moment once you inform someone that they're under arrest when the surprise factor actually works to your advantage and there's a much better chance of compliance. Believe it or not, most criminals don't think you're going to arrest them, or they believe they can talk their way out of it. If you give them any time to think about it, or worse, let them ask questions or challenge the arrest, then the fight is usually on, and you both get all banged up getting them in handcuffs if they decide to resist. So, get the damn cuffs on! It's not like you're going to change your mind and not arrest them. It doesn't work that way! Get the cuffs on before both of you or more, get hurt! This is how people end up on the national news!

So, all cuffed up and he was ready to go. However, I was getting a bad feeling about the entire situation. "Is anyone else with you in the camp?"

"My girlfriend, but she'll be alright here alone for a while." He went on to say that he'd be able to come up with bail money after a couple of phone calls and would be back for her later today. He said she had his cell phone in case of an emergency, so no worries. *Yeah, right. I'm not totally buying this story.*

As I walked him to the cruiser, I carried on the conversation; something definitely was wrong here, but I needed to get this guy to jail before his attitude turned and he tried to bolt or something. As we walked past the truck, I casually asked him about it being in the middle of the road. He said the truck had broken down when they tried to leave earlier in the week and were waiting for a family member to come and help. He assured me that a close relative was on his way to help with repairs and get them on their way.

When we got to my cruiser, I did something I normally didn't do. I put the prisoner in the front passenger seat. I had a plexiglass barrier between the front and back seats and didn't like anyone sitting beside me. The rides to jail were at times lengthy and cuffed or not, the criminals could still cause damage. But I wasn't done talking to this guy, and he was certainly open to chatting. I wanted more information, truth or not.

On the ride to jail, I asked how he'd come to be at the camp. He stated that camp was a "family camp" and was his turn to use it. He said he and his girlfriend had arrived about a week prior, and the truck had broken down when they tried to head to town for supplies. He repeated his story that his relative was on their way to help fix the truck. He talked the entire ride to the jail about this, that, and the other. Very talkative this guy was, which is a sign of nervousness about something. It was also a sign of lying. *Yes, folks, criminals do lie. I realize that's hard to believe, but it's true.*

Something still wasn't right. This guy, who's telling me his life story, by reputation, hates the police. Those who dislike the police don't speak to the police, don't carry on cordial conversations with the police, and certainly don't give up to the police as easily as this guy had. They don't like jail or prison, and they don't volunteer any personal information, ever. Most of the time, if they speak at all, they offer their opinion on what to do with certain parts of our anatomy, which was usually anatomically impossible.

We arrived at the county lockup, and I took the opportunity to check his arrest warrant, which I discovered wasn't a local warrant. This meant that he wasn't simply going to make bail today. He was required to be transported back to the county where the warrant originated from, which would take at least a day to set up the transport and another day or longer to be seen by a judge. And with this guy's record, he knew this when he told me his girlfriend would be fine until his return.

Intuition kicked in completely now. *There's something wrong back at that cabin.* I checked into the ownership a bit further before heading back out. The owner's last name matched my suspect's, so it was a "family" camp, which didn't necessarily mean that he was allowed to be there, however, he apparently hadn't broken into a random camp. I had a strong feeling something was up with the girlfriend.

I drove back out to the cabin in the woods and knocked on the door, announcing myself as an officer. A young girl, probably in her twenties, cracked the door open just enough for me to see her and the room immediately behind her. She was disheveled, wearing dirty clothes and a hooded sweatshirt with the hood up, however, I could see bruising on her face. She looked like she hadn't had clean clothes or a shower in quite a while. The room behind her didn't look any better. It was messy, and dirty, and was apparent that the camp hadn't had maid service in a while.

I introduced myself and asked the girl her name and if she was alright. She provided her first name, and I'll call her Jessica for the purposes of the story. She immediately asked where the man was that she'd been with, looking around and behind me as if he was going to suddenly appear. She was obviously frightened. I explained that I'd taken him to jail, and he wasn't going to be back. Then she asked where she was. *Oh, crap, this isn't good. She doesn't know where she is.* When I explained she was in Bowerbank, Maine, she asked where that was. *Also, not good.*

I asked Jessica where she had gotten the bruises, although it wasn't as if I didn't already know. I assured her again that her "boyfriend" wasn't there and couldn't harm her. After some hesitation, she said the man she'd been with had caused them. At this point, I knew I had at the very least, a battered woman who should not be left here alone and probably needed some type of medical attention. I didn't know yet how dark this was about to turn.

It took a bit of convincing to get Jessica to leave with me. This isn't uncommon for a person who's been the victim of domestic abuse either. They're afraid the abuser will be more violent later on when they discover that their victim didn't stay put and keep quiet. She finally agreed to go with me after I told her I wanted to take her to a hospital to have her bruises looked at. By this time, she admitted to more bruising under the hoodie and on other parts of her body.

We left, and the further we drove from the cabin, the more Jessica opened up to me. She wouldn't look at me, she stared out the passenger window as she spoke. Jessica said she knew the guy as a "friend" whom she'd met very recently. He'd told her they were going for a weekend camping trip to his family camp with other "friends," and she'd agreed. She wasn't from the area and thought they'd be gone for a day or two and would be meeting others when they arrived at the camp. She was from southern Maine, and she quickly discovered that she was being taken far outside of her comfort zone the further north they'd driven. She said when she protested, he became violent and began beating her with his fist as they drove. She had no idea where she'd been taken to and quickly discovered she was being taken and held against her will.

There was no cellular phone. The phone the guy had told me he'd left with her was a lie, so she had no way to call out. Jessica said that after the first sexual assault the very first night, she decided to stop bathing and continually wore dirty clothes in hopes that he'd be repulsed and leave her alone, at least sexually. She also stated she'd been drugged in the first few days and afterward became more cautious about eating or drinking anything that he was trying to give to her.

Jessica said in the first few days she was afraid to simply run away because she didn't know where she was and felt he knew the area and she wouldn't get far. He'd given her the impression that they were deep in the northern Maine woods where, "No one could hear her scream." She also said that after the first weekend, he'd told her they were going home and they did leave, only to discover that he'd once again lied, and they only made it to a "small town" and a store where he bought "more alcohol" and then turned to go back in the direction of the cabin. While briefly in town, he'd threatened her life and the lives of her family, so she didn't protest or try to get away when they visited the store. Jessica said she protested going back once they'd turned around, and he proceeded to beat her repeatedly on the return ride again.

As I drove with her toward the hospital, it became more apparent to me that I had a kidnapping and rape victim in my cruiser. Once I noticed I had cellular service, and while continuing to listen to her story, I placed a quick call to my chief deputy who was also our department sexual assault investigator, and told him to meet me at the hospital in Dover-Foxcroft.

Jessica continued to talk and said she had been told repeatedly that she couldn't get away and there was no one around to hear her or run to anyway. She said she believed this to an extent, not knowing the area and feeling she was very far into the woods of northern Maine.

In reality, Bowerbank is only ten miles from the nearest town of Dover-Foxcroft, however, I understood her mindset where she wasn't from the area and was being told over and over that she was deep in the woods. She was in fear for her life by this time and had nowhere to go.

Jessica said that about two-thirds into the first week, she felt she had an opportunity to try to escape. She had grabbed the truck keys, which he'd left on a counter while he was semi-passed out from alcohol and drugs, and she'd put them in her pocket and waited. She couldn't go right then because he had forced her to drink whenever he did, and she didn't feel she could get to the truck without him catching her if her drink had been spiked. She waited until she felt the time was right and ran out of the camp, jumped in the truck, and tried to drive away. Jessica said he ran after her, and at the point where the truck now sat in the road is where he caught up to her, reached into the truck, and threw it back into park. He pulled the keys out and tossed them into the woods where they'd been lost ever since. She said he dragged her back to the camp where she was beaten again for the escape attempt. She said after that she gave up trying and was in more despair with the only means of exiting the area now gone with the loss of the keys. Jessica said he did try to find the keys once or twice but couldn't find where he'd thrown them into the woods. She said at that point she felt hopeless, with both having no way of leaving and no phone.

Jessica said that in all she believed she'd been at the camp for about two weeks. Her story shocked me, and it took a while for me to realize the totality of what she'd gone through. I also thought to myself how smart of her to remain unbathed. It just may have helped to possibly ward off the repeated sexual assaults, but beyond this, it may have also provided crucial evidence that still existed on her body that the hospital staff might have the ability to collect.

We arrived at the hospital, and I turned the investigation over to my chief deputy and hospital staff. As she walked away towards a safe hospital room, I couldn't help but feel a sense of accomplishment for what I'd done by taking the extra time to follow my instincts. I also couldn't help to wonder what would've happened if I hadn't gone back to that camp. Would she have ultimately tried to walk away and find help? Would she have stayed, not knowing when he'd come back, but after her first attempt to leave, was she far too frightened to try again? And what about when he did finally make bail in two or three days or longer? Would he have made his way back? And if so, what would have been the ultimate end to her situation? Too many "what-ifs."

The suspect was charged with kidnapping, terrorizing, and sexual assault. The case never went to trial, and I hate to think about what the charges were dummied down to get him to plead guilty. I also don't know what ever happened to Jessica. All I can hope for is she went on to live a far safer and happier life.

I was given a commendation for my actions on that day. During the ceremony and in the newspapers, it talked about "officer intuition" and how sometimes we just have that feeling that something isn't right, and it's our responsibility to take the time to follow our gut feelings. As I mentioned, I don't think we all have this intuition, or at least we don't all take the time to pay attention to it or understand what it means or what it's trying to tell us.

I do know that some stories have no shred of humor in them, and there's nothing you can say or joke about to make them any better. This was one of them.

◆ ◆ ◆

It was the spring of 2009, and from late spring into the summer, I noticed a disturbing trend. The town of Dover-Foxcroft had been experiencing late-night burglaries and thefts. Cars and houses were being broken into, and mostly the thieves were seeking cash and prescription drugs. The investigations had revealed the vehicles were almost always found to be unlocked, as were the houses. More and more as time went on, more breaks were occurring, and I found Dover wasn't the only town being hit. As summer went on, I began to notice that other towns in my county seemed to be experiencing the same thing, car and residential burglaries were on the increase, and all similar in detail to the original Dover breaks. Now, the occasional burglary or theft wasn't out of the ordinary, but the numbers we were dealing with were. We had dozens of petty thefts taking place, and the locations were becoming more random.

I put a teletype out on the system asking other departments across the state if they were having burglaries with the similar Motive of Operandi, or M.O., that Dover and the surrounding towns were experiencing, unlocked cars and house burglaries with primarily cash and prescription drugs taken with a pattern of "neighborhood" burglaries. I received quite a few responses that other small towns did have the same issues taking place.

I decided to go back and take a closer look starting with the Dover cases. What I found was that they seemed to all have begun on the same street, and night after night, they "fanned" out to other areas of town further away from the apparent source before moving on to another town, first close to Dover and then again further away. In each town, it appeared the same M.O., with the thefts beginning on one side of town and ending on another, almost in a circular pattern that widened out the further it got from one source point in these towns, almost like a spiral.

In looking at the Dover's cases, I took a look in the area of the first street again where they seemed to have begun, and ultimately located a suspect. It was a guy I'd dealt with in the past on some minor stuff who, at the time of the first burglary, he'd been living with his mother on this particular street. As summer went along though, he'd picked up a girlfriend and was living in another town in her apartment. Coincidentally, he hadn't had a driver's license or car when he'd been living with his mother, however, his girlfriend did, and about the time he hooked up with her the burglaries started to fan out away from his mother's neighborhood and into other towns. I suspected this turd bird might be the guy, however, I had no solid proof yet. The burglar wasn't leaving anything else to go on. No prints, no sightings, no nothing. What I did have though was the usual volatile relationship between my suspect and his girlfriend, which always worked to our advantage in these situations. They seemed to have an on-again, off-again romance, and the off-again usually got pretty heated. When these situations occur, all bets are off. Girlfriends would turn their boyfriends into the police quickly when they were angry with them over something.

I received a call from the girlfriend who said she was tired of her boyfriend's drug use, and she hinted he may have committed some thefts to support his habit. She also said that the two lovebirds were having domestic problems again. Fingers Magee *(not his real name)* had assaulted her the night before, and she'd kicked him out of the apartment. I grabbed Charles from Dover PD where his was the first town hit, and he had a vested interest in solving the local theft ring, and we headed to her apartment in Brownville.

When we arrived, she answered the door and her face showed signs of the prior evening's argument. Charles and I talked to her for a bit, making certain she was alright and didn't need some sort of medical attention. She said she didn't, but you could tell that Mr. Fingers had pissed her off and good this time. Once we were certain that she was physically okay, we brought up the burglaries. Even though she denied knowing anything about the thefts directly and said she wasn't involved, she said Mr. Fingers had committed some burglaries and she allowed us to do a quick search of the apartment for any evidence of his involvement. She even signed a voluntary search form. She was obviously quite upset with this guy.

Now, a couple of things about people who commit crimes and think they can get away with it. One; they usually deny their involvement thinking that you're going to believe them. Two; they feel that they're so good at hiding their crimes that they don't mind you searching for evidence, believing there's nothing to hide. Three; as I said before, a woman scorned will roll over on her lover quickly if she's mad enough and wants to get him in trouble as some sort of punishment. Plus, they feel that if the story is good enough, they won't get in trouble themselves if they're involved in some way.

In performing a quick search of their hallway closet, I found a road atlas. You know, one of those large blue books with maps of the state in it that you kept in your car under the seat and grabbed when you thought you were lost. Do you remember? They were popular before mobile GPS units. Yeah, one of those. *And yes, I know, even mobile GPS units are outdated now!*

I opened the atlas up and noticed something peculiar. In the glossary, some of the names of the towns were highlighted in yellow and some of the highlights had lines drawn through the name. Further, when you looked up these towns on the various maps, some towns were circled, and others had circles with an 'X' drawn through them. I knew enough from my research into my case that the towns with lines and X's on them were towns that had experienced recent burglaries, including Dover-Foxcroft. When I asked the girl about the atlas, she was quick to say that it belonged to her boyfriend, Mr. Fingers, and she knew nothing about it. This opened the door for me to seize it as potential evidence. We also, with this in hand, performed a more thorough search of the apartment and seized a few random items that we believed may have been stolen, mostly jewelry. You see another thing about criminals is that even though they may have a primary focus when they're committing thefts, such as cash or drugs, they can't help but take nice shiny things that catch their eye as well or that they think their girlfriends might like. It didn't take long to match up some of the trinkets we'd seized to various burglaries around the state. It also didn't take long to connect the road atlas to the other evidence seized. I drafted an arrest warrant, and within days we arrested Mr. Fingers on charges of burglary and theft.

Mr. Fingers was charged with multiple, and I mean well over 200 burglaries across the state and was desperate to cut a deal. I'd arranged to have him transported to the Bangor Police Department where I'd reserved a meeting room that was wired for video recording. You know, one of those fancy, technological things we didn't have in the county. I also invited representatives from law enforcement in all of the towns that had outstanding burglary cases that may be connected to our suspect to join us for a sit-down with Mr. Fingers. I'd also spoken to my district attorney who agreed to cut Fingers a deal. If he copped to all the burglaries he'd committed and agreed to provide details, he'd be given a package deal, which would result in a lighter sentence than if he was tried separately in multiple counties for all the burglaries that we could ultimately tie him to. The key was that he had to agree to admit and provide details of all of his crimes to get the deal. The bad part was that under the agreement, any crimes we were unaware of that he confessed to would result in a "get out of jail free" card for him, barring something like murder or a sexual assault. In legal terms, this is referred to as a "proffer."

Now, the one thing I'll repeat about criminals in general, if half of them worked as hard at a real job as they do at committing crimes, they'd be quite successful in life. Mr. Fingers sat down with us like he'd been hired to make a presentation on a topic he'd earned a Master's degree. He proceeded to explain that he had, in fact, started his crime spree in Dover when he didn't have access to a vehicle and "circled out" from his mother's house at night, working his way further away each night until he finished the town while only targeting unlocked cars and vacant houses, at first anyway.

Once he hooked up with a girlfriend and a car, he started burglarizing other towns. He explained that he'd have his girlfriend drop him off on one side of town and told her to park on the other side. Throughout the night, he'd work his way toward her. And here's the astonishing part, Fingers could recall the makes, models, and colors of each car he broke into. Same with the houses, he could tell you the house color and sometimes even the house number. He knew which windows he crawled through, and which ones were locked or unlocked. He knew just what he'd taken from each and he could prove this by also telling us not only everything he took but also where he took it from, so we could match up each and every item to the exact location it was stolen from. It was quite amazing to listen to him describe it all. Over 200 burglaries and he described each in intricate detail. And remember, his crimes occurred at night when it was dark out and difficult to see.

Unfortunately, though, Mr. Fingers had let his drug habit get the best of him. He admitted he was a pill junkie, and once he had access to wheels, he acted as a mule for the local cocaine dealer and would deliver the product in exchange for his preferred drug in payment, which was Oxycontin pills. He'd be sent to a town on a run, and while there, he'd take his opportunity to burglarize the neighborhoods. The one place he wouldn't hit though was the houses he was to deliver the cocaine, although he did say that during one mule run there was a party taking place, and took the opportunity to hit all the vehicles in the yard thinking there'd be money and drugs within them. He admitted this was fairly poor judgment on his part. Go figure.

Mr. Fingers mentioned that only a couple of times did the police come close to catching him, and in one town his girlfriend was questioned by police as to why she was just sitting in her vehicle late at night but nothing further. The cops didn't have anything on her, and she had a clean record. She came up with some excuse, and sitting in a vehicle alone wasn't a crime. Fingers did admit to becoming cockier as time went on and more daring by changing his rule about unoccupied residences when he began breaking into houses with the owners still home sleeping in their beds. He said he was lucky no one ever woke up and found him inside their house.

We all sat there listening like children being told a good bedtime story. We didn't need to ask questions, he was providing everything in detail. The interview went on for hours as he described all the things he'd stolen and where it was all taken from. Now the stupid part. *Well, it's all quite stupid, isn't it?* The one detail that blew us all away was that as sharp as his memory was, the one thing he couldn't remember were the names of each town he'd hit. Remember the atlas? His downfall was that he had to cross off each and every town he'd burglarized for fear that if not, he'd hit the town twice and was sure to find nothing to take, not to mention the increased chance of getting caught if he re-visited a town that he'd already burglarized. In the atlas, he'd highlight the towns he was to perform cocaine runs or simply wanted to burglarize, and he'd cross them out after a night of cleaning out the neighborhoods.

At the end of the interview, Mr. Fingers stood up and shook my hand. He told me he was impressed. He said he never intended to get caught (*they never do*) and he was impressed at my ability to catch such an intelligent mastermind, which it was obvious he felt he was. He expressed that he felt that my mind was as superior to his in my ability to catch him. *Gee, thanks, what a compliment.* In reality, it did involve some luck in finding the atlas in the first place and his stupidity for not being able to memorize the names of towns as well as he could remember every other detail.

In the end, many townships cleared multiple cases off their records. Mr. Fingers was sentenced, through the agreement, to eight years for all the burglaries, mostly to serve out at the Charleston Correctional Facility. I kept the road atlas even after the case was disposed of as a conversation piece. A few years later, when I became a criminal investigator for the state prison system (*more to come on that*), I dusted the old book off, and in plain clothes one day was riding around the grounds of the Charleston facility with the warden. I knew that Mr. Fingers was working at one of the on-site work programs and I spotted Fingers strolling across the work yard and told the warden to pull up next to him. The warden did so, rolled down his window, and called Fingers over to the car. When Mr. Fingers spotted me in the passenger side, it was like an old friend that you hadn't seen in years. I had the atlas down by my side as he approached the driver's side of the car and began asking me what I'd been up to.

I smiled and said, "Not much, same old, catching criminals and all." He smiled and shook his head. I then remarked, "But I'm kinda lost, can you help me find my way?" Just as I raised up his old atlas and opened to a random page filled with circles and an 'X', Fingers peered in at it and recognized that it was his atlas. He cocked his head sideways, smiled, looked up at me, and simply said, "You're an asshole."

Again, sometimes you have to make it a point to have fun at work.

It was around 2010 that this next call occurred. It was during the time that I was working as a Deputy Investigator for the Piscataquis County Sheriff's Department. Piscataquis County, although the least populated county in Maine, is the second largest county, making it very rural. I was on duty one winter's night, along with one other deputy. Our patrol vehicles were permanently assigned to us, typically a Ford Escape police package, so both of us were in separate vehicles and patrolling random areas of the county. Although, when this particular call was received, we both happened to be in the Guilford area. The Town of Guilford was a "central point" to most locations within our jurisdiction and close to our base of operations in Dover-Foxcroft. Guilford, being a "mill town," had a population of around twelve hundred. The call came in described as a "domestic situation" between a father and son.

Upon our arrival at the clean, ranch-style residence, we discovered that a husband and wife, both in their mid to late 20s, had called to complain about the man's elderly father who had been living with the couple in their home. It was explained to us that the father had a history of being 'difficult', which basically meant he had an attitude and was set in his ways. The son described how the rest of his family was unwilling to deal with his father due to his verbally abusive behavior, and on this evening the son and his wife had enough of pops, and they wanted him out.

In many domestic-type situations such as this, which were quite common in that no assault had taken place and no justifiable reason to effect an arrest, it was typically found that removing the "issue" was the best solution for all those involved. This evening was to be one of those cases in which the father had to go or the fighting would only become worse. Leaving the elderly gentleman in the residence would only exacerbate the situation and may very well have led to a divorce for the younger couple.

It was at this point that the problem became twofold. First, the old man didn't have any place to go. There was simply no family left who were willing to deal with his attitude. Plus, we weren't prone to simply turning an elderly person out onto the winter streets in our rural county. We had no "homeless shelters" in the county, with the nearest being over an hour's drive away in Bangor and not really the most ideal of destinations for this guy. We also didn't have much in the area for hotels, again with the nearest being some distance away in either Newport or further north in Greenville, and neither having a guarantee of vacancy and both being many miles out of our way. We also weren't in the business of being someone's taxi service. When a person typically got into our vehicles, it was for a ride to jail or the hospital. Plus, the son wasn't willing to give this guy a ride anywhere, he just wanted him out.

We did, however, have a restaurant and bar in Dover-Foxcroft that had several small cabins that they regularly rented out. After a phone call was made, we found they did have an available cabin.

Now, as I'd mentioned, the issue with relocating this guy came with two problems. The second was how he was going to pay for the room, as the family wasn't willing to foot the bill. However, it quickly became apparent that this wasn't going to be an issue just as long as the hotel was willing to take gold.

Yes, I said gold.

The old timer advised my partner and me that he wouldn't leave without a suitcase full of clothing and essentials, nor without the four large, very heavy boxes that he had in the closet of the room he'd occupied in his son's house. As we'd already agreed to give the guy a ride to the cabins located in the next town over, we had no choice but to take his heavy boxes if we were going to clear this call in a timely manner. So, we proceeded to assist in carrying the cargo to my cruiser. I grabbed the first one and nearly tipped over when it was quickly discovered that the box, average in size, weighed a great deal more than I could carry easily. My partner assisted and as we walked by his son, we asked what was inside the box that was so important.

His answer was, "His gold."

It appears that our "friend" had at some point during his existence converted his life savings into solid gold bars, with each box containing twelve bars of the stuff dreams are made of. The old man, who was quite proud and protective of his bounty, showed me one. With his permission I was able to "handle" the bar, probably the only gold bar I'd ever have in my hands during my lifetime. Now, at an average weight of twenty-seven pounds each, and with four boxes full, we had about 1,296 pounds of gold in my back seat. And, in 2010 the average price of gold was about $1,013.00 per ounce, making his bars worth $437,616.00 for each. The grand total for the entire package, seated within my getaway vehicle, was $26,256,960.00. Yes, that was twenty-six million, two-hundred and fifty-six thousand, nine hundred and sixty U.S. dollars.

So, my first thought was that this old man must be one humungous asshole if his son is willing to let all that gold leave his house, because he wasn't stopping us or protesting in any way. I mean, this guy really must be Beelzebub himself if you're going to allow twenty-six million in potential inheritance to walk out of your house. And, his son was not only not stopping us, but he was also anxious to get the guy out! Not to mention that they hadn't whacked Pops before now and fudged his last will and testament, which they certainly must not have been included within. He was probably leaving it all to his favorite charity, or his favorite brothel.

Which brought me to my next thought; it was a good thing that I was an honest cop, not to mention that I had a partner working with me that evening who could potentially talk me out of driving this guy to the nearest bridge, toss him off, and leave with the booty. Whereas I'd never be seen again, and my cruiser would be discovered days later parked outside of an airport in Mexico after I boarded an airplane to a non-extraditable country.

But I digress.

And, in fact, we did take this guy to the hotel cabin and carried his gold inside the room for him. Again, hoping that his son wouldn't sneak to the hotel in the middle of the night dressed as a prowler, off the old man, and take his gold. *Hmmm, come to think of it, why didn't I do that?*

So, just like most other calls that we responded to, once we pulled out of the hotel parking area, we never heard from the guy again or knew whether or not he returned to his daughter-in-law's house.

He, and the gold, simply disappeared from our memories. Well, until now and I wrote about it in this book. ♦

CHAPTER 12

THE MDEA YEARS

It was 2010, and I had been a Drug Recognition Expert for a while now when the opportunity came up to serve with the Maine Drug Enforcement Agency. Chiefy Charles at the Dover Police Department had put in for a grant for a drug officer, something Piscataquis County hadn't had in the past. The grant was approved on a two-year funding plan with the agreement that the town pay independently for a third year as part of the grant requirements. The base pay for the officer was to come from the grant for the first two years and the grade pay for being an agent would come from the state, making the position financially appealing. If the officer produced in the first three years, the town had the option to continue the position with the state kicking in the extra to keep the pay the same without overburdening the local taxpayers.

The Maine Drug Enforcement Agency, or MDEA, is comprised of officers sponsored by their hired agencies, serving various year terms depending on how their agencies were set up. Some officers serve two-year terms, some longer, some only a year. The Agency is governed by the State Police, and pay is comparable to the state's criminal investigative division.

I wanted this position badly. This went along with my other drug training, and I wanted to work it from the special agent side, performing undercover work rather than uniformed work. There was no doubt that I'd be able to build more solid cases if I wasn't walking around in a uniform and driving a marked cruiser. The problem was I wasn't currently working for Charles anymore and didn't know how he'd feel about hiring me back. I also didn't want to burn a bridge at the Sheriff's Department.

I met with the sheriff and explained my desire for wanting the experience the Agency could provide. He understood and gave me his blessing to go for it and even said that at the end of the term, depending on when that might be, he'd hire me back. I applied for the position, and it was offered to me. I was hired back on with Dover and remained in a part-time status at the Sheriff's Department to stay on the roster and in their good graces. This also allowed me to keep up my road skills for the next two years at a minimum. I'd strictly be a drug agent with Dover and the MDEA and road patrol with the county sheriff. *So much extra time on my hands*.

I was assigned to the headquarters in Bangor and had a satellite office within the Dover-Foxcroft police department. Because I was well-known by this time in Piscataquis County, my primary duties there were to build drug cases and develop confidential informants. For drug purchases, or "buys" as they were called, when I set one up, I had to get an agent from out of the area to perform the buy because I was too recognizable. I was called to do the undercover stuff myself in other locations around the state, primarily in the Greater Bangor area where no one knew my face.

I was sent to the Academy's drug school for new agents where I received all new training that I hadn't had in the past. My tiny brain was filled with knowledge I hadn't yet learned, and I was taking in every bit of it. I was taught to recruit confidential informants and perform potential informant debriefings. I received training in report writing like no other I'd learned in the past, which gave me a special skill that the district attorney enjoyed with my reports being even more highly detailed than before. It got to the point that moving forward the DA would call me for my review and opinion on all major drug cases coming from other officers in the county before even considering prosecuting their cases because of the skills I now possessed.

I quickly developed several confidential informants, or "CIs." And I quickly learned that it truly takes a person living in the drug world to effectively catch a dealer. Through informants, I got closer to the local dealers than I was ever able to when I had the uniform on. Without the uniform, I could look, talk, and act like one of them, gaining their "trust" and obtaining their knowledge of the area's drug suppliers.

CIs were of two backgrounds. Either they were individuals themselves who had been caught with or dealing drugs, and they needed a way out and turned CI, hence the term "rat." Which, by the way, is a term to this day that I despise. Becoming an informant provided someone with an opportunity to better themselves and get out of a situation by assisting the law to get drugs off the streets. The term "rat" comes from criminals who don't want to get caught themselves. The only "rat" is the true criminal themselves. The other type of informants were those who simply wanted to help, to be part of something bigger than themselves, and lived in and around the drug community. In their minds, they wanted to do good, and some wanted the personal satisfaction that went with being an informant. The secrecy of living among the drug community but also helping the police was exciting to them. They weren't necessarily users or dealers themselves, although some were and enjoyed the excitement of a "double life."

In any event, the informants themselves determined whether they were exposed or not. If they could keep their mouths shut to even their families, then they were never discovered. If they blabbed to anyone, including their significant others, whether it be a girlfriend or boyfriend that they told, it took no longer than the time it takes to send a text for the information to get out and they were exposed. Some simply couldn't keep their traps shut, and informants could be their own worst enemies when it came to this. As far as being agents, we told no one. Why would we? Our goal was to be successful drug agents, we needed informants to get us close to the dealers. My informants learned to trust me quickly and none were ever exposed unless they blabbed to someone themselves.

My supervisor at MDEA told me he wanted some quick busts in Piscataquis County to make a name for the agency early on whereas we were "new" in that area, and I did just that. It didn't take me long to get several quick buys into some of the low-level dealers and make some fast arrests while focusing my sights on the actual targets, dealers who had been working the county for several years without having been caught and who dealt in the harder stuff, and in greater quantities.

The Agency wanted at least two controlled buys on a dealer before making an arrest. "Controlled" meaning an undercover agent or informant had to make the purchase while wearing a body wire and using marked cash. Once the buys were complete, we'd wait a few weeks before making the arrest in an effort to put some time between the last buy and the bust. This kept the dealers confused about who the informant was or how they got caught because they typically sell consistently to many more than just the informant. We could go up to a couple of months before making the bust for this reason, to keep the CIs safe and keep the dealers confused and wondering.

It only took a few months for me to take down my first primary target, which was a guy who'd been dealing in the area for years without law enforcement having the ability to get close to him. It was almost a joke how he skirted the law, and he was known to deal in every kind of drug imaginable.

It was also rumored that he had some heavy artillery in the form of automatic weapons on his property, which he liked to take in trade for the drugs.

I had a CI that was in hot water with the feds for various reasons and had an in with this guy as one of his regular buyers. The CI was in deep, and his choices were limited, so he agreed to wire up and make two controlled buys. The buys were within a week of each other and then we sat on the case for a few months before moving in.

On the day of the bust, we raided the suspect's "compound." He lived in a rural section of Guilford, a town of around 1,200 people just north of Dover-Foxcroft. A mostly quiet little mill town with one major route traveling through its village to points north towards Moosehead Lake. The guy's compound was on the outskirts of town and consisted of several acres of junk vehicles and equally junk house trailers. I had drafted a warrant for the entire property, and it was approved by the judge. On the day we executed the warrant, we showed up with several agents from MDEA and deputies from the Piscataquis Sheriff's Department.

Search warrants were always fun to execute, and over my career, I'd written many from property warrants to forensic cellular telephone warrants to warrants for DNA. Over time I'd become quite experienced in drafting and obtaining warrants to the point that other less experienced officers from various departments would seek me out when they needed a quick warrant because they knew I'd written so many successful ones.

We hit the compound hard, and each officer began a systematic search of the various dumpy trailers where random people were living on the property. The property was littered with junk house and camper trailers, cars, trucks, buses, and box utility trailers. Coming out of the target's main house trailer were a bunch of multi-colored extension cords. Follow a cord into the woods and you'd eventually come to another crappy, dirty house trailer with several people squatting in it. The search took hours, but ultimately, we were able to uncover more drugs and I located the guns I had heard about. Hidden inside an unoccupied travel trailer that was literally attached by tar paper and tacks to his main trailer were several semi-automatic pistols, rifles, and machine guns including AK-47s and Uzi 9mm assault pistols. We took the guns, the drugs, and the suspect upon our departure and made several more warrant arrests on individuals along the way living on the compound. It was a successful day.

Of course, the suspect made quick bail and was home again in a matter of hours. One week later, we hit the compound again using the conditions of release, or bail restrictions that I had placed on him a week earlier that provided law enforcement the ability to search the compound at any time without a warrant. Lucky for us, and unlucky for him, he'd gone right back to dealing and we uncovered a drugstore of various types of illegal substances including cocaine, heroin, morphine, Xanax, marijuana, and other types of illegal drugs, which resulted in his second trip to jail within a week.

This bust alone made a name for me and was a good score. This, along with the undercover work I was doing in the Greater Bangor area, made me not only very busy but also gave me training and experience that I'd never thought I'd have which boosted my knowledge even further on drugs and the drug world, and certainly didn't look bad on my resume.

I was amazed at how easy it was for me to buy drugs from people who didn't know me. I looked the part dressed as a "biker," complete with a leather jacket and bandana on my head to cover my short haircut. I had grown facial hair and even had photos taken of me at various motorcycle rallies on my bike to show that I was of the biker world. As long as I had cash to flash, the dealers would sell to me, never having met me one day in their lives.

The CIs would introduce me, the wad of cash would come out of my pocket, and the dealers would ask, "How much do you want?" I also couldn't believe the types of people I was purchasing from.

Hell, one day I bought prescription Ritalin, which as I'd mentioned is basically over-the-counter cocaine, from a sixty-ish grandmother in the parking lot of a little league baseball game that her grandson was playing at. I pulled out the greenbacks, and she dumped the pills out on her car dashboard and let me have my pick. A few weeks later, we'd arrange for two of us, myself and another female agent playing the part of "my wife," plus the informant, to drive granny to the southern end of the state to buy crack cocaine. She never caught on until the arrest that she'd spent the day taking two undercover agents halfway across the state for a load of drugs.

As much fun as I was having as an agent, it was just as much of a headache. The days were long, and the buys were tedious to set up. Drug dealers and junkies aren't the most reliable people. For every ten buys you thought you had ready to go, maybe one would take place successfully. It was all about timing. When the dealers have the dope, they want to get rid of it quickly and make fast cash, so you have to be ready at any time to jump on the opportunities. And it wasn't as easy as just getting a call and then going out to buy the drugs. Being the only agent in a rural county, I had trouble getting enough agents rounded up for the buys with most of them living over an hour away. When we performed a buy, you had to have several agents parked in the area all listening on the wire that someone making the buy was wearing in case something went south. There was also a lot of prep work that goes into the buy, especially if you had to use the CI as the purchaser. The CI would need to be strictly advised on just how they were to act and speak if they were going in alone, and under no circumstance could they take any of the drugs themselves. Try telling that to a junkie when you're handing them free money and letting them go buy dope while all you can do is listen in on a staticky radio wire.

Not to mention that to keep the CIs working, you had to gain their trust, as funny as it sounds, and 'act' like they were your friends. Because they had so few true friends and were depending on the agent to keep them safe, they'd call at all times of the night for no reason because they truly thought you cared about them. Junkies don't keep regular hours. They party all night and sleep it off all day. Getting calls at 2:00 a.m. when they're at their highest and sometimes most alert and want to carry on a conversation with me because they thought I cared was a complete pain in the ass.

Then there was just the fact that everything we did had to be of the highest secrecy for success purposes. There were times that I'd receive a call to pack a bag for several days and report to the headquarters only to be sent on an assignment that I wasn't allowed to tell even my wife about or the location that wasn't disclosed to me until I was in transit. It might be two or three days before being allowed to check in and let my wife know I was alive. Those were challenging times.

One of the other problems was the vehicle they assigned to me. Each agent was assigned an unmarked car to use. There was supposed to be nothing about the vehicle that gave away to the public that it was a police car in disguise. The radios were hidden and all your gear, like rifles, electronic equipment, bulletproof vests, and jackets with police insignia, were kept in the trunk. The cars weren't new, and they were supposed to completely blend in with the surroundings. The problem was mine didn't. Most agents worked in urban areas, so any sedan would most likely work. On the other hand, I was a rural agent, and everyone else in the county drove pickup trucks or junky rust buckets. Everyone except for me.

I was assigned a bright silver Ford Taurus, a four-door sedan that was in fairly good shape. You might as well have painted 'undercover police' on the side of it because it stood out like a sore thumb. There was no such thing as surveillance with this car, it was far too obvious that among the sea of users with their jacked-up pickup trucks, this car was occupied by a cop. Parking this tub in the middle of the woods while trying to perform surveillance just looked ridiculous. Not to mention half the places we had to go required the option of four-wheel-drive, and having to knock on the suspect's door to get a tow out of the muddy field across from their houses where I was trying to spy on them would just be embarrassing. I constantly bugged my supervisor for months to give me another vehicle that would blend in better. Finally, after several months, I was assigned another vehicle.

A nearly new, bright white Mercury Marquis.

♦ ♦ ♦

One of my fellow agents in Bangor, and the person who provided me with my initial training upon joining the MDEA, Jason Warner, had a case that stretched into my area in Piscataquis County. Jason and I worked on the case together and formed a plan.

Jason had developed the CI, and I knew the players, including having had interaction with both the CI and the suspects while doing uniformed work with the county sheriff department. I had arrested the suspect on unrelated charges a couple of years back. He'd resisted the arrest, and we'd fought to the ground during it, so I remembered him well. I had also busted the CI once or twice on some small stuff in the past as a uniformed officer.

The CI could hook us up with the suspect who had ties to a heroin dealer in Lowell, Massachusetts. The CI had arranged to drive the suspect and both their girlfriends to Lowell to pick up a load of heroin to bring back to Maine to sell. The deal was that the CI would have his girlfriend, who supposedly didn't know he was working with us, drive the target car while the CI kept us informed by text as to the progress of the drug run while it was occurring.

It was mid-winter, and most of the run would take place on I-95 from Bangor to the Massachusetts border and into Lowell. We knew the trip to the border was about three hours long in the winter weather and estimated the run into Lowell at another hour or two. Two of us, namely myself and Jason, would follow the CI's vehicle to the border and wait there for them to return with the drugs. From there we'd follow it back to the Penobscot County line and the Greater Bangor area. Once there, several other vehicles with agents and state police would stop the vehicle on the interstate. The reason for following it all the way back to Penobscot County was simple, we knew the prosecutor for that county was more aggressive on drug cases and we'd get a better result in court. Sad but true. So that was the plan, simple enough. Simple if it were to all go as planned. Of course, it didn't.

It was snowing hard, in fact, it was an all-out blizzard, and travel was desperately slow. Jason and I were in separate vehicles following behind the CI at a safe enough distance so as to not be noticed by the suspects. By the time we'd followed the car on the interstate to the York toll booth in southern Maine, where we had planned to wait, we were about four hours into the trip due to road conditions, and it was evening now. The York toll booth, the last toll stop before the New Hampshire border, is about twenty miles from the state line. To reach Massachusetts on I-95, you have to briefly crossover into New Hampshire. Because we were Maine DEA, our jurisdiction ended at the state line. Our plan was to park on either side of the toll booth and wait for the CI to text us that they were on their way back and passing through the toll stop.

Jason sat on one side of the toll gates and I on the other, waiting to hear from the CI and spot the car coming back through, along with the suspect and the drugs. It was expected that the suspect would purchase at least five "fingers" of heroin. A finger being around nine to ten grams of heroin with a total street value of around $5,000.

So, we sat there in the dark, and the storm was picking up with huge, fluffy flakes of snow falling from the sky. The wind was also picking up, and the snow was piling up. The good thing was that the toll plaza was well-lit, and traffic was light, so even if the idiot CI forgot to text us, we should still see the car come through within the two to three-hour window.

Two hours came and went. Then three hours…then four. Jason was frantically texting the CI to get an update. Were they still in Massachusetts? Had they come through already and we missed them? Did the deal go to hell? Were they alive? *That would look bad on our resumes, the CI and his girlfriend get smoked buying drugs that were paid for by the MDEA while we sat freezing our butts off at a toll booth in a snowstorm.*

Finally, after the fourth hour, Jason received a text back. The suspect had picked up the drugs. He not only had picked up the heroin, but he also bought cocaine as well. *Bonus!*

That was the good news. Then came the bad news. The suspect had also bought a little extra cocaine to party with, and he had the CI drive them all to a local motel in Lowell for the night. *Well now, this was certainly a problem.* Apparently, the dude and his girlfriend were now in the room, passed out, having gotten wasted on the cocaine. Supposedly the CI hadn't done any, and due to the fact that the texts were somewhat legible, we believed this was true. The CI didn't know what to do. He had no control over the junkie and couldn't leave, especially without the drugs and the suspect. Jason had no choice but to tell him to crash there overnight with the junkies and our drugs and get on the road first thing in the morning. This, however, created several issues. We had several vehicles and officers waiting at the Penobscot County line that had also been waiting halfway into the night that we didn't know what to tell at this point. Not to mention Jason and I couldn't go anywhere. What if the junkies wake up in the middle of the night and decide that's the best time to make the trip back? What if they stay a number of days and keep partying with the other drugs? This wasn't good.

The decision was made by our supervisor that Jason and I would remain where we were and the others would go home, ready to jump into action if, and when, the suspects were back on the move. *Great, so we're stuck in our cars here at the toll booth for who knows how long in the middle of a snowstorm, and I have to pee.*

For the next several hours, the snow picked up. Jason and I took turns watching and waiting, both having to stay awake by conversing over the radio. We took turns making quick trips into the nearest town for snacks and bathroom breaks. This was also one of those assignments that were hush-hush, so my wife hadn't heard from me for over twenty-four hours, and chances were this was going to go on quite a bit longer.

By the dawn of the following day, the snow had stopped, and the sun had come out. Both Jason and I were tired, but we had to keep at it and remained ready for when the junkies decided to get back on the road again. Sporadically throughout the late morning, we'd receive texts from the CI telling us that the junkies were still passed out from the partying the night before. *Don't most hotels have early check-out times?* The fear now was becoming greater that these idiots would stay longer and start using the drugs we'd intended to bust them for. *Junkies can be so unreliable.*

In hopes that the plan would be back in action on day 2, the posse began plans to form again on the interstate at the Penobscot County line some two hours away from us. There was an abandoned truck weight station just after the Penobscot County line near Pittsfield where a few were waiting and the rest at the nearest on-ramp in Newport, a town about twenty miles south of Bangor.

It would be late morning when we finally got word from the CI that they were back on the road, this time with the CI driving, making it difficult to receive updates. Apparently, the CI's girlfriend was in no condition to drive, most likely having partaken in the prior evening's goodies, leaving only the CI in any condition to operate the car.

It was early afternoon when we finally spotted the car coming back through the toll stop, and both Jason and I took up positions behind it a few vehicles back so one of us could consistently keep the target in sight. We'd take turns passing each other and letting other cars go by us to make certain one of us was never directly behind the CI's car for too long but also always keeping the target vehicle in sight. We were both beat, so playing shuffleboard on the interstate helped keep us both awake and alert. When we got closer to Newport, we radioed ahead, and the posse got into the ready positions. The plan was for Jason and me to back off as we passed the weigh station and a marked state police unit would get in behind the target, follow for a short distance, and make the traffic stop on the interstate.

As we passed by the weigh station, I noticed the vehicles tucked in behind the bushes that separated the on-ramp from the interstate. I looked in my rearview and watched the wagon train pull out behind us. Jason and I both slowed to allow them all to make the pass and get in behind the CI's car. Once we went by the Newport on-ramp, more marked and unmarked police units joined the train. It had to be obvious to the suspects at this point that something was about to happen, and it did. The command was given, and the line of police cars lit up like a string of blue Christmas lights. A pursuit stop was initiated, which is when marked units box the vehicle in on all sides and guide the vehicle to a stop in the breakdown lane, so a travel lane can be kept open, and so the suspect can't drive away and initiate a chase.

It was an impressive sight to watch all the uniformed officers, guns drawn, exiting their cruisers, taking stances behind the cover of doors and vehicles, and commanding the occupants from the target vehicle from a safe distance. In performing these types of busts, everyone gets arrested, including the CI, so as not to tip the suspects that anyone in the car is an informant. The CI gets treated the same as everyone else.

We searched the suspects roadside, and the heroin was found packed inside a condom in the jacket pocket of the suspect's girlfriend. This surprised us greatly to find the drugs so easily discoverable and quite unhidden. Most times the dealers are at least smart enough to anticipate some sort of interaction with law enforcement and either hide the drugs on their bodies or have a "hide" in the vehicle. I've searched cars and found drugs under the dash, inside rocker panels, and under the hood before, so why was the heroin in a jacket pocket where we could so easily locate it?

I had the glamour job of searching the primary suspect himself. The only satisfaction I had was that I had dealt with him as a uniformed officer and now he knew I was the one to nab him as an undercover agent. Those are satisfying moments. I found the "eight-balls" of cocaine wrapped in tin foil hidden in his underwear. There were several packages each about the size of a large marble. *Small packages next to a small package.*

We arrested "everyone" and took them all back to the headquarters in Bangor. We separated them all and proceeded to question the suspects and debrief the CI. As it turned out, the CI had an explanation for why the cocaine was well-hidden, but the heroin wasn't.

The CI explained that the plan had been that the suspect's girlfriend was to hide, a.k.a. "pack" the heroin-filled condom in her *hoo-hoo*, using petroleum jelly as a lubricant to help make it easier to insert. *Yes, friends, this is where most dealers hide their drugs, in a body cavity.* The problem was they remembered the condoms but not the lubricant, and the condoms weren't the "self-lubricating" kind. *Someone didn't know how to shop smartly.*

The CI said that when they saw the cops pull in behind them on the interstate, all he heard from the back seat was, "Push harder, push harder," from the suspect and, "It won't go in, it won't go in," from the suspect's girlfriend. *Picture that.* He said he didn't want to turn around to see what was happening, but he had a good idea of what wasn't happening, the drugs weren't being hidden in their intended location. Ultimately, she had to shove the drugs into her jacket pocket because she couldn't *shove* them anywhere else. I can imagine just what the expression was on Jason's and my face as we were being told this "dry" tale of woe and desperation. A Kodak moment it wasn't, I'm sure.

From start to finish, Jason and I put in well over forty-eight hours without sleep and pulled off a good bust with drugs in street value of over five grand having been kept off the streets. It wasn't major by any scale, but it did keep some drugs out of the hands of others, which ultimately was always the goal. And it did put the dealer and his girlfriend away for a couple of years, not nearly long enough, but that part was always out of our control.

And as for the suspect, I'm certain he wished he'd bought that lubricant once he got back to prison.

I've always wondered why on earth anyone would want to snort something up their nose or inject into their veins that came from someone's sweaty underwear or other body cavity, front or rear, literally, of some junkie.

It never made sense to me.

◆ ◆ ◆

Speaking of confidential informants, here's an amusing little tale about the level of intelligence some of them had, or lack thereof. If you recall, I mentioned that an informant was either someone who's gotten themselves into trouble and trying to help themselves out. Or they're someone who enjoys living the "double life" of living amongst the drug population and most likely being a part of it, but also assisting the police because of a greater feeling of being part of something good. This story is one involving the latter, or two to be exact.

The other quirk to being a voluntary informant was that they could get paid for their services. Not much, maybe $50 to $100 a score, but it was something for their efforts. We didn't want to make buying drugs a lucrative venture for the CIs, but we also didn't want them to walk away with nothing, especially if their motivation was personal. It was almost like having another person on the payroll that you didn't perform a background check on in advance before hiring them.

There was a low-rent apartment building in Milo, and many of the residents were involved in the drug trade to at least a minor extent. I had two confidential informants who lived in separate apartments in the building. Both had been informing for the sheriff's department on and off before I had become the local MDEA agent, and both had been "handed over to me" by the S.O. to help build cases in the area. Both informants proved to be reliable, each having separate and strong ties to local dealers. I managed to build a couple of good cases using each separately, as both had contacts of their own. And both CIs enjoyed the few bucks we'd throw at them each time they scored a buy for us. It was a win-win for a period of time.

For purposes of this story, we'll call one of them Nitwit One and the other Nitwit Two (*obviously not their real names*), but as circumstance would have it, this is basically how we identified informants in reports, minus the 'Nitwit' part. Confidential informants, for purposes of anonymity and protecting their identities, were provided numbers in place of their actual names so no one would have the ability to identify them through our reports.

Several months into my assignment, I was contacted by Nitwit One who explained he'd met a guy in the Milo area who was willing to sell his prescription Oxycontin pain medication to him. He said the guy preferred to trade the pills in exchange for his preferred drug, cocaine, however, he thought he'd take cash if that was all that was available. I told Nitwit One to keep working the angle and see just how much the guy was willing to sell and how much he wanted for each pill. You see, prescription drugs commonly had a street value equal to their strength in milligrams. Meaning if the strength of a pill was thirty milligrams, the pill was usually worth $30 each on the street, give or take. We needed a cash transaction to set up the buy, no trades. I told Nitwit One to dangle the angle with cash and see if the guy bites like a fish. I didn't hear back for a few days. And then about a week later, Nitwit Two called me on the telephone. He said he'd found a guy in Milo, who was willing to provide him with some cocaine. When I asked about the quantity and how much he wanted, Nitwit Two said there was a "catch" to the deal.

"What catch?" I'd asked.

"The dude says I gotta sell him my Oxys before he'll sell me his cocaine."

Being that I was working more cases than just this one, I didn't immediately catch on until about this same time I received a call from Nitwit

One, who said that he'd managed to talk his connection, a.k.a. Nitwit Two, into selling his prescription Oxys for cash.

Now you can probably imagine the look on my face that I must have had as I was listening to these two idiots. You know, that, "I'm dealing with two complete morons," look as I'm holding the phone receiver and realizing my two confidential informants are working each other, both hoping to score a deal on the other, trying to impress me and each getting a couple of bucks in their pockets for their troubles.

I let the charade play out for a few days only because I knew that Nitwit Two had the prescription to sell, however, Nitwit One had never divulged that he was holding any cocaine that he was willing to sell. Not to mention that Nitwit Two wasn't supposed to be selling his pills either. I wanted to see how far both would go to make themselves look good to me, not realizing that I knew they were both willing to sell drugs in order to buy drugs for the MDEA and that they had no idea that the other was an informant. I was also simply getting a chuckle out of the whole situation.

When the deals were closer to being finalized, I called it all off, coming up with an excuse to do so that wouldn't cause either one to figure out that they were both informants working each other for a score. I also stopped using both whereas they'd just proven not only each to be dumber than dirt, but neither was deemed reliable anymore where they both were willing to sell drugs to the other one. ♦

CHAPTER 13

A BAD DAY

This next part was a bad day all around for everyone involved. This tragedy is the reason that I've changed most of the names of the people in this novel because again, some wouldn't want their real names used, and there are victims and families involved that may not want their real names mentioned. Like all before and after, this is a true story. And to clarify before we get into it, once all was said and done and the investigation was completed by the Attorney General's Office, there would be only two officers who were on scene this particular day that was told, in their opinion, they were completely honest in their depositions on what occurred. I was one of them.

I also want to mention one of my pet peeves. It upsets me when someone who wasn't present on a high-risk scene, or any scene for that matter, offers their opinion on what occurred. Even worse, tries to tell you what happened when they weren't even there. I've been asked many times about this day, and depending on who I would be speaking to, someone always tries to tell me how it actually went down. *Duh, people, I was there.* There are those who actually enjoy saying things like, "Why didn't you do this, or why didn't you do that…" Here's a hint, if you weren't there, then don't try to tell people who were what happened, and don't tell them how they should have acted or reacted. I'm certain many of you reading know what I'm talking about. People's opinions are like…well, you know the rest of the saying. *By the way…are you all still reading, or have my opinions turned you away from the book? Don't answer that.*

It was a fairly early morning in November of 2011, and I was in my MDEA satellite office on the second floor of the Dover-Foxcroft Police Department. I was dressed in my normal T-shirt, jeans, and sneakers, the standard uniform for an agent who may be called at any time to perform a buy or meet with an informant. I wasn't doing anything in particular, other than deciding what cases to work on that day when the radio traffic on my scanner made my ears perk up. "*…Dispatch to Dover 3, reported shots fired at Pleasant Hill Manor…*" Now, normally the report of shots fired, 99 percent of the time, turns out to be kids with fireworks or something along those lines. However, this transmission got the "second glance" from me. There was something in the tone of the dispatcher's voice, not to mention Pleasant Hill Manor is a home for the elderly, and it was too early in the day for fireworks. But again, it could be the fact that work was being done at the facility and maybe a pneumatic hammer was being used and it sounded like gunshots to one of the elderly residents.

Then came the immediate second radio transmission. "*…Shots fired at Pleasant Hill Manor, one man down..!*"

I leaped from my chair and headed to the Taurus. Uniformed officer Sgt. Darrell Saunders, a.k.a. "Dover 3," was out the door just ahead of me. Other officers from both the Dover Police and Sheriff's Department were scrambling as well. Something serious and out of the norm was definitely taking place.

We were informed by radio through dispatch that a man had been shot in the parking lot of the group home. No further information was available at that time. No other details on the shooter or anything else yet. And to be specific, Pleasant Hill Manor was less than a quarter mile from the station, so not a lot of time for information gathering.

Darrell arrived just ahead of me. I could see several people standing in the parking area. I didn't have a good feeling because who's to say one of these guys wasn't the suspect, or all of them? As we arrived, the people in the parking lot were also pointing to a man lying on the ground, and at the same time, dispatch advised us to be on the lookout for a white pickup truck with specialty firefighter license plates. I didn't immediately see any vehicles matching that description in the parking area, so I assumed the suspect had fled.

Darrell leaped from his car and ran up to the victim. He checked for a pulse and looked back at me, giving me the "nope" look. This guy was done. I was barely out of my car and got right back into it to leave to begin searching for the white truck and the shooter.

So, the back story so far, was that there was a work crew at the group home performing repairs to the building that morning. A white male, unidentified as of yet, arrived in a white pickup truck and shot one of the workers, Perry Schmidt, to death in the parking lot. It would later be determined that the shooter had "hip shot," meaning as soon as he got out of his truck, he immediately began shooting with the first several rounds from his .45 caliber semi-auto pistol hitting the ground leading up to Schmidt, and the rest of the clip into and up Schmidt's body, killing him instantly. A total of sixteen shots had been fired. This guy had really wanted Schmidt gone for some reason, and he'd achieved his goal.

Believing that if the minimal information so far was correct, we had a local volunteer firefighter who had committed the shooting and had left the area in a white pickup truck in an unknown direction. I radioed that I was going to the local fire station to check for the truck, and I took off in that direction, the center of town. I could hear that other officers were responding from various locations throughout the county, however, at the moment, there were only a small handful in Dover, and I didn't want this guy getting out of the area if I could help it.

Another piece of information we hadn't realized as of yet was that the suspect was, in fact, a Dover firefighter and had a portable radio with him that had the capability of scanning the police band channels as well as the fire frequencies, so he was also hearing the radio traffic as it was being transmitted to us.

As I pulled through the fire station, I didn't see the suspect's truck. I overheard traffic that it may have been spotted heading out of town on Route 6 towards Milo, another small village a couple of towns over to the east of Dover about nine miles away that also had its own small, local police department. I did know that the Milo Police were headed our way on Route 6, so if the vehicle was headed that way, it would most likely be intercepted by the Milo cops if it didn't turn off somewhere in between.

I was headed out Route 6 when, on a hunch, I turned down a side street, Fairground Avenue, in case the shooter was trying to hide locally or change directions. Again, if he's listening to the radio, he knows where we're looking.

As the name indicated, the county fairgrounds were located on this side road, and the fairgrounds ran parallel to the road almost the entire length of the short street with three entrances onto the grounds. I passed by the first two entrances slowly enough to get a good look at the far back of the fairgrounds, but no vehicle matching the white truck's description. I pulled into the third entrance enough to see the grounds, and in the far back in a field where the horse-pulling usually takes place, I spotted the white truck.

Now the next bit of information that I hadn't been aware of yet was that the shooter was actually known to me and all of us. He was one of our emergency 911 dispatchers. Mitchell Chambers was a long-time employee who was very experienced at dispatching police, fire, and EMS calls. Another fact that I wasn't yet aware of was that once he parked at the rear of the fairgrounds, Chambers had initiated a radio conversation with the county dispatch center on a fire frequency that I didn't have access to in my car, so I was unaware that he had called into the dispatch center himself and was talking to the dispatcher on duty. He hadn't provided his location, but he was distraught and told the dispatcher that he had committed the murder. As it would turn out, Mitchell was intoxicated, and Schmidt was the target of his anger. For whatever reason that only Chambers was in control of this day, in his moment of despair and fueled by alcohol, he'd murdered Schmidt in a fit of rage.

I pulled further into the fairgrounds and took up a position behind the antique tractor barn, parking my car in between two of the tractors, which allowed me a bit of cover. It was estimated that this put me over 200 yards away from Chamber's location at the far end of the field, just close enough to confirm this was the suspect vehicle. I radioed that I had located the vehicle, so other units could quickly respond my way.

As I opened my driver door and used it for more cover, taking out my .40 caliber semi-auto handgun, I could see that the truck was pointed away from me and that the suspect was standing at the rear of the truck, leaning against the bed and was looking in my direction. Because I was so far away, it was difficult to make out the suspect's hands or face, and without the knowledge of who he was yet and the fact he was speaking on the radio to dispatch on a channel I didn't have, I couldn't make out who he was or that I even knew him.

Now several dilemmas were facing me at the moment. One, and most importantly, I'm alone here and I'm not driving a marked unit. This guy, whoever he was, had no idea that I was a cop. For all he knows, I'm someone who knew the victim and I'm coming to take revenge. Secondly, I can't see his hands. I know he has a gun, but where is it, and is it pointed at me? I just didn't know. Third, I needed two more hands. I needed my weapon out and ready, I needed to keep dispatch informed of my situation by radio, and I needed a set of binoculars to see exactly what this guy's hands were doing. I also really, really wanted my bulletproof vest, which not only would offer me some protection if bullets began to fly but also had a nice, big "Police" insignia on it. The problem was that was in the trunk of my car. One thing I did know was that this guy was exactly where I wanted him at that moment. The field was bordered on two sides by woods, and in the rear by the wood line was a large berm before you came out onto a woodlot of a local mill. This guy couldn't get off these grounds by vehicle without going past me, and he was no threat to anyone else where he was right then.

Luckily, though, the binoculars were under my front seat, so with gun in hand, I could at least use my other hand to switch between the binoculars and the radio. I peered through the glasses and saw that the suspect was standing with his hands crossed on top of the tonneau cover on the bed of his truck. I couldn't see his hands under his arms, but I surmised that in one hand was the gun. And unbeknownst to me yet, in the other hand, was the portable radio he was using. I still couldn't make out a face, he was too far away for that, even with the binoculars. What I did see was a shirtless, disheveled man whose identity I couldn't determine as of yet.

Now the next bit of information that none of us knew yet, but would later be determined, was that between the Pleasant Hill Manor and the fairgrounds, about a mile or so, the shooter had managed to reload his weapon, fifteen rounds in the magazine and one ready in the pipe. Even without this information, I had to assume he had rounds in that gun and was ready to shoot at me if I posed a threat.

Still, only moments in and continuing to be alone when I briefly put the binoculars down and picked my mike back up to make a radio transmission and update dispatch when I heard the shots ring out…

"Bang…bang, bang, bang!"

Shit, I'm getting shot at! "Shots fired! Shots fired!" I screamed into the mike, my adrenalin going through the roof. I immediately dropped the mike and picked the binoculars back up to see where the gun was pointing. The shooter was back with his hands folded on the bed of the truck, no gun was pointing at me at the moment. I didn't know exactly what had just occurred. Had he shot at me with the intention of killing me too? Had he shot at me as a "warning" to stay back or to try to get me to leave? I just wasn't certain.

"…Shots have been fired. Repeat, shots have been fired…" was the echo from the dispatcher over the radio to all other responding units. Now I didn't currently have holes in me, and I didn't hear the "ting, ting, ting" from bullets striking either my car or the cast iron on the nearby antique tractors, so either this guy is a terrible shot, or he's too far away and his bullets fell short. I quickly thought, *"If he's too far away to hit me, then no matter what kind of a shot I am, I may not hit him on return fire."* This isn't something that I was willing to risk; if I shoot back and miss, then the war might be on, and I didn't want him closing the gap between us. I'm safe and unharmed, and I wanted him where he was, so I wasn't returning fire unless circumstances changed. Keeping in mind only mere moments had gone by since locating the shooter, and anything could change quickly.

Adrenalin still high, the next transmission I heard over the radio was from Lt. Baker to dispatch, "I'm at the first entrance to the fairgrounds, waiting here for additional backup!" *Are you kidding me right now!? I'm getting shot at in here! Get your ass over here and help cover me!*

I was just a bit, just a tad, upset by what I'd just heard, not to mention the shooter probably heard it, too. I determined that I definitely needed more protection on my body, so carefully, with a gun in one hand and the glasses in the other, I slid towards the back of my car and retrieved my vest from the trunk. I also could hear more sirens and engines finally approaching.

The first cruiser to nearly drive over the top of Baker's car was Deputy Stephen Wickle of the Sheriff's Department. He quickly took up a spot near me amongst the tractors and he, too, had a pair of binoculars, so now we had two good sets of eyes on the shooter. Quickly behind him, a wagon train of cruisers from both the Dover- Foxcroft Police and Sheriff's Department arrived, not to mention other departments were on their way. Both Charles and Sheriff Jerry Robinson also arrived on the scene.

Now with that said, you need to picture the dynamics of the situation. I technically was the superior officer on scene with my title being MDEA, which meant I worked for the state, and that typically trumped everything. But I also had a police chief and a county sheriff on the scene, and that's a recipe for disaster. Too many captains on this boat. Additionally, you need to know the relationship between Charles and Jerry at that time, it wasn't good. These two were constantly at odds with each other over who had final jurisdiction in Dover-Foxcroft. Plus, the situation itself, the shooter was an employee of the county, and known to all of us, making this a unique, if not terrible set of circumstances.

I was finally advised of who the shooter was, and I was stunned, to say the least. Not that Mitchell was a good friend or a friend at all, however, I'd obviously had professional interactions with him, and he was a damn good dispatcher. This didn't make any sense, nor did it change the situation. Mitchell had just killed someone. The only question was how he was going to react to all his fellow officers who were now all pointing guns at him.

I now had knowledge of who the shooter was, and that Mitchell had been talking to dispatch on the fire channel, and the on-duty dispatcher had been doing an excellent job keeping him calm. Obviously being very familiar with Mitchell was helping that situation. Sheriff Robinson took over negotiations on the scene over a portable radio that we all could now hear. This is very important to the story. We were now all able to hear the radio traffic between the two from the hand-held that Sheriff Robinson was speaking through, and Wickle and I were keeping the information flowing by both using binoculars to keep a close eye on Mitchell's hands. He never left the position he was in, arms folded over the truck bed looking at us with the gun in one hand and radio in the other, both tucked under his folded arms.

More officers arrived, and Lt. Baker finally arrived at our location, taking up a position to my immediate left. We had several officers in the immediate area under the tractor barns and others flanking to the left and right of the scene. It was a confusing scene at first with one officer from another local police department pulling up right in front of us, not realizing the logistics of the scene, and we had to waive him back out of the way. However, after a few short moments, we finally had a relatively safe, controlled scene on our hands, and negotiations were taking place between Mitchell and the sheriff. Everything was as calm as could be for the moment.

You could overhear the conversation with Mitchell apologizing to the sheriff for all he'd done. He admitted openly to the killing, saying he'd done what he came for and wasn't going to hurt anyone else. The sheriff doing his best to keep the conversation calm and trying to talk Mitchell into putting the gun down and walking off the field toward us. All the other officers, including Charles, were behind cover ready in case it all went bad. Darrell was still at the scene of the original shooting processing that area, and an ambulance was dispatched to our scene just in case of anything.

After a few minutes, a state police cruiser arrived, and out popped Trooper James Cross, an officer whom I had gone through DRE school with and who'd recently returned to work after a tour overseas with the armed forces in Afghanistan. I knew him fairly well, well enough to realize immediately something was wrong. He came up to me in a very excited state, holding his assigned AR-15 rifle up against his chest, and began pacing back and forth in front of me asking, "Where's the shooter, where's the shooter?!"

My eyes grew wide as I told James to calm down and pointed out into the field, "Right there." *The guy wasn't hiding.* The thing I noticed about James immediately was that he was looking through me. Not at me, through me. I'd seen this look before, all seasoned officers had, and it scared the hell out of me. We call it the thousand-yard stare when the person speaking to you isn't able to focus on the situation. We see this a lot in drug cases when the person is experiencing extreme paranoia or in people who've experienced some sort of mental or emotional breakdown. Cross wasn't "with me" at that moment, he wasn't *with* any of us right then. His mind was technically somewhere else.

Later in the day, one of the lead investigators from the Attorney General's office would confide in me personally that in their opinion, Trooper Cross wasn't "there" on this day, he was back in the battlefields of Afghanistan, experiencing extreme PTSD. In his mind, he was, during those moments with us, on the battleground in a combat situation and not able to discern the difference. The truth was, I had never encountered anyone experiencing PTSD in this way.

"He's killed someone, we need to take him out!" Cross repeated to me several times, still pacing in front of me. I realized quickly that we had another serious problem on our hands. My focus was now off the shooter and on James, trying to calm him down and bring him back to reality. My focus needed to be back on the guy in the field, not here with a law enforcement officer who was not in this moment of reality.

"James, there's a negotiation taking place. You can hear it. You need to calm down!" Other officers began to take notice of the immediate problem I was dealing with.

"He's killed someone! We need to take him out! Where is he?!" Cross kept yelling at me, wide-eyed, staring straight through me.

"James! You need to calm down right now! Everyone is safe at the moment, he's right out there and we're talking to him! You need to pay attention and listen to the negotiations!" I was directly in Cross's face, trying to get him to focus.

Suddenly the trooper dropped to a prone position and pointed his gun out at the field. I breathed a brief sigh of relief, believing James had snapped out of it and come to his senses and was taking up a safe position directly between me and Baker to wait for the outcome of the negotiations. I focused back on the field. Mitchell was in the same position, and the talks were continuing via radio between him and the sheriff.

So, to be clear for those of you who may be wondering, no matter what crime has taken place, you don't interrupt active negotiations that might bring the situation to a peaceful and safe ending. There's more to consider than just what the suspect has done. There are other lives in jeopardy, namely ours at that moment, and nobody wanted to see a gun battle take place. The suspect was where we wanted him, in a place that he couldn't get out of and nowhere near the public at that moment. We didn't want him to drive or run away to a place that put him back among the public and a greater danger to others.

The negotiations continued, *"Now, Mitch, no one's going to hurt you. We know you didn't mean to do it,"* the sheriff was reassuring the shooter in a calm voice via the radio. We were all listening intently.

Well, most of us were…"Put the gun down and your hands up! This is the state police! I command you to put the gun down now!!!" Came a loud voice from between me and Baker. My eyes nearly popped out of my head as I looked down at Cross in astonishment.

"Shut the fuck up!" I commanded the trooper, almost at the same time that Baker yelled the same at him. "The sheriff is negotiating with him! Keep quiet!" The command fell on deaf ears as the trooper repeated his commands as if only he and the shooter were in their own solitary little world at the moment.

I dropped to my knees, and without hesitating, told the trooper exactly what I was going to do to him if he interrupted the negotiations again. It involved my boots and his ass! Baker was right there with me backing me up. The trooper said nothing and just kept staring blankly through his gun sights onto the field. I stood back up and tried to refocus back on the field and the actual emergency we came here for. Luckily, through the binoculars, I could see that Mitchell hadn't moved a muscle.

"No one's going to hurt you, Mitch, as long as you don't hurt anyone else," the sheriff kept repeating over the radio. *"We just need you to put the gun down and walk to us. You'll be safe."*

BANG! BANG! BANG! Came three quick, distinct sounds of gunfire from between me and Baker. "Ting, ting, ting," came the sounds of the rounds bouncing off the truck parked in the field. *Jesus Christ!* We were all in shock. Cross had just attempted a double-tap-plus, and not that that wasn't bad enough, he'd missed! He'd hit the truck instead of the shooter. Slow motion literally took over as everyone on the scene stopped what they were doing and looked at the trooper in total astonishment. Baker and I were both out of our minds yelling at him. In this instant, this officer had become more of a threat than the guy who had just committed murder, and all focus was now off the original shooter and on the new one. We were in a total mess of a situation. Everyone joined in yelling at Cross, and the scene was out of control. The next radio transmission snapped us back to attention and made us all realize we were focusing on the wrong problem.

"Stop shooting at my truck!" Came from Mitchell over the radio. I quickly used several expletives while ordering Cross off the scene. Both Baker and I commanded him to get in his car and leave immediately, or he may be the first person to go into cuffs that day. Finally realizing he might be the next person to get shot, Cross got in his car and backed out of the area. We thought we were done with Trooper Cross. We thought he'd left the area. We'd soon discover that we were wrong.

Focusing back on Mitchell, the Sheriff reassured him no one else was going to shoot at him again, and luckily the negotiations continued. Lt. Wickle and I were back on the binoculars making certain that even though Mitchell wasn't putting the gun down, it also wasn't moving from underneath his arms, which were still crossed and resting on the tonneau cover.

A few minutes later, after a few more failed attempts to convince Mitchell to put the gun down and come to us, the sheriff then came up with the terrible idea that if Mitchell wasn't willing to walk off the field toward us, he would walk out to Mitchell. The sheriff felt that he knew Mitchell well enough to trust that he wasn't going to get hurt if he went out to get him. Again, bad assumption. No matter what we thought of Mitchell as a fellow employee, he'd still just killed someone. That's proof of someone not in their right mind. It didn't matter if he was crying and saying he was sorry, he'd still just committed murder, and walking onto that field was an incredibly bad idea. The sheriff tried, quite unsuccessfully, to get one of us, including me, to go out on the field with him. Everyone attempted to talk him out of it.

Finally, the sheriff radioed, *"Mitch, I'm coming out to get you. I want you to put the gun down, and you're going to walk back off this field with me."* With all of us shaking our heads, we watched as the sheriff started out onto the field, without a gun in his hand, towards Mitchell. Tensions mounted, and there was nothing else we could do but watch Mitchell's hands carefully and be ready.

Now, what we didn't know. *There seems to be a lot we didn't know that day.* What we didn't know was that Trooper Cross hadn't completely left the area. He'd backed his car off the scene just enough so that he was out of our site. He then grabbed the next officer to arrive on the scene who didn't know what was going on and commanded that the officer go with him. The officer was from another neighboring police department and had just arrived on the scene, completely oblivious. It wasn't his fault that he wasn't privy to what had taken place just minutes earlier. A state trooper was giving him an order, and he was following it, unaware of what was about to happen.

Just before the sheriff decided to walk onto the field, the trooper had taken the newly arriving officer, and they worked their way up into the wooded area just to the left of the rest of us. The fairgrounds had a wooded camping area just to the west of the tractor barn that paralleled the field where the shooter was standing in. No one had seen them sneak into the empty campground and take up a flanking position as they crept through the wood line to a location that put the trooper closer to the suspect, facing the shooter's back.

The sheriff was about a hundred yards, about halfway out between us and Mitchell, when the shot rang out. One shot and Mitchell went down. The sheriff stopped in his tracks, stunned, not knowing what had just happened. We, too, were all in shock to see Mitchell go down. It took a moment or two for us all to realize what Cross had done and where he was; he was hidden somewhere to our left in the woods and had shot the suspect. I had actual fear in me that a second shot might come, and the sheriff might be the next to go down. Cross wasn't in his right mind, and this wasn't Afghanistan. Regardless, I was the first to take off running across the field with another officer, Deputy Duncan, right behind me. I didn't have a good feeling, not knowing exactly where Cross was and what state of mind he was in.

In fact, when I started running, I yelled toward the woods where the shot had come from, *"James, It's Wilson! I'm coming across the field! Don't shoot again!"* I ran past the sheriff, who was still standing dead in his tracks, attempting to clarify the situation in his mind. I got out to Mitchell, who was down but still barely alive. One look and I knew he wasn't going to make it. He was gasping for air that he wasn't going to get. His lungs were filling with blood. I yelled for the ambulance. Both Duncan and I began telling him he was going to be okay, only because that's what you do. You tell people that they're going to be okay, even if you know they won't be, so their bodies will fight for some grasp to life.

Everyone back behind cover had also finally realized what had just occurred. Everyone but the sheriff. He surmised that the shot had come from one of us behind him. He had immediately assumed that Charles had ordered one of his Dover officers to shoot. When the sheriff finally regained his ability to take another step, he got out to us in a less-than-happy demeanor. By this time, all the officers, including Charles, were there watching Duncan and me attempting to keep life in Mitchell's body.

The sheriff began yelling at Charles, accusing him of causing the shot that brought Mitchell down. Charles immediately became upset, having no time for the sheriff, and began to defend himself, which only fed fuel into the fiery situation, and they started arguing back and forth. The ambulance that had been waiting nearby drove quickly out to the scene, and two attendants began working on Mitchell. Duncan and I backed off, still down on our knees, ready to assist if we were needed while others stood by. Charles and the sheriff kept arguing, which was becoming quite a distraction. They were literally arguing right over us while the ambulance crew was struggling to keep a person alive.

Finally, one of the ambulance attendants looked at me and said, "Can't you do something about them!?" I truly didn't know exactly what to do. I stood up behind the sheriff and told Duncan to grab Charles. The sheriff was very animated in his arguing with his arms flailing, so I grabbed one arm from behind and put him in a half-nelson just as Duncan grabbed onto Charles, and we separated the two. The sheriff turned around on me with his other hand up and clenched in a fist as if he was going to take a swing at me, probably believing it was a Dover officer who'd grabbed him. When he saw it was me, he pulled his punch back.

"It wasn't Charles!" I yelled at him. "James Cross is over in the woods somewhere. He took the shot." I could tell by the changing look on the Sheriff's face he'd realized he'd been wrong and took in what I said as he looked over to the wood line. I realized in that moment that we still had a disillusioned officer hiding in the woods somewhere and I felt none of us were safe in that field. And as if my words had some type of telepathy, all of a sudden Trooper Cross emerged from the tree line and began to walk our way. *A really bad idea!*

The sheriff spotted him first. "Murderer! You're a murderer!" He began pointing and yelling at Trooper Cross. I immediately started to push the sheriff in a direction off the fairgrounds and shoved him straight into the sheriff's chief deputy and told the chief to get the sheriff off the field, which he did but not easily. He tugged and pulled on the sheriff, all the while the sheriff trying to get away and yelling, "Murderer!" in Cross's direction.

Luckily, at some point, someone must have notified the state police barracks of what had occurred minutes earlier because just at the same time Robinson was being dragged off the field, my academy classmate, Corey Smithers, who had recently joined the state police, came running towards us across the field and grabbed Cross, escorting him quickly off the field and drove him away from the area without saying a word.

With both the sheriff and Cross out of the way, and the ambulance crew working on Mitchell, I was finally able to get on my cellular phone and called my supervisor at the headquarters in Bangor, who obviously knew nothing of the incident as of yet. I quickly explained the shit show that had taken place, and he told me to stay put on the scene and he'd start the boys from CID, or the state's Criminal Investigative Division, as soon as he could. Mitchell was finally taken to the hospital, and within the hour, the suits were on the two scenes, the fairgrounds and Pleasant Hill Manor, and started to reconstruct the day's events. Most of the officers remained on the scene, coming down off their individual adrenalin rushes and trying to make sense in their minds of what had taken place.

Every officer on the scene, beginning with me, was to give depositions over the next few days. Mine was right away that same day as I was the sole officer to have dealt with the entire incident from start to finish and was the only one to be alone with Mitchell at the fairgrounds before other officers had arrived. One by one, each officer that had been involved in the incident was to be questioned, each interview recorded and transcribed for compilation into a final report that would come out many months later.

Trooper Cross, as it turned out, would state that he was "protecting" the sheriff in shooting the suspect. This, and many other statements in general, would make it into the final Attorney General's report as truth. But then again, as I mentioned at the beginning of the story, I was told that mine was only one of two accurate and completely truthful accounts of what had taken place that day in CID's opinion. In actuality, I was the impartial witness, being employed by all three major agencies at the time, the state, the Dover-Foxcroft Police Department, and the Sheriff's Department. I wasn't biased towards anyone and received a paycheck from all three.

One thing I found out later on after all was said and done was that once Mitchell realized he'd shot at me, he could be heard on the radio recordings saying, "Tell Dave I didn't mean it. I didn't know it was him." The dispatcher talking to Mitchell had told him who the officer was on scene that he'd shot at just moments after he'd done it. Mitchell had only one target that day and he was sorry that he'd taken shots at me.

As it would turn out, we'd lost two members of our community that day, and a family with ties to both would be forever changed, not to mention other lives wouldn't be the same either. Mitchell would pass away shortly after being taken by ambulance to the hospital in Dover-Foxcroft, and Perry Schmidt was dead before the final bullet entered his body at Pleasant Hill Manor.

There's no happy ending to this story, and trying to add or find humor in it would simply be wrong.

After this incident, I would finish out my tour with MDEA. Ultimately, towards the end, I would be pulled more and more into cases further away in the Greater Bangor area where the agency chose to focus on and needed agents, and less for Piscataquis County where I was initially assigned. ♦

CHAPTER 14

PRISON POLITICS

In 2012 the Piscataquis Sheriff's Department was experiencing a hiring freeze, and I had to find another avenue in the interim once my time with MDEA had come to a close. I was certain that at this point in my career that I didn't want to return to full-time road work. I had a good deal of experience under my belt, and it was becoming time to set my sights a bit higher. I received a call from a friend who worked for the Mountain View Youth Development Center, a maximum-security facility and detention center for youths. He told me there was an opening as a Criminal Investigator for the Maine Department of Corrections and asked if I'd consider it. During my time with MDEA, I'd worked with the Department of Corrections on a case of smuggling drugs into the prison, and apparently, it didn't go without notice, and now it seemed they wanted me full-time.

The position they were offering was basically a detective within the prison system. The Maine prison system consists of five facilities from minimum security to the supermax facility in Windham, Maine. Four criminal investigators were assigned throughout the state to combat the influx of drugs and other felonies within the prison system, which included sex-related crimes. The investigators were, for the most part, in charge of each facility's Special Response Teams, or SRTs, however, we were the only four officers across the state allowed to carry weapons anywhere inside the prison walls, other than armed guards who were only allowed to carry in certain areas, or situations.

I was hired into the northern division, which primarily covered the Charleston minimum security correctional facility and the Mountain View Youth Development Center. However, I would end up being sent state-wide for various assignments as needed.

Both the correctional facility and the youth development center were located on the same grounds in Charleston, Maine. A small town with a large mountain, hence the title "Mountain View." The town of Charleston is in Penobscot County, and the facility is literally on the Piscataquis County border line. The facility itself sits on top of this mountain, about one mile above sea level. In fact, when I was a kid, there was a restaurant right beside the facility called the "Mile High Restaurant." It's gone now.

The youth facility had higher security than the adult side. This housed the worst of the youth offenders and the ones that as an adult you knew weren't going to make it. The kids were housed in pods with each pod having a common area surrounded by eight cells with four kids in each cell. Ages varied up to eighteen and as young as twelve or thirteen.

On my very first day on the job, I was called to handle their first-ever hostage situation. A kid in one of the pods held another at bay with the sharp edge of a drop-ceiling support he'd ripped from the ceiling after jumping up from one of the four steel picnic-style tables bolted to the floor in the common area. I was to investigate how the situation was ultimately handled. Luckily no one was hurt, and it ended peacefully after the kid demanded a McDonald's burger and fries. The only casualty was the ego of the kid he'd grabbed who'd pissed himself in fear of having this throat cut. It was a rough place at times.

The adult side consisted of several minimum-security units. This was designed to be the facility where inmates were housed toward the end of their sentences. The truth was though, those inmates were shuffled constantly, especially if they broke the rules in another facility. A minimum-security prisoner could find himself in the supermax unit just because they had room available, or possibly he'd done something to get sent there regardless of his time left or threat level. In turn, the minimum unit could have a supermax prisoner if he was transferred for not playing by the rules. It seemed this was the prison system's form of punishment, sending them somewhere else and making them someone else's problem, so it was occurring regularly. The issue, however, at the Charleston facility was that unlike the other higher security units around the state, it had no barrier protection. No walls, no fences, or anything other than an imaginary line that prisoners weren't supposed to cross, otherwise they'd be considered to be off the grounds. Charleston was just a series of billets and outbuildings that included work areas, the chow hall, and a small med lab.

The Charleston facility also had both on-site and off-site work programs. Unless you were convicted of murder or a sex crime, you were required to participate in the off-site work program as part of the rehabilitation process. This meant that inmates left the facility on a daily basis to perform work within the surrounding communities.

The actual truth was that no matter what the crime, the prisoners had nothing but time on their hands to think up ways to break the rules. Drugs were the main problem at every facility, and the inmates spent their days finding ways to get drugs inside each of the five state facilities, usually through off-site work programs or family visits.

Coincidentally, one of the most intricate drug cases I ever dealt with was inside the prison system and connected to every one of the state facilities. It was tied to a guy who used the system itself to move money and bring drugs inside to the inmates. He was also frequently shuffled between the facilities, so he had a drug racket tied to all five facilities by the time I'd caught him.

Slick Stainpanties (*not his real name*), I'll just call him Slick. Slick was in his twenties and was serving time on a drug charge. *Go figure.* Slick had set up a commissary account, where anyone could deposit money on his behalf on an account at the prison, and he could use it to purchase things at the commissary, such as snacks, soda, and phone time, as any inmate could. Deposits could be made by anyone, and the money technically belonged to the inmate. If an inmate wanted to cash out their commissary and send it to someone on the outside, they could. Hence one of the problems with the system, which made it easy for someone to make or receive a payment for drugs, which the inmate could check by simply seeing if someone on the outside had deposited money into his or her commissary account. *You would have thought that the facilities would start to wonder why an inmate would have a thousand dollars on their account, now wouldn't you? Oh, no, they didn't.* You would have also thought the prison system would wonder why so many people wanted to "give" Slick so much money on his account. Again, they didn't.

Anyway, if an inmate serving time along with Slick wanted drugs, they'd have money deposited into his account. In turn, he'd request his commissary be cashed out, have the prison cut a check, and he'd send the check to his mother. *Yes, I said his mommy. This was a "family" business.* His mother would, in turn, hold the money for him and she was, in fact, the key to the entire operation. You see Mommy had a prescription for Suboxone. This is a drug I simply detest, and it also amuses me at the same time. Suboxone is a drug prescribed to an opiate user. It's an "anti-antagonist," that is it's meant to suppress the withdrawal symptoms of opiate use, such as heroin addiction. The problem, like any other drug, is that an opiate abuser commonly obtains a prescription for this stuff not to kick the habit but to simply suppress the withdrawal symptoms between scoring a fix, so they don't get sick waiting for their next heroin hit. The amusing part is that even though this drug is categorized as an opiate, it's an anti-antagonistic drug, which means it has no opiate qualities within it that would cause the user to get high. Unlike methadone, which is an actual opiate only at a lower dosage, Suboxone literally does nothing for the user except suppress symptoms of withdrawal. These brainiacs all thought they were getting high when in actuality they weren't. *Okay, you can stop laughing now.*

Inside prison, however, Suboxone served its purpose because it was difficult to get opiates into the prison system quickly enough, so all the abusers would potentially be "jonesing" while serving their time. Jonesing by the way, for those that aren't familiar, is a term for people suffering the withdrawals caused by the user coming off their high and their body is detoxing, and they can't obtain more of the drug fast enough to prevent the withdrawals their body is experiencing. This also basically sums up drug addiction. The body becomes so accustomed, or dependent to the drug, that the body "needs" the drug to simply feel normal. This is also known as drug tolerance.

Suboxone would make the user feel better by suppressing those withdrawal symptoms. So, they all thought it was getting them high by making them feel better, which made the street value of the drug in prison extremely high. The other part of this is that this particular drug came in a thin, sublingual form much resembling an orange breath strip. This was the dumbest thing I'd ever seen a prescription drug maker do was to create a medication in this form. In fact, in the first year of its use in this form, the Poison Control Centers were blowing up with junkie parents calling because their children were finding and taking these things thinking they were sucking on a breath strip or piece of candy. *Great idea, makes a great commercial ad campaign, doesn't it?* Due to their sublingual strip form, these could also be "quartered" into four cuts with each cut being worth at least $20 in the prison and $100 for a full strip.

Slick's mother, who was also an opiate addict, had a prescription for Suboxone. She could get upwards of 100 individually packaged strips for a whopping $3, with the remainder paid for by the state Medicaid program each month. *Yes, folks, paid for by you and me, Mr. and Mrs. taxpayer!* $1,000 worth of drugs in street value for a massive $3 co-payment. *Quite the profit margin, don't you think?*

After the money transfers were complete, Slick would provide his mother with an address over the prison phone system to where she was to send the drugs, which was quite easy. You could put a dozen of these things in an envelope between a holiday card, and no one knew the difference. Slick would attempt to cover the recorded call using codes that both he and his mother recognized. He'd tell his mother that he needed her to send a birthday or holiday card to someone, and that was her signal to send some drugs. He'd tell her how many by referring to the receiver's age.

"Send a birthday card to so-and-so, they're gonna be twenty this week." *You get the idea.* The drugs were sent to the prisoner's outside contact, usually a girlfriend or wife, and then they'd have the responsibility to sneak the drugs into the prison during a contact visit after the payment was made and the drugs were sent.

Getting the drugs into prison was done in one of several ways, primarily through contact visits. Contact visits are when the inmate can visit with someone without a barrier between the two. In Charleston, for example, there was a large, crowded visitation room. Within the room were vending machines. The visitor was allowed to purchase soda, chips, and whatnot to share between the visitor and the inmate. The visitor usually had the drugs in tightly wrapped small packages, hidden in their panties or socks, and could easily retrieve them and slip them into the chip bag. The inmate would then take the package and quickly swallow it, pretending to be munching on the potato chips. Later they'd crap out the drugs in their cell toilets and voilà, instant drugs. *A bit soiled perhaps, but junkie inmates aren't picky.*

We uncovered one instance at the Supermax facility where the girlfriends or whatever would go out and purchase the same size and brand sneakers that the inmates were issued. They'd hollow out the soles, hide the drugs in them, and glue them back together. They'd then come to visit wearing long garments, like a dress that covered the shoes, and when they played footsies under the table, they'd switch shoes and as easy as that, the inmate made it back through a search post-visit and had the drugs inside the prison.

Anyway, over the course of several months of listening to Slick's recorded telephone calls, I was able to pick up on all of his secret codes he'd given to his mother. Amounts of drugs, who to send them to, how to package them, addresses, etcetera, etcetera. It was fairly easy to decipher any inmate code system after listening to a few calls. Inmates were pretty simple-minded, and they used simple code words.

I was working with one of the local United States Postal Inspectors on the case. These folks had more power than even I had as a criminal investigator. They could track packages and perform searches under circumstances that would take me days or weeks to obtain a search warrant. After a few months of monitoring the calls, we felt we had enough evidence, and after one of Slick's plans to move drugs for several inmates at one time, which was to be one of his biggest scores to date, we made our plans to move in.

The mother had three shipments to send out, all placed inside separate Christmas cards of all things. It was August, and not too many people were sending holiday cards that time of the year. Not to mention prisons didn't celebrate Christmas in July. We had the names and addresses of each person that she was to send the cards. On the morning she was due to send all of them, we moved in and checked her mailbox without her realizing it. She lived in a mobile home park, so her box was at the end of the road with several others. We discovered and seized the target letters from her box. As I said, this guy from the Postal Service had far more power than I had to take the mail from her personal mailbox without a warrant.

We then took three of the suspected letters to a local police department that had a K-9 trained to detect drugs. We had the K-9 sniff out the drug-filled letters from a stack of mail. The dog was fantastic and hit on just our three packages, proving the drugs were inside the envelopes. Now we couldn't open the letters yet without a warrant, but there was a legal way around that which would work to my advantage in the case. If the postal inspector presented the letter to its intended recipient, and they accepted it, he didn't need a warrant to open it. Their acceptance would prove the letters were intended for them and no one else, and no need for a warrant at that point under their rules. If they refused the letter, then we had to fill out the paperwork and find a judge.

We started out across the state to the addresses on the letters. At every stop, the inspector knocked on the door of the intended recipient, and luckily, they all answered. He told all three that the letter had been "misplaced" in the mail carrier's vehicle and that he was delivering them personally. Each one bought the charade and accepted the letters. The inspector would then take the letter back, open them, and out fell the drugs that old Saint Nick was holding in each card. We'd intercepted and seized all the drugs in one day. By the end of the day, we'd seized over 200 strips of Suboxone with a prison street value of over $2,000.

We returned to where we'd started, arrested Slick's mother, and brought her back to headquarters for questioning. She folded instantly and admitted to her part in the entire operation. The next day, the inspector and I traveled to the Supermax facility in Windham where Slick had recently been transferred to, again, and met with him.

Slick didn't initially know why we were there, and we played the game right along with him. I accused him of drug trafficking, and in his sarcastic, egotistic demeanor, he denied the whole thing. That is until I told him we'd arrested his *mommy* the day before and had all the drugs in our possession, along with all the telephone recordings. He reluctantly folded but only momentarily. Before trial, he'd deny the whole thing again, and mommy dearest would end up doing three years. *What a good son he was.* His denial didn't work with the judge though, and he ended up getting convicted as well, and Slick didn't see daylight for another three to five on top of his existing sentence.

By the way, in case you're wondering, the answer is yes. All prisoner telephone calls are recorded with a nice announcement at the beginning of each call stating this fact that can undoubtably be heard by both the caller and recipient. Slick's drug profits ultimately paid for the same recorded telephone calls that convicted him.

◆ ◆ ◆

During my time as a criminal investigator for the DOC, I did manage to have a state statute changed for the better. There was an issue at the Charleston facility in which inmates were sneaking in contraband, mostly tobacco products at the time. Most would arrange for a "drop" at their off-site work location, and in turn, they'd "pack" the product in their keisters to bring back into the facility. *Butt-flavored smokes, the preferred brand of inmates. A bold, manly flavor!* It always amazed me just how much tobacco a dude could fit up his own ass.

Some, on the other hand, would have the product dropped just off the prison grounds. As I'd mentioned, the Charleston facility, being of minimum security, had no walls or fences. It was surrounded by woods and privately owned land. It wasn't tough for an inmate to sneak just off the grounds, pick up a drop package, and get back to his bunk house before being discovered. This was happening quite often, and I was getting complaints from guards who were having trouble catching them. Like any other state facility, the staff was minimal and far outnumbered by the prisoners. There were also several outdoor workstations with each work crew overseen by one or two unarmed guards. The guards, by statute, had only minimal enforcement capabilities, even if they noticed something taking place. I was becoming fairly popular with the staff with my drug experience and harsh attitude towards the offenders. My nickname had become Sledgehammer or 'Sledge' for short. I brought the hammer down.

Not to change the subject, however, the incident that truly made a name for me was when I found that a woman was planning to bring in drugs hidden on her infant child. During the visit, the daddy-prisoner would change the baby's diapers, or so the charade, and take the drugs from the diaper. *No kidding, people, this is the level criminals go to. I never wanted any of them back on the streets after my stint as an investigator for the prison system!*

Once again, I learned of the switch through the recorded phone system. I listened intently for hours covering weeks' worth of calls planning this event. On the evening of the visitation, my warden and I sat outside in an unmarked car, looking like any other visitor, and waited for the target vehicle. It was our lucky night. With the entire large parking facility to choose from, the target parked directly in front of us in an adjacent parking space. While waiting for the visitations to begin, we watched the mother change the baby in the car and put the drugs in the diaper. She had a car full of scumbags, and some were known out-of-state gang members, so caution was utmost to us, not to mention there was an infant involved. We had other guards waiting, and I wanted them to be part of the production as the rural and relatively small prison had never seen a bust like this. The facility was anxious and excited to show other inmates that they were paying attention. When the gatehouse began allowing the visitors to enter the visitation parking area from the general parking area, we followed behind the target vehicle. Once through the gate, we stopped the car. I exited and rushed the target vehicle, my gun drawn, and I made a scene out of it that the prisoners could see from the visitation windows. The prisoners had never encountered a bust like this at Charleston, and it scored me points with the guards who were at times seen as no better than the inmates they watched over. One of the guards removed the child from her mother, and the child was taken to a safe area and searched. The drugs were found on the child, and more drugs were located during the search of their car.

The rest is history. You know, the inmate got nearly no extra time, the mother got a fine and time served, and the child remained in the custody of the junkie, dealer-parents. The usual.

Anyway, I strayed off-topic, my apologies. Back to our story. One evening near dark, the prisoners were standing in the medical line at the dispensary building, waiting for their turn to get their prescriptions for whatever they pretended ailed them. One guard was outside watching the line, which was fairly long. One of the inmates, who'd pre-arranged a tobacco drop just off the prison grounds, bolted from the line and headed for the woods. The guard watching the line spotted him and ordered him to stop, which the inmate hadn't really planned on doing, and he didn't. He continued running up a small ridge to a wood line. The guard, who couldn't run after him due to the rest of the inmates he was required to keep watch on, continued to yell commands for him to stop and radioed for assistance.

The inmate, who was now off the grounds and trying to navigate the wooded ridgeline to find his way to the drop site, fell off the ridge top. He tumbled down a steep embankment and banged himself up fairly badly, injuring his face, legs, and arms. He was limping and bleeding and had a decision to make. *Not that he had the ability to make good decisions, to begin with.* He couldn't run anymore and felt he wasn't going to get to the drop site before someone caught up with him. He decided he'd double back and attempt to sneak into the prison billet, hoping he could accomplish this without being seen or caught by those who may be chasing him. This is the kind of idiot he was, he truly thought that if he could get back into the bunkhouse without being caught, nobody would notice that the limping, bleeding inmate might just be the guy they were looking for.

The inmate did manage to double back and sneak into his billet, forcing his way through a rear door as the guards were looking for him off the grounds. However, it didn't take the guard assigned to the building long to locate him in the bathroom, tired, dirty, with torn clothes, and bleeding. I was off duty at the time and was called in to make the formal arrest and levy charges. *I always found it amusing to have the ability to arrest people who were already in prison.* I charged the inmate with failure to stop for an officer and escape.

My District Attorney, or DA, denied the charges. He said we couldn't charge him with failing to stop because prison guards weren't police officers, and only a police officer has the authority to make a person comply with that type of command.

"Are you serious? What are they supposed to do? They're the prison guards! Are they supposed to say, oh, wait, please wait while I call a real cop...no, really, please wait? Hey, why aren't you waiting!? You do realize, don't you, that they're the *only* people that *can* make the prisoner stop?!"

The DA also didn't want to bring the escape charges. His theory was that the prisoner came back, so he didn't really "escape."

Now I liked the DA. He and I worked together for years on various cases. Since I had first become an officer, this guy was my primary prosecutor, and he was very good at it. Over the years though, I'd find that if he said no, in actuality that translated to, "Give me a reason," and often I'd have to convince him to take a case, much like he had to convince a jury that the defendants were guilty. I didn't mind doing this. I was only one of very few officers that had the expertise, and cahones, to challenge my prosecuting attorney, and I believe he enjoyed that about me.

It took a couple of months of back-and-forth bantering, but ultimately, I was able to get the DA to agree to send the escape charge to a Grand Jury. I argued that it didn't matter if there were walls or fences, or if the prisoner had returned. Under the state statutes, leaving the grounds of a prison without permission was an escape, period, and he should be made to answer to the charge regardless of the circumstances.

By the way, a Grand Jury, for those unfamiliar, is simply a group of everyday people who are gathered to very briefly hear the facts of a case to determine if there's enough evidence to send the case to a formal criminal trial. The prosecutor has only a few minutes to explain the case to the room of twenty-three people, and they're allowed to ask the arresting officer questions to help them make a determination. They decide within minutes if the case will go to trial or not. It's all very fast-paced; most of the time the process is over and done within a matter of minutes.

So, there we were in front of the Grand Jury. They were hearing the escape case only, as the law didn't allow prison guards to make the commands for the inmate to stop, so the "Failure to Stop" charge was out the window to begin with. More on this in a minute. When the DA was finished with his brief presentation, I could see confused looks on some of the Grand Jury's faces. When question time came, a hand went up from a gentleman in the back row.

"Am I to understand that the prisoner opted to break back into prison after he'd escaped?" A few jurors began chuckling to themselves.

"Yes, sir. He did," I calmly responded, trying not to smile.

All of a sudden, the quiet chuckling turned to all-out laughter from several of the jurors. I realized at that moment we had a case headed for trial.

The inmate was ultimately convicted of escape, and as a result of this case, we set a precedence for these types of circumstances from that point forward.

As it pertained to prison guards and their limited enforcement, at the next state legislative session, a law was passed that under certain circumstances, namely an escape attempt, guards have the same powers as a police officer and can effectively command the inmate to stop and lawfully detain the inmate for failure to do so. *Imagine that, a prison guard can detain an already convicted and incarcerated inmate. Go figure.*

Score one for the good guys.

♦ ♦ ♦

The mother and son drug bust I mentioned previously was one of the largest drug cases the Maine Department of Corrections had seen up to that point. Normally the department didn't enjoy the publicity of the public knowing that criminals can continue to commit crimes while still in prison. *Even though we all know they can.* On this bust though, we looked like we'd headed off the drugs before they got inside, so they were riding the coattails of that success story, and I became fairly popular with the higher-ups in admin. After this, my boss would run cases by me quite often, no matter who they were ultimately assigned to across the state. This, however, wasn't always a plus.

I received a call one afternoon from my boss in Augusta, Maine. Augusta, being the capital of the state and the headquarters of the Maine Department of Corrections, lies in central Maine and was about a two-hour drive from my office in Charleston. My normally very calm and collected boss, Larry the Suit (*not his real name*), sounded frantic with obvious panic in his voice. He said he had a situation at the Farm. The "Farm" was the nickname of another minimum-security facility also known as the Buldoc Correctional Facility, located in the Mid Coast area of Maine in the town of Warren. This facility, too, had both on and off-site work programs. Larry said that he had a situation and needed me to look into it immediately. He said that morning an inmate work crew had gone out to a site in the City of Augusta, and a serious problem had occurred. For those of you who are still wondering, and to provide more detail, inmate work crews typically consisted of several prisoners who are believed to be trustworthy enough to be allowed out into the community to perform the work being required, and they do receive compensation and good-time credit for their efforts. Work crews are transported and overseen by a "crew boss" who isn't necessarily a guard and also isn't armed. In my experience, there was nothing trustworthy about work crews, and most did it just to get out of their cells and try to get contraband back into the prisons. *I'm a fan of the old roadside chain gangs that are overseen by armed guards. We need to bring those back.*

Larry said that a woman had shown up at the work site claiming to be a probation officer and had told the crew boss that she needed to meet with one of the inmates who was also her client. The inmate, Dumont Sh:ttake, (*not his real name*) a.k.a. Dumb Shit, was allowed to leave with the woman. Yes, this was my first indication while listening to Larry that something had gone horribly wrong. Inmates don't just leave their work sites, and the crew boss should've known this woman wasn't a probation officer. *Apparently, he'd never heard of asking for credentials.* Regardless, the crew boss didn't even bother to make a call back to the prison to see if this had been approved, which he should've had brains enough to know in the first place that things like this just don't happen. In fact, the crew boss didn't tell anyone that the inmate was gone. In my mind, Larry had an escape on his hands, but as I was listening, I was also to learn that it was about to get much worse.

Larry said that apparently the woman had taken the inmate to a local hotel in Augusta. *Uh-oh.* A couple of hours later, the woman was reported running from the hotel room, naked, down to the lobby past the front desk clerk and out the door with the inmate chasing her the entire distance, naked as well. And, just for clarification, it was the inmate who was naked, not the desk clerk. I thought I should explain that point. Sorry.

Holy Shittake…

The clerk then watched as the inmate, obviously not wanting to cause too much of a commotion on the street, like naked people chasing each other through a hotel lobby isn't normal, returned to the room and left again minutes later, this time clothed and was seen jumping into a taxi. Inmate Dumont then arrived back at the work site and finished out the day, and apparently, this all seemed kosher to the crew boss. However, when the crew arrived back at the Farm, the sergeant on duty noticed the odor of alcohol coming from Dumont and questioned the crew boss, who then proceeded to tell the story of his inmate having left with the woman earlier in the day.

I'm guessing that at this point during the telephone conversation with Larry that I probably had the deer-in-the-headlight look on my face with my eyebrows raised in amazement and maybe trying not to giggle at the ridiculousness of what I was hearing. So, the prisoner escapes, gets drunk, gets laid, (*apparently not a good lay either, by the way*), and then, while still naked himself, chases a nude woman out of the hotel. He then goes back to get dressed again and hops into a taxi back to the work site. Very odd behavior, even for an inmate. *I do believe there's more to this story than where he got the cash for the taxi ride.*

Larry also mentioned that even though the naked woman didn't grab her clothes before running from the hotel room, she did grab her purse, which she was dumping out in a trail behind her throughout the hotel hallways while running away, coincidentally dropping her identification which the hotel clerk had picked up. During the time I was listening to my boss tell this story, I was also pulling up the inmate's file in our department computer system, known as the "Corus" system (*To this day, I have no idea what that stands for*). On

Dumont's face sheet was a list of people he wasn't supposed to have contact with. Can you guess who was number one on that list? You're correct, the woman he was in the hotel with, according to the name on the identification card she'd dropped in the hotel lobby.

So, I didn't even need to be a good investigator to figure this one out. My guess so far in listening to Larry was that this woman was a former lover of the inmate, probably a victim or witness in a case against this guy. Over time he'd been having telephone conversations with her and had convinced her she was "still the one" and to meet with him, dreaming up this entire probation officer scheme, which by some miracle, at least initially, had worked.

"Um, Larry? I have some more bad news for you," I explained what I was seeing in the Corus system and that someone, or multiple people at the Buldoc Facility, had allowed Dumont to have telephone and possibly even visitation contact with this woman that he was supposedly restricted from having any contact with. *From where I was sitting in my office far, far away, I could literally hear the "whoosh" of Larry's career flashing in front of his eyes at that moment.*

"What are we going to do!?" I could hear Larry's voice crackling.

"What do you mean 'we', Larry? At the very least you have an escape attempt on your hands, plus whatever happened in that hotel room to make the girl run out of it naked, which by the way occurred in Augusta PD's jurisdiction. You need to call the state police and get CID involved. If we handle this case ourselves, no matter the outcome, we're going to look very bad and as if we're trying to hide something. Which I'm guessing you'd like to do right now."

Larry definitely didn't want to take my advice. He didn't want this kind of thing going public. He was beginning to realize just how amazingly stupid this made the Maine Department of Corrections appear. "Dave, just track down this woman and see if she'll talk. We'll decide from there, *please*?" There was pathetic desperation in Larry's voice.

I agreed to see what I could find out about the woman, what role she played, and why she was on this guy's no-contact list. *And why she doesn't own more clothes?* I told Larry I'd get back to him as soon as I could. I repeated several times though that we needed an outside agency to take this case.

The woman's address was listed as Hampden. I called one of my buddies at my old stomping ground at the Hampden Police Department and asked if they'd see if her address was still good. I explained the situation and asked if they'd go talk to her if they could even find her. Just because her license had a Hampden address didn't mean she hadn't moved several times. In the meantime, I did more digging in Corus and discovered that the woman was a victim in Dumont's case and maybe even the reason he was in prison. It seemed he'd been convicted on arson charges for burning her house down. *Possibly some relationship issues here?* It was fairly clear why he was to have no contact with her. It was also clear they'd been involved in a relationship at some point in the past. It became apparent that he'd used his *wits* and *charm* during prison contacts to convince her that all was well in the universe and to pose as a probation officer to pick him up for an afternoon of booze and sex at the very least. He'd obviously had a lot of contact with her to convince her to do all these things, and it had obviously taken some time to achieve. Something, however, had gone horribly wrong in that hotel room.

A couple of hours later, I got a call back from my buddy in Hampden. He said he'd caught up with the woman at her apartment and she'd had time to put some clothes on, but she had refused to divulge any information about the day's events. She simply wouldn't talk. Thinking about it, this was probably smart on her part realizing that she might be up on charges for aiding an escape attempt at the very least.

The officer then filled me in on a tidbit of information I hadn't been aware of. "Do you remember the double homicide at the Commodore Hotel in Bangor last year?" I did recall the case. It was rumored to be drug-related when two people were found dead and burned up in a car in the parking lot of the sleezebag hotel. It was also rumored that the bodies had been found decapitated in the vehicle with their heads placed in their laps, a tidbit of information that hadn't been released to the public at the time. He went on, "This Dumont guy is a suspect with ties to the gang from New York that's reportedly connected to those murders, and your girl here is listed as a witness for the prosecution in the case." *Well, this changes things just a smidgeon, now, doesn't it?*

I quickly concluded that this wasn't just a case of a horny inmate who had a fight with his on-again, off-again girlfriend. He was trying to eliminate a witness in a pending case that involved more than just arson. He's managed to coerce her into an afternoon of inappropriate behavior and most likely intended to end it in murder if she didn't agree to not cooperate with the prosecution on the parking lot killings. It appears he thought that if he got her drunk and he "performed" well, then they'd be friends again and she wouldn't testify against him, which obviously hadn't happened, hence the streaking in the hotel lobby. *I wonder, was it bad booze or bad sex? You had to give him an 'A' for the effort though if nothing else.*

I called Larry back and told him the 'good' news. I also told him that no matter what he chose to do, I wasn't going to be involved in the case, even if it meant he'd fire me. I wasn't about to be part of this mess. I explained to him that no matter what came from this case, we'd end up looking like we'd covered something up, even if we hadn't intended to. This needed to be investigated by an outside agency.

Unfortunately, as it turned out, Larry would initially agree with me just to end the phone conversation and then he would assign the case to a new investigator who couldn't say no because he was on probation and needed his job. I heard very little about the outcome of the case after that, nor did I ask too many questions. I do know that it was kept very quiet, and to this day, I'm not certain that any action was taken against the inmate or the woman.

It was soon after this that the hiring freeze at the sheriff's department was lifted, and I was back with them, leaving the Maine Department of Corrections in my rearview mirror, not to mention a bad taste this all had left in my mouth. ♦

CHAPTER 15

RETURNING TO THE SCENE OF THE CRIME

I left the Department of Corrections as soon as the hiring freeze was over at the Sheriff's Department and returned with the understanding that I'd primarily be working drug cases in the county again. However, I soon found that being back with the S.O. was far different than it had been before. The administration had gone through some changes, and the patrol division wasn't receiving backing from the admin like we'd had in the past. I'd been asked back by the new chief deputy to focus on drug cases with my expanded background from MDEA, but it soon became apparent that I wasn't being allowed to work the cases like someone with my experience should have been. Other deputies weren't able to focus on their particular skill sets either. It felt very restrictive, not to mention we were still on the same seven-day-on schedule. Seven on, three off, two on, two off. No matter how you looked at it, an overtime shift caused an eight-day stretch with little time off in between. Also not to mention, the virtual twenty-four-hour on-call you had to take whenever you were scheduled on duty. The shifts were grueling. It wasn't a good situation, and with the minimal staffing, the pressure was always on to take extra shifts. I was back going from one call to the other with little time to work drugs, even if I'd been allowed to, which I wasn't. I was back on doing arduous, short-staffed rural patrol.

Wickle had been promoted to lieutenant, and without any background in drug investigations, he fancied himself a drug expert, which he certainly wasn't. He created a rule that no one other than himself was to have contact with either the DEA or MDEA. *Really?* I was fairly fresh out of the MDEA with enhanced training and experience, and I couldn't even place a call to them. And I wasn't "privy" to information that the now-promoted lieutenant wasn't sharing. It made working drug cases very difficult, if not impossible.

There was little support from admin, and the sheriff wasn't paying much attention to what was going on, as he was nearing retirement anyway. Poor decisions were being made, and the bad relationship the department had with other smaller, local municipal departments and the state police was deteriorating even worse than before with the attitude of admin that the S.O. was the only "real" law enforcement agency within the county. Still, we had to do our best, and the relationship I had personally with other area departments remained strong.

◆ ◆ ◆

It was 2014, and I was on evening patrol. Recently we'd had an issue in the county with two want-to-be, or "wannabe" as we called them, gangs. Two factions of young adults mostly were between the ages of 18 and 22. I think this is called "late adolescence," however, it should maybe be called "that stupid age for boys." The "gangs," I think one was called the green boogers and the other the crippled crips. Well, not really, but that's about all they were to us, a bunch of very immature kids who thought each one owned the "neighborhood" in Guilford. They started the two groups at the local high school level and then just continued on after they graduated, assuming they graduated and decided rather than further their education or get real jobs they'd just run around with spray paint and tag things. I'm certain they thought there was a much better future in that. That's about all they did, too, a bit of vandalism and creating a public nuisance now and then but not much more. That is until the night I got the call of the shooting.

I knew some of these kids. I'd obviously dealt with them since they were younger. A few of them had consistently gotten themselves into trouble. I'd been fair when needing to deal with them, which their parents appreciated, and created a bit of trust between me and the kids in that they didn't mind carrying on a conversation with me every now and then, even though I was "the man."

I'd heard on the street that something was brewing between the two groups but just rumors here and there. I had nothing solid, and these weren't real gangs, so that's all it was, talk.

On the evening it occurred, I was patrolling through Dover- Foxcroft, having just left the office on my way to Guilford. This is where most of the little darlings were from. And lately, we were staying close in the area because chances were if you ventured further into the county, you were sure to get called back at some point during your shift to chase the little jerkoffs around town for something they'd done.

Dispatch radioed to me there had been a report of a shooting in the parking lot of a small, empty warehouse that sat on the banks of the Piscataquis River in Guilford. I knew the location well and knew the parking area had a wooded walking trail behind it that led to where a couple of the wannabees lived. The caller had reported a group of "kids" had been involved in the shooting. I knew who they were talking about right away, however, the 'shooting' part certainly wasn't expected.

As was the norm, I was on duty alone, so I quickly radioed for backup which meant having other local agencies respond and waking up other off-duty deputies to quickly switch their jammies for a uniform and come out. I hit the blues and siren and started racing the five miles or so to the scene. I asked dispatch to get me as much information as they could. How many people were involved, what other kinds of weapons were reported, and how many people were still on the scene? Dispatch advised from the reports there was only one handgun mentioned and that everyone had fled the scene, some in cars and some on foot. Dispatch also had the description of two vehicles that had left the area. As I was racing towards the scene, with my heart beating to the wail of the siren, I saw the two cars go by me in the opposite direction. I radioed the Dover Police to stop the vehicles and I continued on. Just before I got to the scene, I heard one of the Dover officers call in the traffic stop and requested backup as well.

I arrived at the location of the shooting. The parking lot being right on the banks of the Piscataquis River. The road, Route 15, crossed over the river near the entrance of the parking area. Behind the lot were the walking trails and a small, wooded area that ran along the banks of the river. A couple of people who appeared to be the witnesses were the only people left on the scene. Their presence made me feel a bit better in that there were probably no people left here waiting with guns or other weapons, or still fighting.

I parked on the roadway, jumped out, and looked over the parking lot. There were baseball bats, clubs, and knives lying scattered in the lot. A small amount of blood could be seen as well. As soon as I got out of the car, the two witnesses approached me, one man and one woman. At about this same time, I received a radio transmission from dispatch.

"*…Dover Police have two suspect vehicles stopped on Route 15. They're holding everyone at the scene. Well, everyone except for the guy with his face gnawed off…he's headed to the ER…*"

"The big dog did that," the woman said to me when she overheard the radio talking to me. The woman appeared to be in her twenties, and I thought I recognized her as a local from the area. She continued to explain she'd been walking to the corner convenience store when she came upon the commotion and had watched it all unfold. She described two groups of young adults, one group arriving in the two vehicles and the other group arriving on foot coming from the walking trail. The group on foot was led by a guy who had a large Pitbull mix in tow on a heavy chain leash. The two groups of boys squared off in the lot, mostly yelling and taunting each other at first. The guy with the dog seemed to be the leader of one group while the other group's leader squared off on him and pulled a handgun from his pocket. He'd pointed the gun straight at Dog-Boy's (*not his real name*) head, pretty much touching the barrel of the gun to his brow. She said another guy who was with Dog-Boy swung a bat and hit the one holding the gun on the wrist hard enough to cause him to drop the gun, but not before getting a shot off and hitting Dog-Boy in the arm. She said this caused Dog Boy to let go of the chain leash that was holding *Cujo* at bay, and the dog lunged at the guy with the gun, sunk his teeth in the dude's face, and wouldn't let go. She said this sparked all the others to begin fighting each other with fists, knives, and bats.

The woman said she didn't want to see anyone else get shot, so in the melee of the dog gnawing on the shooter's face and others either fighting or trying to pull the dog off, she jumped into the group, grabbed the gun from the ground, and tossed it into the river. She said once they got the dog off the guy's face and saw the damage, everyone stopped fighting and scattered. She also confirmed what I had suspected, she was a regular and knew some of the players in the battle and named off as many as she could. I was fairly familiar with them all.

As other officers began to arrive on the scene, I radioed dispatch and asked them to contact the ER to be on the lookout for a gunshot victim and warned that if he landed in the same spot as the guy whose face had been used as a chew toy, there could be trouble at the hospital.

I assigned another officer the duty of scene control and evidence collection while I proceeded to attempt to track down others who'd been involved. I knew that Dog-Boy lived in an apartment just off the walking trail, so I began there. When I arrived, I found he'd initially run home from the scene, however, had since been taken to the ER by his girlfriend after she'd crudely bandaged his gunshot wound. I drove to the ER and discovered upon my arrival that he was in fact at the local hospital, however, Chew-Toy (*not his real name*) had since been airlifted to Bangor to the Eastern Maine Medical Center due to the extent of his missing face and desperate need for a plastic surgeon, and this small hospital hadn't the resources to deal with it.

During this time, the Dover Police had searched the two vehicles they'd stopped and found ammunition and other hand-held weapons inside the two cars. They'd also dragged everyone to their station for questioning and temporarily impounded the two cars.

By the end of the night, through the witness and other information, we'd identified most, if not all, of the people involved for later questioning. We'd also found two cellular phones in one of the vehicles, which I seized as evidence, plus most of the weapons that they hadn't dropped at the scene. All except for the gun, which was probably in the river somewhere, and the dog, which we'd heard that the owner had handed over to a relative before leaving to go to the ER. He'd told them to get the mutt out of the county, which they'd apparently achieved in doing.

I was able to interview Dog-Boy at the hospital in Dover-Foxcroft. He had a gunshot wound to his left forearm that went straight through. He hadn't realized just how lucky he'd been that his buddy managed to strike the shooter in the wrist just as he was pulling the trigger of the gun that had been pointing straight at Dog-Boy's forehead. Thus, causing the gun to drop and the shot to go through his arm instead of through his tiny little brain.

Chew-Toy had to wait to be interviewed, as much of the left side of his face was missing. The dog had managed to get a good mouthful, which caused quite a bit of damage. It came as no secret that Dog-Boy had trained his cuddly pet as a fighting dog, and quite the weapon if need be. He was also great at hiding him; we were never able to locate where he'd sent the dog. His tight-knit family would move the dog's location often, and we never saw the mutt again.

Many weeks of investigations including interviews with all involved had taken place in the aftermath. I ultimately drafted a search warrant on the cellular telephones that were located in the suspect's vehicles. As luck would have it, one of the phones did belong to Chew-Toy. In the text messaging, I'd discovered messages from that very day to his fellow cohorts in which he'd, and I quote, promised to, "Shoot me a Dog-Boy tonight." Plus, all the text chats about the planned fight itself. You can't get much better evidence than that.

During my initial interviews with Dog-Boy's "right-hand man," the guy who'd had the bat, he'd ended up running from the scene with the weapon in hand, and I managed to retrieve the life-saving instrument to enter into evidence totally by coincidence. Seems this moron, the day after the event, had been using the bat to hit rocks in the air in his front yard which were striking his neighbor's vehicles, and they were none too happy about it and reported it to the Sheriff's Office just about the same time I'd planned on interviewing him anyway. He had the bat in his hand when I arrived. I believe the saying goes, "You can't fix stupid."

I also, during the investigation, contacted the Maine State Police Dive Team and asked them to search for the handgun that the witness had tossed into the drink. It took the diver only minutes to retrieve it from right where she said she threw it into the slow-moving river. In retrospect, I never knew if this had been brave of her to jump into the middle of the two fighting groups or if she'd done it to keep local kids she was familiar with out of trouble, but it didn't matter, someone got shot and the evidence was apparent.

Chew-Toy survived only to turn out to be a bit less handsome than he was before, and Dog-Boy ended up with a permanent peephole going through his forearm. *Should've been in the middle of his forehead.*

Who knows what the two were originally fighting about? Turf, I suppose, or maybe who had the better-looking underwear on that day. It's all fairly foolish when I think back about it.

So, from this little story, one would think that this one might have a good ending, punishment wise I mean. I'd spent a good deal of time putting the reports together, hoping that Guilford's first and only shooting that I know of would end in a justifiable punishment on both sides of the two groups and send some sort of message to future wannabees. On the one side, we'd had a definite and pre-meditated shooting that nearly killed someone. On the other side, we had a guy who'd trained his pet dog as a deadly weapon and obviously brought him to the fight to use him in that manner. Plus, we had one guy with a hole in his arm and another who doesn't get the response he'd like from then on when he asks the magic mirror, "Who's the prettiest of them all?" We had a pre-meditated rumble in the Bronx, evidence up the wazoo, and witness testimony. It seemed like enough to get a few convictions such as attempted murder, felony assault with a deadly weapon, aggravated assault…carrying a concealed weapon…disturbing the peace?

Jaywalking?

How about nothing at all?

Yes, that's right, the DA wouldn't levy one single charge on the entire case. He didn't even have a reason why he wouldn't do it. I mean we didn't even need an admission of guilt or even cooperation, we had the physical evidence, text messages from that day, a witness, and two guys with reported and documented injuries. What else did we need?

This, my friends, is unfortunately what occurs all too often when the system is overrun with cases and people don't want to take the time to fight for inadequate sentences. You get crimes that don't fit or don't even receive the punishments at all.

The moral of the story is that as an officer of the law, you can't allow actions, or inaction as in this case, to get to you. A seasoned officer once told me early in my career to, "Just make the arrest and then walk away." Meaning, that if I worried about what the punishment might be, I'd eat away at myself and become just a shell of an officer. You can't let the end result get to you, even though all too often when the punishment doesn't fit the crime, the community sometimes lays the blame on the officers, even though we have nothing to do with the prosecution or the outcomes.

◆ ◆ ◆

Along came mid-winter of 2015, and I was on the day shift with another deputy named Cameron. He called me and said he'd been given a "No Trespass" order to serve on a guy in Monson, a small town north of Dover-Foxcroft in the Moosehead Lake Region.

It seems this guy was making threats to the local town office staff and had left a particularly threatening message on their voicemail the night before, and staff was getting nervous about his intentions. The order was to keep him away from the town office and off the town property altogether.

Initial reports were that this guy was a hermit who lived off the main road, off the grid, and possibly had a screw loose. In his threats, he made mention of using firearms. Other than this little bit of information, we really didn't know much about this guy or why he was pissed at the town office staff. We'd never dealt with him before that I had known or been made aware of.

I wasn't going to allow the other deputy to go alone, and our newly appointed lieutenant, who had handed down the assignment and who now despised and avoided any road duty, which he felt beneath him, wasn't offering to go so I told my partner I'd meet him in Monson and we'd arrive at the house together. I would also find out later that the LT also knew more about this dude's violent history and problems with mental illness and hadn't bothered to pass the info on to us.

Cameron and I arrived at the same time at the mouth of a dirt road off the main road on Rural Route 15 where this guy supposedly lived. That's one of the problems with rural areas, not everyone has a formal address. A short distance in on this wooded road we came to an old, two-story house where a vehicle was parked. Not having an exact house number or description to go by, we decided to try this place first before moving on further down the road. As soon as we exited our cruisers on this chilly morning, a scruffy-looking man appeared at a window from the second story of the house. He opened the window and pointed further down the road, "That place down there, that's the one you're looking for."

It seems the bigger story was that the guy we were looking for had also been harassing his neighbor here and had made threats to him as well. It also became clear that the only two houses on this road belonged to this guy we were talking to and our suspect, who lived only a stone's throw away. The dirt road took a sharp turn and slightly downward dip from here, and there lay the house that we were seeking. Cameron and I decided to leave our cruisers here and walk the short distance.

As we started walking away, the man in the window yelled out one last bit of advice, "Watch out for the flying lead." *Oh, great.* I knew immediately what this meant. It meant the rumors were true, our suspect did have guns and enjoyed shooting them, possibly at people that got too close to his property. So, even more alert, we proceeded to the end of the road, literally.

At the end of the woods road was parked a green Jeep Cherokee. This detail will be important a bit later on. At the end of the drive was a snowbank about two feet high. On the other side of the bank, there was a slight downward slope, and a few steps over the bank lay the suspect's house. From the top of the bank looking down, we were able to see the small cabin made of old, decaying logs and graying lumber. We could see two sides of the cabin including the front porch and door. The cabin itself didn't have the appearance of being overly welcoming. A hand-written sign on the front door that I could make out from the top of the bank warned against trespassers, especially cops. *Yes, it's true, some people just don't like cops in general, go figure.*

As we walked by the Jeep, I peered into it, a standard practice. You can figure out quite a bit about a person from the condition and junk they keep in their vehicles. There wasn't anything overly suspicious that would give us any clues in the Jeep. My partner said he'd go knock on the door, and I stayed at the snowbank at the top of the knoll where I could see down at the two sides of the cabin in case this guy decided to jump out a window and take off on us, which happened quite often in our business. I had a particularly bad feeling about the situation that day. That damn intuition again.

Cameron approached and knocked on the front door and waited briefly for the suspect to open it just enough to speak to the officer. I couldn't see what the guy looked like, he remained inside the doorway, but I could hear my partner address him, "Excuse me, sir, we're here to…."

Slam! The door shut in Cameron's face. The wind from the door seemingly pushed Cameron back an inch or two. The younger officer looked back at me with one of those "I dunno" looks on his face and turned back to the door. Just as he began to raise his fist to knock on the door again, I yelled out, "Get back up here now!" It's difficult to describe the feeling I had, but I knew something was going to happen that neither of us would enjoy. That intuition thing was now kicking into overdrive. Something was about to go down.

And it did.

Just as Cameron turned to come back up the knoll, the front door opened just a crack, and a rifle barrel began to emerge from the opening.

"Gun!" I yelled as I drew my duty weapon from my holster. Cameron didn't even look back, he scurried and slid up the snowy hill and dove to my side of the snowbank. As he did this, the suspect completely emerged onto the porch holding a 30-06 hunting rifle in one hand and the ammunition clip in the other, which he was attempting to jam into the gun.

Now if you're not familiar with what a 30-06 round is or what it can do, it's fairly powerful and can take down a bull moose in one, well-aimed shot. This, nor any firearm, was anything to mess around with, and this scumbag was loading one right in front of us.

"Drop the gun! Do not load that weapon!" I screamed, pointing my semi-auto square at his chest. Cameron quickly got up, covered in snow, and stood directly to my right with his weapon pointed at our target as well.

Now, when I say that tunnel vision, which I spoke of earlier, is a real thing, here's the proof. Cameron was standing literally within arms-length to my right, and I know for a fact that he was yelling the same commands to this guy that I was, but I couldn't hear him, and I was unable to see anything other than a man standing in front of the sights on my gun trying frantically to jam a clip into his rifle. I couldn't hear anything other than my own voice yelling over and over the same command, "Do not load that weapon!"

My focus was on this guy's right hand, which was trying to jam the clip into the chamber of the rifle, and I also watched the barrel of the gun, which was pointing up in the air and away from us. If either the clip goes in and he racks a round or the barrel comes around, I was ready to put two in his chest and one in his head.

Now, just like always, only milliseconds had passed, and the tunnel vision didn't allow me to hear the shot. Out of the corner of my eye, I saw Cameron bolt over the bank while yelling, "Call an ambulance!" *Excuse me? Do what? Call an ambulance for who?*

I didn't realize what had occurred yet. The suspect was still standing and holding the rifle, so why was Cameron yelling for an ambulance? Is he hurt? This guy hadn't shot his gun. It's not even loaded yet. And why is my partner jumping over the bank toward this guy? Who needs an ambulance? What is happening?!

What I hadn't realized as of yet was that Cameron hadn't waited for Grizzly Adams (*not his real name*) to load the gun. Cameron had taken one shot that I'd never even heard, and he felt he'd hit his target. The only problem was this guy was still standing up. It hadn't been an immediate kill shot as was most likely intended.

Cameron, sprinting and sliding, got about halfway to this guy and finished the job with his taser rather than shooting him again. I honestly don't think Cameron expected this guy to still be standing at that point, but he was. It wasn't long before the combination of the bullet, which did, in fact, hit the guy, and the taser's charge that finally washed away his adrenalin, that our suspect started to go down. Now keep in mind, I still don't know what the hell had happened at that point, so I'm still recapping in my mind. Cameron's gone nuts and charged at an armed suspect while yelling for an ambulance…and he tases the guy on the way! *You couldn't just stay back here with me and keep your gun on this guy? You had to rush up and tase him? That seems peculiar.*

Finally, just as my partner got down to the suspect, I saw the guy drop the gun and collapse. I jumped over the bank and slid down to the porch, on the way gabbing my radio off my hip and calling for an ambulance. I got down to Cameron and the suspect, who was now face down on the ground.

"What the hell just happened!?" I yelled at Cameron.

"Did you call the ambulance? I shot him!" Cameron shouted back at me, even though we were face to face over this guy now.

"You did what? Where?! You tased him! You didn't shoot him." We both dropped to our knees and began to turn the suspect over in the snow.

"I tased him after I shot him!" *Oh, thank you for clearing that up.* We turned the guy over, and I held his head up. He was still alive, luckily, and awake.

"You shot me!" The suspect looked up and yelled at us. I could now see the blood beginning to pool. Cameron had shot the suspect in his right arm. And with the angle that the guy was standing, the bullet had gone clean through the arm and entered his chest, and again, traveled straight through and out the side of his torso. One shot, four holes, no waiting.

"Why'd you tase him?" I yelped.

"Because he didn't go down after I shot him!" *Okay, that makes sense.* "Why didn't *you* shoot him?" Cameron looked at me and asked.

"Well, seems kinda silly now, don't you think? I don't think I needed to. You shot him, and he has four holes in him. Plus, you tased him. How much do you think this guy can take?"

I propped the suspect up and began paying close attention to his breathing. I knew an ambulance was at least twenty miles away in any direction out here in the middle of nowhere. I began talking to him to keep him alert. "Why didn't you put the gun down when we told you to?"

"I was trying to scare you. I wanted you guys outta here." The suspect moaned and he began to shiver.

"Do you have a blanket inside your house? Do you mind if I go get it for you?" I asked his permission. He gave it, and I went into his house to get anything to keep this guy warm and alive. Upon entering the cabin, it looked pretty much like I'd envisioned. Unkept, a mess, hoarded, and the usual bad odors. I did notice almost immediately another rifle close to the front door. I quickly found a blanket and went back out to put it around the bleeding man.

By this time, Cameron had called into dispatch and informed of the officer-involved shooting. We kept the guy warm, awake, and calm until the ambulance arrived. It wasn't long before the property was swarming with officers and the State Police Crime Investigative Division (CID) was on its way to begin the investigation into the incident. I was told to stay on the scene while my partner, who had taken the shot, was immediately placed on administrative leave pending investigation and removed from the scene, a standard practice.

My chief deputy began to type a search warrant for the cabin as the state police arrived and started their investigation outside of the ramshackle residence. While I was standing around, I decided to check the Jeep. *Remember the Jeep?* I called in the registration plate number and was informed by dispatch that the vehicle had been reported stolen the evening before.

Excuse me? The evening before? Unfortunately, the day shift, primarily me and Cameron, hadn't been informed of any stolen vehicle. Now, this might have been nice to know beforehand. This dirtbag had stolen this Jeep the night before we arrived. Most likely he thought we were coming to arrest him for vehicle theft instead of just giving him a piece of paper. Not to mention if we'd been able to serve the notice and left, we probably would've never known about the Jeep or ever seen it again. He probably would've dumped it quickly after we'd left in one of the several deep rock quarries in the Monson area.

I'm a big fan of communication, for obvious reasons.

So, ultimately the guy survived. We were probably sued, too. Cops are sued so often by scumbags that half the time we're unaware of it. We did, however, recover a stolen Jeep quite unexpectedly. And because Cameron was on leave for several weeks, and I was the only other officer in Cameron's rotation and nearing my days off at the end of a seven-day stretch. I ended up working fourteen days straight and switching mid-stream to the night shift on day number nine before demanding a day off. By day fourteen, I was so exhausted that I fell asleep at the wheel of my cruiser in the middle of the night and plowed over three trees on a sharp curve at seventy miles per hour. An accident that should've killed me but only served to make me angry that it happened. Not only had I been dead tired from the shift and callouts, but I was also dealing with a muscle tear in my left shoulder from a young punk a week earlier who had been caught amid a home invasion, resisted arrest, and decided to fight with me and tore my shoulder up in the process. All in a day's, or fourteen day's work, actually.

Anyway, on to the reason why my partner had shot, and I hadn't. Two different variations of the situation. Cameron decided he wasn't going to wait for the rifle to be loaded before taking action. He'd felt that the initial warnings were enough and the guy, once loading the weapon, intended to shoot us. I, on the other hand, didn't feel the guy was a threat yet. Until the clip was in the gun and racked, or the barrel came down and around, I wasn't going to shoot the suspect. All shots we take as law officers are intended to kill our targets, that's the point. At the point we're prepared to shoot, we believe our lives are in imminent danger and someone intends to kill us. We need to stop the threat, period, and go home safe. So, when I take a shot at a suspect whom I feel has the same intention to kill me, I don't intend my target to have the ability to return fire or put up any more of a fight of any kind.

Not to mention, I'd rather not shoot a guy, make four holes, and watch him walk away afterward. That's just embarrassing. Bad shot, Cameron. Try harder next time.

♦ ♦ ♦

As difficult as it was being back with the county, I did manage to score at least one good drug bust. And with that, I'd just like to say there should always be a lesson to learn in everything we do in life, and there's a lesson to be learned in this story. And to my defense, I don't think I'm the only one to ever have done this.

I was working for the sheriff's department and had developed a case against a woman that I'd suspected was growing dope on her mother's property where she lived in Ornville, a very small village just outside of Milo. The woman was in her fifties and was a lifelong doper. She claimed to have a lot of medical issues, and marijuana was one of her self-prescribed medications for her self-diagnosed problems. The problem was she was also selling to anyone who had cash, and some of her buyers were school-age kids. *And keep in mind, marijuana, at one time, was illegal, so stop with the opinions on why we busted potheads!*

Anyway, I had an informant who had seen and described to me the grow operation this woman had on the property. Her mother owned quite a bit of land, and I was told that marijuana was growing all over it. I'd also been told she had developed a cocaine habit to go along with the marijuana. *I'm not sure what medical issue the cocaine was supposed to cure, but I'm certain she did.*

Another deputy and I had managed to get close enough to the property to get a photo of a few of the marijuana plants growing just behind the house, and I drafted a search warrant. We planned to hit the house late in the afternoon, and I rounded up the entire department, meaning all five deputies, and we landed in her yard.

Now for the record, I really enjoyed executing search warrants. The adrenaline rush from planning how to strategically execute a warrant, to the potential dangers, to actually rolling up and knocking down doors was exciting and culminated in a great deal of prep work. Up to the point of a warrant's actual execution, a lot of work takes place. Investigations can take weeks, months, and even years to build a case to the point where you're ready and prepared to take someone down. Failed searches, even though they did occur at times, were not in my vocabulary. I wanted the product in my hands and the suspect in jail, so I put a lot of time and effort into each warrant that I drafted.

So back to the adrenalin rush, we rolled into her, or a better term would be "her mother's" yard, and executed the warrant. We did, however, take into account that her elderly and innocent mother was the homeowner, and we didn't want to scare her into having a heart attack, so we politely knocked instead of grabbing the ram and taking down her back door.

We began the search with half of us checking the several acres of property and woods behind the house and the rest of us, including me, searching the farmhouse and adjacent barn. The officers checking the property found a recreational vehicle trail behind the house and many, many marijuana plants growing along it beginning right behind the barn. We also found a nice, nearly new ATV that had been used to check the plants that we seized as evidence, thus adding to the adrenalin rush. I always enjoyed it when I could tie a car or expensive piece of equipment to the underlying crime and was able to seize it, it added to the satisfaction of taking the bad guys down.

In searching the barn, a small crack-cocaine operation was discovered, and some of the actual product was found. Again, this was getting better as my information was panning out, and we were finding more evidence of drug crimes.

Inside the house, where I was, we were finding even more drugs and drug paraphernalia. It became apparent she'd been dealing in prescription drugs, some that she had managed to be prescribed along with others she hadn't. Bonus! Now we had weed, crack cocaine, and other illegal prescription drugs. The best part was that we located several firearms inside the residence. When you have a drug case and find guns, it's an automatic win-win for the good guys because guns go along with drugs and makes for a stronger case. As you can imagine, I was very excited by this point, I had a damn good case on my hands. My heart was pounding, and the adrenalin was streaming through my veins. Now, I keep mentioning 'adrenalin' quite frequently for a reason, and here it comes.

It was getting to the point of dusk, and I was making frequent trips in and out of the farmhouse with armfuls of evidence and taking it to the cruisers parked in the yard. I entered and exited through the front sliding glass doors, which the elderly lady kept nice and clean. Very clean in fact. Too damn clean. Are you getting my point here? The glass was clean!

Each time that I made a trip to the cars and back, I picked up speed in my stride. More evidence was coming into and from the farmhouse, and as it was being cataloged, I was picking up speed and nearly at a jog going in and out of her open glass door, anxious to see what had been discovered next. It was getting darker as I trotted in and out, ultimately with only the lights inside the house to guide me back as the darkness of night quickly approached. Now the key phrase in the next to the last sentence was "open glass door," please keep that in mind.

I don't know which asshole it was that slid the very clean glass doors closed on me during one of my runs to the vehicles, but on my return trip to go inside the residence, I didn't notice that my path back into the house was now blocked by a thick wall of glass that was so clean, it didn't even look like it was there. My nose met the glass first before the rest of my jogging body slammed into it, and I bounced backward on her porch deck. The force from my hitting the glass so hard sent me backward nearly four feet, took me off my feet, and landed square on my back. I must've looked like a cartoon character as I landed with my vision going spotty and hearing little tweedy birds ringing in my ears. I damn near knocked myself out for a few moments, not realizing what the hell had just happened. The noise of me smacking against the glass with all my gear on and then landing hard on the deck caused everyone to stop and look.

Now, the adrenalin part. I was so "high" on it that I didn't immediately feel the pain of what I'd just done to my nose. Blood didn't rush from it immediately, and I was too embarrassed to notice the swelling that would get much worse in the minutes to come. So, there I was, lying on the deck, and wouldn't you know it, the first person to come to my aid would be the suspect herself, asking if I was alright. I almost felt bad that I was about to arrest her in the way she appeared to express concern, probably hoping that I wasn't going to sue her mother, as well as arrest her for my new injuries. And I was somewhat surprised that she didn't offer me some pain medication, Lord knows she had enough of it lying around the house. Obviously, my fellow deputies got a good laugh at my expense, but they also knew I'd hit the glass hard and apparently had done some damage to myself.

My chief deputy asked if I wanted to go to the hospital, to which I quickly said no. Again, I wasn't feeling any pain yet, however as we continued to execute the warrant and we got closer to wrapping up, I began to feel the throbbing and could see my nose swelling and felt it pounding to my heartbeat. When I finished up and finally arrested my suspect, I headed back to the station where I fully intended to process the booty into the evidence storage area. By the time I arrived in Dover, I couldn't take the pain any longer and had to take a trip to the local emergency room where I was told I'd received two compound fractures to my nose. I'd gone twelve rounds with a glass door and lost big time. I'd end up looking like I'd been beaten with a baseball bat with a huge, swollen schnoz and two black eyes for the following several days. I suppose I could have told everyone a colorful story that I'd been in a fight with a suspect who'd resisted arrest, the only problem was the entire department was there when it occurred and had seen me plant my face into a defenseless glass door.

It was a good bust though. I mean the drug bust, not my nose. I suppose it was a good bust to my nose, too.

♦ ♦ ♦

So, to stop and recap my career as a cop in terms of injuries over the twenty years thus far; one broken nose, a severely torn shoulder, whatever I got out of that accident I mentioned, high cholesterol (around 380 at one point), along with two clogged arteries that nearly caused a heart attack that doctors tell me was caused by the stress of the job. Carpal tunnel in both hands and two blown knees, probably from that ridiculous running the academy had made us do, and a mangled L-5 disc from wearing my cuffs on the back of my gun belt for so many years that doctors described to me as looking like a "train wreck" in my lower back. You know, the usual stuff as a result of a successful career as a cop. ◆

CHAPTER 16

TIME FOR A COOL CHANGE

The bust I'd made in Milo was relatively small, and I was still not being allowed to work drug cases as I'd desired to. This wasn't going unnoticed, and in 2016, I was contacted by the chief in Milo and asked what it would take to join his department and be back to investigating drug cases that primarily affected his area. I made an offer, and the chief met my request. I was now with the Milo Police Department, and I hit the ground running with renewed energy. *However, I made certain there were no plate glass doors in my way.*

I had information that the local heroin pusher was living in Milo, and I targeted him first. This guy was selling all over the county and not just heroin. Mr. Pusherman (*not his real name*) was a virtual pharmacy on wheels. If you wanted it, he could get it, and it didn't matter what type of drug you preferred, he had connections. Pusherman had a girlfriend who acted as his "mule" or delivery driver. This was primarily because Pusherman's license was suspended and he didn't need that kind of attention while selling illegal drugs all over the place, but it also gave him an alibi as you'll learn in a moment. She drove the car, and he sold the drugs.

Two weeks into my new gig with Milo, I was working the night shift. I got a tip that Pusherman and his girl had left a house in Brownville, a small village that bordered Milo to the north. Beyond that is the Mount Katahdin region. Mount Katahdin, which is the centerpiece of Baxter State Park, is 5,269 feet high and the starting point of the Appalachian Trail. Brownville is basically the gateway to the Katahdin region.

Pusherman and his mule were reported headed back to Milo on a secondary, back road. The town of Brownville had a small police department, and I contacted their Chief, Ward Clarke, who was working that evening. I told Ward what I had, and we made plans to come in from both ends of the road they were rumored to be traveling and find our target, get them pulled over, and search the car. We suspected that he'd scored a boatload of drugs and was on the delivery trail that evening, looking to sell as much as possible before the night was over.

With both Milo and Brownville being very rural, however very spread out, and it being late at night, we expected the traffic on this back road to be virtually non-existent except for our target. And this assumption was correct. I quickly located the car on my end and got it stopped for having a headlight out. Ward showed up from his end soon after, and we approached the vehicle together. Pusherman was in the passenger side of the car and his girl was behind the wheel as usual. It didn't take long to find a marijuana joint out in the open, which was our way into the car. In Maine at that time, marijuana was still illegal, and Maine had a "plain view" law which meant if something illegal was within our view within the car, we owned it at that point and could perform a warrantless search.

We got both Pusherman and his girl out of the car, separated them, and I questioned the girl away from Ward and our intended target. She was the weak link that I needed, and she began to cry almost immediately. It didn't take long to get her to confess that Pusherman had spotted my cruiser and had handed her the drugs to hide on her body before I was able to get the car pulled over. She handed me two vials, each about the size of a small flashlight. Inside each was filled with a variety of pills and substances. Cocaine, Oxycontin, Xanax, Suboxone, Vicodin, Methadone, and weed. *Jackpot!*

We arrested them both, impounded the car, and brought them to the county jail. Because the girl had the drugs on her, she was obviously facing higher charges, and I wanted her cooperation. We acted as if we were going to book them both, however with the girl, it was mostly shown to make it look like they were both receiving the same treatment. Once we arrived at the jail, I had the guards put Pusherman in a separate cell area and "on ice" while I kept the girl with us in the booking area. Ward and I took her to a debriefing room, and I laid out the situation to her. I played on her sympathies and emotions, explaining how her boyfriend had purposely planted the drugs on her knowing he'd ultimately roll on her and walk away from the charges and that she was facing five to ten on the possession. It was all true, and luckily, she knew enough to realize it. She agreed to cooperate in hopes of receiving a break on the charges.

We also had found enough drugs on Pusherman and in his car to get a decent possession charge on him as well. Enough anyway that it allowed me to stack on a pile of bail conditions that would allow the law to stop and search him at any time, which helped. Plus, the arrest didn't stop him, he was right back at it as soon as he was released. It was just two days later with the girl's cooperation that we caught him again with a load of fentanyl-laced heroin, and a second arrest resulted.

After this second arrest, I got a call from Lt. Wickle, whose voice was a bit distressed, and he asked me, "What do you think you're doing?"

"Please explain," I replied calmly. I knew what he was calling about, but I played the game with him.

"That's my case! I've been tracking Pusherman for two years!" Anxiety and anger in the LT's voice.

"Two years? It only took me two weeks. What's your problem?" There may have been a bit of sarcasm in my voice.

"I was waiting for the right time! I was waiting for my probable cause! I was waiting….!"

"Waiting?! Waiting for what?" Cutting the LT off and definitely some sarcasm now.

"He wasn't easy to catch! I was waiting for my opportunity!"

"Not easy?! Ever hear of a traffic stop there, LT? That's how I did it, it wasn't rocket science. Just involves you doing your job and getting out of your office! Oh, and knowing what you're doing, that's helpful!"

Needless to say, the conversation didn't get any better, and I wasn't about to listen to someone who wasn't my supervisor any longer. I terminated the call and proceeded with my case.

During the second arrest of Mr. Pusherman, I'd seized two cellular telephones. I quickly drafted a search warrant for both and got it signed by the local judge. I sent the phones to the state crime lab for forensic examinations and patiently waited for the results. What I got back was more than I expected. It became apparent that Pusherman did all his business through text messaging. By the time I read through everything I was able to identify 163 (yes, that's 163) drug contacts in the area. Pusherman would advertise, sell, and plan meetings all through text. Lucky for me, he used real names for his contacts and not nicknames or code words. I had printed out two large binders full of transcriptions of texts to include names, dates, drugs, prices, and locations of the transactions. I don't think this guy even had a real voice, just text. This was a huge jackpot with all of the texts documented on paper and no way to deny it.

I spent the next several weeks tracking down everyone who'd been part of a text conversation that had anything to do with purchasing drugs from Pusherman. Many names were not surprising as they were the local users you'd expect to see if you knew the area, however, some were a bit of a surprise. Drugs don't discriminate, there were representatives from all walks of life on the list. I tracked down and met with them all.

I had one question for each, "What would you rather be in court, a witness or a defendant?" I spelled out every charge that I had on each of them, depending on what type of drugs they'd purchased, how much, and how often. Most were buyers, however, a few were the connections and sources to Mr. Pusherman. These were my major targets, along with Pusherman himself. I stayed away from the ones I felt were his sources for drugs, for now, to make a case against them later, especially if Pusherman decided to save himself and cut a deal. The texts dated back at least a year, so I had the ability to show the intent and history of his dealings. And, I had also found something else, Pusherman had caused an overdose death. *Bonus! Well, not so much for the dead guy.*

I had known of a guy who'd died recently, and drugs were certainly suspected as the cause. I had texts showing that the day he died he'd texted Pusherman and asked for drugs, which Pusherman said he had available. The texts named the time that Pusherman was to deliver them personally. I knew this guy had lived with his family, so I interviewed his sister who confirmed that just minutes before they had found her brother dead in his bedroom, Mr. Pusherman had visited him briefly. Between her testimony and the texts, I had Pusherman dead to rights, so to speak. She was more than willing to testify, and I was ready to throw Pusherman away for a long time.

I spent many weeks building a solid case of Aggravated Trafficking in Scheduled Drugs, the Maine charge for this type of crime, and it was of the highest level. Pusherman had also opted not to cooperate, which was fine with me. No deals meant he'd take the entirety of what was coming to him, and he was certainly due.

Ah, well, punishment for crimes. Yeah, sort of an oxymoron in the State of Maine, to say the least. In fact, it's quite a fairy tale now. As I'd mentioned earlier about that seasoned police officer who once told me early on in my career to, "Make the arrest and then walk away." This means that you're far better off not paying attention at all to the punishment; if you do, you'll lose hope quickly in the system. No truer statement was ever spoken to me as a law enforcement officer and drug agent. Especially as it relates to this case.

By the time the deals were done at the state level, the case was over before it was even scheduled to go to court. Mr. Pusherman was offered a plea bargain on all the charges, and he agreed to a five-year sentence, out in three, and any sort of murder charge was out the window. Go figure. Another one of those, "Make the arrest and walk away," situations that I should've paid attention to. Either that or you're certain to go crazy in this line of work.

Coincidentally, the outcome of this was the case that would frustrate me the most in my career. I was used to punishments that didn't fit the crime, but I allowed this one to get to me with the ridiculous sentence and dropping of the murder charge. By this time, I was a well-seasoned officer, however becoming increasingly hot over the lack of punishment that the offenders were receiving for their crimes. I was also frustrated at the lack of responsibility being placed on those committing the offenses. It seemed no one was ever to blame, except the victims or the police. It was all "society's fault." I suppose, just like anything else, it just gets tiring when every single day you go out and do your job to the best of your abilities just so the offenders can play a game, plea to lesser charges, and be back out on the streets wandering around society just so they can violate again.

I think all police officers go through a phase in which they evaluate their careers in this way. And I'm pleased to say that I don't regret my decision to choose law enforcement as a career. I've experienced it all, pride, pain, happiness, sadness, stress, anger, and frustration. But, most of all, a sense of achievement.

◆ ◆ ◆

It was in 2016 when I made the decision to leave the road work to the younger, more energetic officers. To this day I continue to teach for the academy and universities, offer my skills part-time as a field instructor for fresh officers, and I still go out on the occasional call for a DRE because there are so few of them, and I've spent so many years training and instructing the skills that I feel I still have to make myself available to other officers. I do get asked quite often to come out of "retirement" and go back on the road. Officers are always in high demand, and a seasoned officer who's any good and has any common sense is worth their weight in gold to law enforcement agencies these days, especially with everything going on in our nation right now and in recent history.

Police officers, by virtue of their job, are the decision-makers. They're forever going to be called to respond to people who commit crimes, it's unavoidable, it's life. And, of those who choose to commit crimes, there will be the ones who choose to fight with the police and resist arrests. The police will always be needed, and called to respond, and not always treated the way you and I would like or expect to be treated as a result. The job isn't glamorous, it won't make you rich, and chances are you'll get hurt someday as a result of choosing the profession. Hopefully, you're training and common sense will keep you safe. So, my advice is to pay attention and stay alert, especially if you pick public safety as your career of choice, which I still highly recommend and I'm still proud to be a part of to this day.

Over my years and career in public safety, I've seen many disturbing trends nationwide that have affected the profession as a whole. And with this statement comes one final opinion; people in general need to stop blaming law enforcement for the problems in society, and yes, I specifically mean the issues of racism and alleged police brutality. I realize that it occurs, however, it's not a reflection of the profession as a whole.

I believe I mentioned before that I'm not racist. I see everyone as equal, and I don't see skin color or cultural background when I look at someone. I suppose this is why it disturbs me as much as it does when I see things occurring in our nation that paint law enforcement in a less-than-favorable light.

Many instances have occurred during my career that have affected us as a society in various ways. From Rodney King and Reginald Denny to Nicole Brown Simpson. The 9/11 attacks. Trevon Martin, Mitchell Gray, William "Billy" Simpson, and George Floyd. There are many others, some of the ones mentioned include racial implications, and some don't. Some included the police, some didn't. In the end, to me, the common denominator wasn't necessarily race, but the abuse of power as an underlying factor.

Take the Nicole Brown Simpson case for example. I don't think there's a doubt, many years later, that O.J. Simpson murdered her. Even Johnnie Cochran and Robert Shapiro had to believe this as they were defending him, but that was their duty to perform, and it continued to add to their fame and fortune. The case itself was about power over another human being, not the fact that Nicole was white, and O.J. was black, but it still divided those who saw it this way at that time.

Fast forward to the George Floyd incident. I don't believe it mattered what color or ethnic background Mr. Floyd was. I believe that Officer Derek Chauvin, by virtue of the amount of time he knelt on Mr. Floyd's neck, was going to result in the death of whomever he was attempting to arrest in that moment due to the suspect's size and physical condition, regardless of his skin color. And the fact that Mr. Chauvin was on a power trip to completely control his "suspect." This was a clear case of abuse of power, which has harmed law enforcement in a way that it shouldn't have. Don't get me wrong, this was a case of homicide, there's no doubt, but it didn't mean that law enforcement as a whole required the bad reputation that it's received as a result. It only serves to put a nationwide stigma on an otherwise respectable occupation and against many thousands of individuals of all colors and backgrounds who choose to be a cop as a career.

It's not fair to say that just because we choose this or any career, that we're "accepting" the chances that come with it. I didn't choose to put on a blue uniform thinking that every day I'd be spit upon, yelled at, disrespected, physically assaulted, or even killed at any given moment. Sure, I realized that I'd be treated differently, and I hold police officers to a higher standard. But, as the saying goes, "We're all human." Which, by the way, that statement has absolutely no racial undertones at all. It makes us all entirely equal.

And again, it's not fair to say that I "knew" that by choosing this occupation I might be injured or die as a result. The same as it's not fair to say that anyone joining the military openly acknowledges that they may die in battle someday. That's not why people join the armed forces, and it's not fair to place that stigma on them. They join for a sense of duty, to gain education, and experience, to be proud, and to have a solid future. But certainly not to "die."

Every job nowadays seems to have its threats. If we're going to say that every officer should expect to be harmed, then we might as well say that the individuals at the Fed Ex in Indianapolis on April 15th, 2021, should have gone to work knowing they may die, or the same for the young students at Columbine High School on April 20th, 1999. Or any other tragic occurrence over the years in between these two incidents. It's not a fair statement.

The same goes for law enforcement. It's not fair to say that an officer should go to work each day expecting they may be harmed or die, or that all police officers are racists because they're required to arrest those of other skin colors or backgrounds. Or, if their suspect is confrontational during the arrest they must resist using a higher level of power to subdue the people committing the crimes. Those few instances that make the newspapers or television where cops do abuse their power, or obviously (*and yes, I use the word obviously because not every incident in the media falls into this category*) abuse their power, whether they're racist or not, shouldn't be used as a global excuse, or platform, against racism or to say that the law enforcement community as a whole is racist.

When individuals, or groups, call for nationwide reform in law enforcement because of these very few occurrences, they're not being fair to those dedicated officers who are performing their job to the best of their training and abilities each and every day. All they're accomplishing in these circumstances is laying blame for an existing issue that goes far beyond law enforcement, and taking away tools that police officers require to make certain that they can perform their job, and go home safe every single day. If we continue to take away tools that a well-trained officer should have at their disposal, then we're either going to leave them completely powerless to the criminal who intends to cause harm, or we're going to leave them only with the one weapon that kills every time it's used, and neither is a good idea. More training and less blaming are what's needed.

I truly believe we're all equal, and we can't begin to fight the issue of racism if we limit it, or blame it, on one profession and turn a blind eye to all the other factors. We seem to forget too easily that even in a circumstance of a "bad cop," (*and certainly there are, in fact, bad cops*) the media attention this brings doesn't make the profession itself inherently racist. We also tend to forget that if the individual that's being arrested had simply complied, right or wrong, there wouldn't have been a confrontation that very well ended up with someone dying. Police officers still need to make arrests for the suspected crimes, and the crimes will continue to be committed. We can't and shouldn't ignore crime, or pass judgment on the types of crimes. The law clearly states when an arrest is or should be made. It's not the officer's fault when someone defies that order and decides to resist, fight, or even deliberately attempt harm against an officer who must then defend themselves accordingly to effect that arrest. And remember, an arrest is not only to protect themselves but other innocent people in the area of the arrest who don't necessarily understand or agree with the actions the police are taking.

I've never in my career made a "bad arrest." I've also never fought with a suspect that didn't start the fight themselves. I suppose that's what makes me upset about how police are too often labeled as "racist" or accused of "brutality" when it's apparent that wasn't the situation at all, regardless of the outcome. The media adds hype to the situation and many times paints a picture of something that simply wasn't as it seemed. Again, I'm not saying there aren't bad cops who make terrible decisions, there certainly are. It just seems that there are times that we jump to conclusions, and end up making poor decisions, based on politics and pressure. And, that we're making hasty decisions that ultimately make it tougher for the police to simply do their job. And, without cops, we all know where our society would be.

Well, it turned a bit somber in here for a few moments, didn't it? I can almost hear myself humming Kumbaya to attempt to bring us back to a friendly place. My apologies, that wasn't my intention. However, I'll say it again, I've never regretted my career choice and given the opportunity, even in today's society, I'd do it all over again.

So, as the time draws near to an end to this book in whatever chapter in my life I'm in, and whatever chapter we're in here together *(I've lost count)*, there's one more short story that I'll offer as an example of how this job can be rewarding in one of those rare moments that someone actually took the time to thank me for showing up. ♦

CHAPTER 17

A PROMISE KEPT

I thought of several ways to end this book, and I didn't like any of them. I don't think it's easy ending a book about yourself, especially when you're still alive. *That was a dumb statement, wasn't it? How would I write the ending if I were dead? Someone would have to hold the pencil and move my arms for me.*

I could just stop here and say, "The End," but then I'd be breaking a promise that I made in the beginning, to explain what "Death by Peanut Butter" actually meant.

So, the question is, how do you bring an ending to a story that isn't over yet? As I said, I remain close to law enforcement with my instruction and DRE requests, and I certainly could tell more stories, but this is a book and not an encyclopedia. *Again, please keep the "old guy" comments to yourselves.*

I decided, as melodramatic as it may be, that I'd like to tell a brief story that details how one person showed their appreciation and highlights the best "thank you" that I ever received. *And no, it didn't involve soft music and lubricant, so get your mind out of the gutter.*

Let's face it, as police officers, the majority of the people we serve don't typically verbally thank us and for the most part, don't even like to see us coming. They know they're probably in for an arrest, a citation, or a lecture that won't necessarily go over well with them. Even those individuals who place the actual calls to us become upset when they realize someone's potentially going to jail as a result. So, the words "thank you" don't necessarily get spoken too often to us or with any degree of sincerity. Possibly with a lot of sarcasm though.

◆ ◆ ◆

The year was somewhere around 2007, and I was working for the sheriff's department. The season was early spring, and there was still a bit of snow on the ground, but temperatures were on the increase and the snow was melting. On the roadsides were the ugly mud-covered brown snow and ice that lined the town streets and rural routes throughout the county.

I was on patrol on Rural Route 150 in Parkman near the county line when I came upon a disabled pickup truck on the side of the road truck with its hazard lights flashing. The vehicle had a flat tire on its passenger rear side. Down on his knees in the snow and mud was an older man, maybe in his late sixties. He was what you'd call somewhat overweight and appeared to be having a difficult time attempting to remove the flat tire from the hub.

I rolled up behind the vehicle, activated my blues as we always did to protect and bring attention to whatever was obstructing the roadway, and I exited my vehicle. The roadside ditch had a bit of snow runoff flowing down it, and the man's tattered flannel pants were getting wet as he tugged on the tire iron to remove the rusty lug nuts. His breathing was a bit heavy, and he was sweating badly as he struggled with his task.

I peered into the passenger side of the pickup and saw two bags of groceries on the front seat. It appeared that he'd just been to the store and was heading home when his nearly bald tire went flat. From what I could see of the groceries, from the frozen TV dinners to the bag of hard candy on the top, I was able to determine, and what I'd guess was fairly accurate, was his current life status at that moment without having to ask. This gentleman was retired, and from the amount of effort he was making and how hard he was trying, he'd obviously worked all his life. How did I know this? Because he didn't give up immediately on that tire when I pulled up, and in fact, didn't even look up at me when I arrived, even though he knew I was there. He kept right on tugging on that tire iron. He was independent and proud, and as many his age do, having a hard time dealing with the fact that he couldn't get that tire off by himself, but he also wasn't giving up. He was probably divorced or maybe even widowed as told by the type of groceries he'd purchased and the limited quantities. He was now retired and earning a limited income, and this was most likely his only trip to the grocery store for the entire month. Lastly, and most importantly, he was too proud to ask for help and needed to prove to himself that he still had the strength and determination to succeed at the task of changing that tire himself.

As I peered into his truck and saw that bag of hard, root beer candy on top of his groceries, it reminded me for a moment that this exact brand was also my dad's favorite candy. We had never taken a trip to camp together without Dad having included in the pack of supplies this very brand of candy. I recall thinking how funny it was that little things like seeing this bag of candy can take us back to such great memories in time.

Now my biggest mistake at that point would have been to say something like, "Hey, old timer, looks like you're having trouble there. Let me do that for you." Or worse, if I'd moved in without asking his permission to change the tire. This would have been a mistake and sent the wrong message and thus would have offended the man and belittled his efforts. I knew, however, that he was struggling and needed assistance. Not to mention, if this tire was going to be changed successfully or without calling roadside assistance, or worse, an ambulance for the heart attack it may have caused this man if he continued to sweat and tug on that tire iron, that I needed to help him.

Instead, I knelt down, and my initial greeting was this, "I tell you what, when you get tired, I'll take over for a bit, and between the two of us, we'll get that tire changed out for you." That's all I said, no more, no less. The man didn't look back at me, or answer. He didn't need to say anything, but he did hear what he needed to trust that I wasn't insulting his age or his usefulness.

The man struggled for about a minute more and then simply got himself up out of the watery ditch, using his truck to steady himself as he stood, and handed me the tire iron, not saying a word. He also didn't stop there; by the time I was able to remove the lug nuts and tugged to get the rust-solid metal rim off the hub, he'd dug into the covered bed of his pickup and wrangled the spare out for me to put back on. After a few minutes, the fresh tire was on, and we were both ready to be back on our separate ways.

As I said my departures and headed back to my cruiser, the man said nothing, he simply walked back to the driver's side of his pickup truck and got in. I got back in my cruiser, a bit wet and muddy, and was preparing to pull away when I saw the man exit his vehicle again and walk towards me, this time with a small bag in his hand. He approached my side of the cruiser, and as I lowered my window, he reached in and handed me the bag of hard root beer candy.

Now, remember, this gentleman was obviously on a fixed income and had just completed probably the only trip to town for groceries for the entire month. He purchased little more than two small bags of groceries, barely enough to get him through the next thirty days, and he had just handed me the only bag of his favorite hard candy. This was his "thank you" to me. To have refused it due to any existing policies about not accepting gratuities would have been insulting and simply wrong. I accepted it happily, smiled, and nodded my head. He smiled, nodded back, and then walked back to his truck, not having uttered a word the entire time. He had no idea of the nostalgic value of that candy or how significant the gesture was to me. To this day, this incident has stuck with me as the best and most thoughtful thank you that I've ever received as a law enforcement officer. Possibly it was the sacrifice itself he'd made to show his gratitude. Maybe because it reminded me of my dad and our times together at camp before he passed away. Either way, it meant more than any "thank you" was ever uttered and meant far more than just saying the words.

◆ ◆ ◆

And then there was that call that came one early summer afternoon in 2004 when I was a Dover cop. I, along with another officer were responding to a guy who'd reportedly overdosed, no further details were available or provided to us. We were the closest unit to the call and responded to assist the ambulance if we could, which was fairly routine in rural areas. Unlike larger cities where there's plenty of help nearby to respond, in rural areas, there simply wasn't. When you heard a call go out, whether it be police, fire, or ambulance, if you could help, you responded.

When we arrived first on scene, we discovered that the guy who'd "overdosed" wasn't high or drunk. He'd just been really, really hungry. Apparently, to satisfy his cravings, he'd foolishly grabbed a wooden cooking spoon, stuffed it into a jar of peanut butter, and shoved the overloaded utensil which had far too much peanut butter on it into his mouth all at once. As a result, it was apparent that he immediately couldn't breathe, nor could he manage to swallow the tasty, big gob of goo, and he apparently also hadn't the ability to hack it back out either.

When we arrived, we found him on the floor, quite dead, a wooden spoon in one hand and an empty jar of peanut butter in the other…and seemingly not very hungry anymore.

So yes, friends, just as I stated in the beginning, it was in fact, "Death by Peanut Butter." ◆

THE END

ABOUT THE AUTHOR

David Wilson is a veteran law enforcement officer, having served his community for over 20 years. He's acted in various roles to include routine street patrol for both local municipal and county departments, to serving as a special agent to the Maine Drug Enforcement Agency, to being a Criminal Investigator for the Department of Corrections. All the while choosing to live, and serving in his home state of Maine.

While never downplaying the seriousness of calls he's responded to, David uses humor and story-telling as a means to cope with the situations he's seen and dealt with on the unique road of choosing to be a police officer.

David continues to live and work in Maine, and continues to write while using Maine, and humor, as his inspiration.